PARTICIPATORY VISUAL AND DIGITAL METHODS

DEVELOPING QUALITATIVE INQUIRY

Series Editor: Janice M. Morse
College of Nursing, University of Utah

Books in the **Developing Qualitative Inquiry** series, written by leaders in qualitative inquiry, will address important topics in qualitative methods. Targeted to a broad multi-disciplinary readership, the books are intended for mid-level/advanced researchers and advanced students. The series will forward the field of qualitative inquiry by describing new methods, or developing particular aspects of established methods.

Series Editorial Board

Volumes in this Series:

PARTICIPATORY VISUAL AND DIGITAL METHODS

Aline Gubrium
Krista Harper

Walnut Creek, California

LEFT COAST PRESS, INC.
1630 North Main Street, #400
Walnut Creek, CA 94596
http://www.LCoastPress.com

ISBN 978-1-59874-488-0 hardback
ISBN 978-1-59874-489-7 paperback
ISBN 978-1-61132-711-3 consumer eBook

Library of Congress Cataloging-in-Publication Data:

Gubrium, Aline.
Participatory visual and digital methods / Aline Gubrium, Krista Harper.
  p. cm. — (Developing qualitative inquiry; 10)
  Includes bibliographical references.
  ISBN 978-1-59874-488-0 (hardback) —
  ISBN 978-1-59874-489-7 (paperback) —
  ISBN 978-1-61132-711-3 (consumer eBook)
  1. Visual anthropology—Methodology. 2. Visual sociology—Methodology.
  3. Video recording in ethnology. 4. Motion pictures in ethnology. 5. Digital
  media. 6. Ethnology—Research. I. Harper, Krista. II. Title.
  GN347.G84 2013
  301.01—dc23
                  2012049077

Printed in the United States of America

∞™ The paper used in this publication meets the minimum requirements of American National Standard for Information Sciences—Permanence of Paper for Printed Library Materials, ANSI/NISO Z39.48–1992.

Contents

Illustrations

Figures

Tables

To our families, with love

Acknowledgments

Six years ago this summer, we met for lunch for the first time in downtown Amherst. Aline had just arrived at the University of Massachusetts as a new faculty member in Community Health Education and was launching a new participatory action research (PAR) project with a digital storytelling component on women's reproductive health in Western Massachusetts. Krista had just returned from six months of fieldwork in Hungary, where she had just carried out the Photovoice project described in this book. We knew immediately that we wanted to write together. This book is a collaboration of equals, passing the baton back and forth on the long race to the finish line. As authors, we have listed our names alphabetically to reflect this.

We have benefited from a number of grants that helped us to develop this project. Aline received a Faculty Research Grant (FRG) and fellowship grants from the Center for Public Policy and Administration and from the Center for Research and Education in Women's Health, and Krista received an FRG and a grant from the Center for Research on Families at the University of Massachusetts Amherst, all of which provided time and resources for research and writing. Both of us benefited from presenting our work as part of the Interdisciplinary Seminar in the Humanities and Arts (ISHA) led by Stephen Clingman. A grant from the College of Social and Behavioral Sciences enabled us to host a seminar on visual and digital research.

Earlier versions of some sections were previously published in a 2009 *Practicing Anthropology* issue on "Participatory Digital Technologies in Research and Action"; this material appears by permission from *Practicing Anthropology* 31(4).

We thank Mitch Allen, Janice Morse, and Jennifer Collier at Left Coast Press, Inc., for their encouragement, patience, and expertise in guiding us throughout the process of writing this book.

Several people read parts of the book at different stages. We thank Jean Schensul for taking an early look at our project and Cathy Luna, Roberta Garner, Kamela Heyward, and Jessica Carrick-Hagenbarth for providing helpful feedback on chapters. Dana Johnson deserves special mention for her keen editorial eye, fresh perspectives on what we wrote, and assistance with preparing the index.

The authors offer special thanks to the researchers who shared their core stories with us in interviews, discussions, and correspondence:

12 | Acknowledgments

Darcy Alexandra, Peter Biella, Carroll Parrott Blue, Sarah Elder, Leonard Kamerling, Charles Menzies, Thaddeus Guldbrandsen, Garth Harmsworth, Kate Hennessy, Amy Hill, Claudia Mitchell, Marty Otañez, and Nancy Ries.

Our colleagues have made the University of Massachusetts a welcoming place for scholarship on participatory visual and digital research. Aline thanks her colleagues in the Department of Public Health. Special thanks are due to David Buchanan, Gloria DiFulvio, and Lisa Wexler. Aline owes much gratitude to Idalí Torres, who shepherded her into the Community Health Education program and a community-based participatory research approach. Krista warmly thanks her colleagues in the Department of Anthropology and the Center for Public Policy and Administration, especially the following: Jane Anderson, Whitney Battle-Baptiste, Lee Badgett, Elizabeth Chilton, Julie Hemment, Elizabeth Krause, Kathryn McDermott, Joya Misra, David Mednicoff, Charlie Schweik, Neil Silberman, and Jacqueline Urla.

Our collaborators and co-researchers in the projects described in this book merit special acknowledgment. Aline is grateful to Anne Teschner and Ana Rodriguez, who have provided her a wonderful venue for conducting participatory arts-based ethnography on youth sexuality and who serve as shining lights in the field of alternative education—this is how education should be for everyone. Krista is forever in debt to Judit Bari and her team of six co-researchers for courageously agreeing to collaborate on a Photovoice project in Sajószentpéter, Hungary. She also thanks Catherine Sands, Molly Totman, Diego Angarita Horowitz, Lee Ellen Reed, and the youth of Holyoke and Williamsburg, Massachusetts, who have been co-learners on the path of participatory digital methods.

Aline thanks her husband Vince, twin sister Erika, and parents Jay and Suzanne, who have supported her throughout this work, and much loving thanks to daughters Marit, Lily, and Malin, who in their own ways urge her to consider new ways of seeing and being seen. She also thanks Cara Page for first introducing her to the digital storytelling approach and to Amy Hill and Joe Lambert as true visionaries in conceptualizing participatory visual and digital methodologies. Finally, much thanks to Jaber Gubrium, Sinéad Ruane, Betsy Krause, and Jeff Peterson for nudging her in new theoretical directions.

Krista would like to thank her parents Victoria and Bruce and sister Cynthia, who have always inspired her to grow as an anthropologist and as a person. The Sammet men—Reed, Cliff, Jared, and Thatcher—are a source of encouragement and humor, and Jared even lent a hand during fieldwork in Hungary. She is grateful to the Ash and Garner families for their moral support. Most of all, she is grateful to and for her partner in life, Michael, and sons, Ezekiel and Rafael, the thread of love and sheer joy running through all of her projects.

CHAPTER 1

Introduction

WHAT IS PARTICIPATORY DIGITAL AND VISUAL RESEARCH?

Emergent digital and visual methodologies, such as digital storytelling and participatory digital archiving, are changing the ways that social scientists conduct research and are opening up new possibilities for participatory approaches that appeal to diverse audiences and reposition participants as co-producers of knowledge and potentially as co-researchers. Given the shift in the social sciences to more participatory forms of research, participants are increasingly conceptualized as collaborators in the process. In the field of public health and other applied fields, as well as much of contemporary feminist studies, participatory action research (PAR) and community-based participatory research (CBPR) have gained prominence as an approach to scholarship and advocacy. Through digital representations of their experiences in YouTube videos, the taking and sharing of visual material online through interfaces such as Facebook and Flickr, and mapping their own environments in collaborative blogs, such as in "orange: a just and beautiful city 07050" (jbc07050.blogspot.com), research participants are now positioned as producers of veritable social research data that, in turn, can be repurposed as material for community mobilization and advocacy. Participatory digital and visual methodologies produce rich multimodal and narrative data guided by participant interests and priorities, putting the methods literally in the hands of the participants themselves and allowing for greater access to social research knowledge beyond the academy.

More than 20 years ago, feminist and postmodern anthropologists led a discipline-wide discussion of the ways that we produce and provide access to cultural representations through ethnographic fieldwork and writing (Clifford & Marcus, 1986; Fox, 1991; Harrison, 1997; Marcus, 1995; Marcus & Fischer, 1986; Rosaldo, 1989; Tedlock, 1991, 1995). Calling for the reinvention of anthropology, these scholars challenged the disciplinary norm of the detached "lone ethnographer" and invited

Participatory Visual and Digital Methods by Aline Gubrium and Krista Harper, 13–25. ©2013 Left Coast Press Inc. All rights reserved.

the "natives" to talk back in scholarly texts. Few of these critics, however, challenged the notion of the written text as the central medium of anthropological knowledge. More recently, we have witnessed calls for a shift in the ways we train social researchers, including revision of the ways we produce text in these fields, and a frank acknowledgment of the ways that ". . . as fieldwork has become multi-sited and mobile in nature, subjects are more 'counterpart' than 'other'" (Marcus, 2008, p. 7) and that younger practitioners may aspire to conduct more "activist" research, such that their work can have useful applications.

Arjun Appadurai (2006) trenchantly argues for a "de-parochializing" of research, "for opening it up as a genuinely inclusive and universally available capacity" (p. 169). In this manner, research can be positioned as an endeavor with "democratic potential" and as a "right" fundamental to full citizenship that should be available to all human beings as they have the capacity to serve as researchers, "since all human beings make decisions that require them to make systematic forays beyond their current knowledge horizons" (Appadurai, 2006, p. 167). Appadurai's work with subaltern youth through the organization Partners for Urban Knowledge, Action, and Research (PUKAR) emphasizes a "documentation as intervention" approach. In reviewing the approach, Appadurai notes:

> [T]hese experiments in documentation have opened a double path for many young people; one is a deepening of skills they desperately need; the other is the recognition that developing the capacity to document, to inquire, to analyze and to communicate results has a powerful effect on their capacity to speak up as active citizens on matters that are shaping their city and their world. (p. 175)

This 'double path' is key to our enthusiasm for the potential uses of participatory visual methodologies—uses that derive just as much from the research process as they do from produced outcomes.

In response to the critique of ethnographic representation, visual ethnographers have begun to embrace participatory approaches. While written texts remain a central practice in the discipline, they are increasingly turning to new/digital media for scholarly production (Pink, 2007). By digital, we refer to methods that are often computer-based or "virtual," whether this relates to the mode of production—such as with the editing of digital stories on laptops—or with how the outcomes of production are disseminated, such as with digital archives. We are quick to point out that digital methods are not always necessarily participatory in nature and have in many ways become online or computer adaptations of traditional qualitative inquiry methods, known as "online/Internet research methods" or "virtual methods" (Fielding, Lee, & Blank, 2008;

Hine, 2005; Johns, Chen, & Hall, 2004), such as in the use of online interviewing (James & Busher, 2006; Salmons, 2010) and virtual ethnography (Hine, 2008). That said, "digital ethnography" or "digital anthropology"—in the sense of studying online social life—is not a special focus of this book. For cutting-edge research in this field, see the work of Chris Kelty (2008), Gabriella Coleman (2010, 2012), Tom Boellstorff (2008), Boellstorff et al. (2012), Michael Wesch (2009), Whitehead & Wesch (2009), Amber Case (2012), and Jillian York (2012).

Shifts in the everyday use of digital visual technologies increasingly challenge the centrality of the written text in anthropology. Having grown up with the Internet, laptops, Facebook, and YouTube, today's undergraduates and graduate students are particularly drawn to the use of digital technologies in conducting social research. Indeed, many of our research participants also use these technologies in their daily lives. The emergence of more "open source" technologies and methodologies has resulted in new venues and networks of knowledge production.

CORE STORIES: A COLLABORATIVE APPROACH TO CASE STUDY CONSTRUCTION

The impetus for this book began when we co-organized two conference panels in 2008: one, "Visualizing Change: Emergent Technologies in Social Justice Inquiry and Action," at the Society for Applied Anthropology (SfAA) Annual Meeting in Memphis; the other, "Emerging Methodologies: Public Anthropology and the Challenge of Community-Based Participatory Research (CBPR)" at the Northeastern Anthropological Association Annual Meeting in Amherst, Massachusetts. The intent of both panels was to cast new imaginings of the ways that social and applied researchers might include collaborative visual and digital methods in research projects. We subsequently took part in another conference session, "Public Anthropology/Public Culture: Image, Voice, and Participation in Public Visual Culture," in 2009 at the American Anthropological Association (AAA) Annual Meeting, where we focused on ethical issues pertaining to participatory visual and digital research methodologies and future possibilities for engaging with them. The warm reception we received at these sessions prompted us to co-edit a special issue of *Practicing Anthropology* that same year on use of participatory digital research methods in applied anthropology. Our discussions surrounding these events led us to conclude that a book that introduced anthropologists and other social researchers to participatory visual and digital methods would be of interest to many and was increasingly needed in the field.

So what do we mean when we use the term "participatory," in conjunction with visual and digital methods of qualitative inquiry? By participatory, we refer to methodologies, approaches, or techniques that afford the "subject," "community member," and/or "field site" greater narrative latitude when it comes to ethnographic knowledge production and a larger role in determining why and how research outcomes are produced and received by lay and academic audiences alike. There are several terms for research methods that integrate the active participation of community members in the co-construction of knowledge: CBPR (Minkler & Wallerstein, 2008), collaborative anthropology (Lassiter, 2005), and PAR. Although each term has its own history of development, we choose to use the term "PAR" throughout this book because it is widely used and places emphasis on "action" as a research goal.

At least in concept, the increasing use of community-based and participatory approaches has led to the assertion that social research is shifting toward a new paradigm premised on achieving equality, not only on the basis of "the distribution of predetermined benefits but also in the status and voice" of historically excluded stakeholders (House, 2002, p. 633; Peterson & Gubrium, 2011, p. 2). In the field of public health, Green and colleagues (1995) describe CBPR as centered on community–researcher collaboration, from developing research questions through the dissemination of findings. In practice, uncertainty remains in relation to conflicts over the perspectives, priorities, assumptions, values, beliefs, and language of "participation" and "research," as well as over its conceptualization of "community" (Israel et al., 2005). We also recognize inherent discursive and practical challenges of participation. As Cooke and Kothari (2001) note, participation often "remains a way of talking about rather than doing" research (p. 32).

We began writing this book with the idea that we would assemble a simple text to be used both in classroom and field settings. Our intention was that it would be written so that students and social researchers alike, who were interested in using participatory digital/visual methods in their own work, could access the book as a resource in considering the planning, design, implementation, and analysis of a project employing these methodologies. However, as we began writing we realized that for a book about participatory approaches, who else better to inform the story of these approaches than their own practitioners?

Our approach to writing was thus very much aligned with a participatory approach to knowledge construction. When we began to collect material for the specific methodology chapters we realized the "collaborative" wisdom of drawing upon the perspectives of key scholars who have driven the field of participatory visual research, beginning in the early 1970s. Reviewing the work of key visual anthropologist Timothy Asch,

Sarah Elder's (2001–2002) articulation of the concept of "core stories" is very much in line with our modus operandi for considering case studies in this book:

> . . . [A] "core story" [is] the kind of identity story each of us tells about our lives. These stories are as much a part of us as our fingerprints. Our stories give form and meaning to the inchoate details of our experiences, allowing us to make sense out of life's raw footage. Core stories are signifiers for where we have been and where we might be traveling. They teach our listeners the intricacies and valences of our values, values of which sometimes even we are unconscious. In the various telling[s] of this . . . story, particularly [under certain circumstances], Tim laid down a framework for our understanding of what was important to him. He gives us a map of where he came from and where he might be heading, a place and space inscribed by his life's process. (Elder, 2001–2002, p. 91)

Interviews we conducted with prominent practitioners in the field were crafted into case studies: core stories that reflect the methodological sense-making trajectories of these scholars about their own work and the forms of participation and knowledge created and invoked in their work. These stories allow the reader to see the ways in which practitioners' academic and ethical values infuse their approach to collaboration, such that participation takes on a variety of contexts depending on the type of visual medium used, the multiple applications for the methods, and the pathways drawn by practitioners in terms of developing a program of research surrounding the methodologies.

We began with interviews (many, perhaps ironically so, conducted through a fairly new digital technology, Skype) asking scholar/participants to describe their history of engagement with participatory methodologies. Engagement was framed in terms of participants' epistemological, ontological, and ethical perspectives on participation and/or collaboration in the field, and then how these perspectives have shaped use of the particular technique in their work. We also asked participants to describe a project (or projects) in which they had used a participatory visual approach and the process and outcomes resulting from this work. Finally, we asked them to describe the benefits and challenges of using these methodologies, with many participants highlighting ethical implications, as well as the affordances of using the approaches to conduct truly engaged research that might serve the needs of communities involved. Participants also relayed how they saw the methodologies adding to the field(s) of social research.

We digitally recorded these interviews and transcribed them, with copies of audiofiles or transcripts emailed to participants for review. Participants were asked to provide any corrections and suggestions that they wished to make. Similar to the approach outlined in a number of the case studies, participants were also given the opportunity to delete or change anything in the transcript that they felt uncomfortable including in the case study or that did not properly capture their story. Finally, upon receipt of the "member-checked" file, we assembled a core story from the interview, and then returned these narratives to participants. Just as with the interview transcript, participants were given the opportunity to review the core story and provide elaboration, comments, and edits to their stories. We have also included our own "core stories" of using a particular methodology. Gubrium's core story focuses on her use of digital storytelling for reproductive research and justice purposes in her work as a medical anthropologist in the field of public health, while Harper's story focuses on her work as a cultural anthropologist using Photovoice as a research and advocacy method for environmental justice among the Romani in Hungary. This book, then, is just as much a collaborative (auto)ethnography of participatory digital research as it is an introduction to the methodologies, with the dialogic process of core story construction very much reflecting on our own research projects and the growing interdisciplinary literature on participatory digital and visual research.

Participatory visual methodology case studies featured in this book include Photovoice, digital storytelling, participatory GIS (PGIS), participatory forms of digital archival research, and collaborative and participatory film and videomaking, as well as those focused on the ethical implications of participatory visual research and dialogic/participatory data analysis. While we do try to give an overview of the current state of affairs for each methodological approach, for some areas such as participatory videomaking, visual anthropology, and science and technology studies, there are more exhaustive surveys available than what we present here. Other participatory digital methodologies gaining traction in social research fields, but not reviewed in-depth in this book, include collaborative blogging (Downey et al., 2012; Fish et al., 2012; Forte et al., 2012), interactive multimedia (Young & Barrett, 2001), and digital ethnography in its own right (Dicks, Soyinka, & Coffey, 2006; Murthy, 2008; Wesch, 2012).

Although we provide overviews of each methodology "in practice," we do not provide detailed technical descriptions of how to use specific software programs in the methods chapters. We suggest that interested readers seek out the most current user guides and groups online. Finally, we readily acknowledge that while we have tried to be inclusive in our review of the various approaches, there is much "madness to the method" of trying to write about participatory visual and digital research approaches, as much of the literature on this work appears online, with libraries and information systems straining to keep afloat of how to catalog all that is out there. Indeed, the terminology and practices related to these method-ologies are constantly shifting, with "emergent" techniques and areas of research constantly springing to life.

ARE WE GOING TO LET THE TIDE TURN WITHOUT US?

Just as a sea change is occurring in social research to include participa-tory visual and digital methodologies (Gubrium & Harper, 2009), the relevance and social justice potential of ethnography is also reaching pol-icy and activist settings, with social researchers having a responsibility to respond to new approaches to fieldwork and new conceptualizations of just who or what represents the field, who directs meaning-making in the field, and who sets the agenda for research (Checker, Vince, & Wali, 2010). Participatory visual methodologies are proliferating in the human sciences, as well as in applied fields such as public health, education, nursing, and social work (excitement that we may gauge from the sheer number of graduate student committees we are asked to serve on, often due to our interest in these methodologies).

Digital and visual approaches to participatory research offer oppor-tunities to open up the ethnographic process and to share research with a diverse array of audiences. We recognize that some of these methods have been used in prior iterations since at least the 1960s. However, today's academics have to reckon with the cultural impact of virtual media, and especially the way we must reconsider text as the primary object we produce. In this we agree with Marcus (2008) that graduate students earning social science PhDs today are entering a new academic terrain. The entire landscape of academic production is changing and with it, the publication and dissemination of ethnographic research. Our participants themselves have come to expect more than just reports of findings, encouraging us to address the relevance of the findings to their communities. Furthermore, while these approaches have been readily taken up and applied in different settings, scholars have not yet drawn out the theoretical implications of emerging methodologies.

WHY ARE YOU HERE?

We hope this book will be useful to a range of readers. Some readers may be graduate students in the classroom who are intent on learning about more participatory approaches that they might take in their research and/or activist endeavors. Others may be established academics, ready to begin a new project and already knowing that they would like to integrate participatory visual and digital research methods into their project design from the outset. Other readers, having conducted more traditional ethnographic research in a specific setting, may now wish to introduce participatory approaches to "give back" to the community and to foster more collaborative research relationships. Participatory action researchers who have not yet used visual or digital technologies will learn about using these methods to engage participants and to reach policymakers with their research findings. Others may simply be trying to decide whether participatory visual and digital methods match the goals of community collaborators and their own research agendas.

SETTING SAIL: PREVIEW OF THE BOOK

In this book, we explore some of the reasons motivating researchers to consider the ethical and power issues invoked in the social research process and outcomes, the ways this work is disseminated to diverse audiences, and how participatory visual and digital methodologies fit into all this. We explain how to start applying participatory approaches, from project design, through data collection and analysis, to presentation and dissemination of research to multiple audiences. Each stage of the research process brings with it new questions about the nature of participation, the appropriate use of visual and digital technologies, research ethics, and the goals of our knowledge production (Table 1-1). We begin by reviewing the theoretical foundations and ethical implications of these methodologies, and then review the various methods as they can be used for social research purposes.

In Chapter 2, we look more in-depth at the foundations of participatory visual and digital methodologies. We review critiques of traditional ethnography put forth by postcolonial, feminist, and postmodern scholars. From the perspective of applied social science, we discuss the ways that ethnographic field methods have been applied in international and community development work, contexts which serve as the wellspring for many of the methods reviewed in this book. We also look at the ways digital and visual methods have been informed by more academic settings, especially in the humanistic disciplines. Science and technology scholars, in particular, are well known for taking a critical perspective to the use of digital and other communication technologies as "shiny new objects" brought on board to conduct ethnographic research. We end this chapter by examining the social implications of incorporating new digital visual and communication technologies in social research.

In Chapter 3, we examine ethical issues involved in conducting participatory visual and digital research. Especially where these potentially public methods are concerned, it is extremely important to expand our ethical considerations beyond those of merely obtaining participant consent forms or fulfilling the expectations of a university human subjects' board. As Bourgois (1997) notes:

Table 1-1 Charting the participatory visual/digital research process

	Research Design/ Preproduction	Data Collection/ Production	Data Analysis/ Postproduction	Dissemination and Application
Collaboration and participation	Partnership as starting point of research Developing research questions together Research as a practice, as collective action	Community-based teams or collaborative dyads Involvement of wider group of participants	Team discussion of visual documentation Participatory editing of media or texts Opportunity to include wider community, in person or online	Multiple research products Multiple authors Discussion of audiences and outcomes Exhibition as opportunity for further research
Technology	Appropriate technology Partners value technical and research skills as "capacity building"	Training and use of digital or visual technologies: digital photography and video, multimedia archives and stories, GPS/GIS, blogging	Digital image circulation "Opening the archive" through Internet	Modular units versus "whole stories" Challenges of presenting complex multimedia projects in journals
Ethics	Ethical principles after Said, *Writing Culture*, and feminist anthropology Decision to pursue PAR IRB process Community IRBs	Training research teams Consent in visual research Learning the local ethical landscape Despite efforts, some researcher/subject distinction persists Ongoing reflection in situ	Who participates in PAR discussions? How are these facilitated? Discussion of how data will be presented and used in next phase of research? Role of the anthropologist?	Image ethics: attention to the context where images are consumed "Circulatory regimes" (Ginsberg, 2008): hard to maintain control in digital environments Internet: uneven access, may not be inclusive

(*Continued*)

Table 1-1 (*Continued*)

	Research Design/ Preproduction	Data Collection/ Production	Data Analysis/ Postproduction	Dissemination and Application
Knowledge production	Research goals: intentions in tension What is "interesting and important"? Funding and planning, especially in international	"Emic" perspectives in focus: participants choose where to point the lens Metaresearch: participant observation of participants' observation Interplay of perspectives: inside/outside academic/activist anthro/ interdisciplinary	Description-analysis-action Visual documentation Visual elicitation A place for stories Negotiated meaning Member check for validity	Multipronged approach Accessibility, language New venues and forms Room for affective and aesthetic elements Informed action as a research outcome Academic recognition

[t]he problem with contemporary anthropological ethics is not merely that the boundaries of what is defined as ethical are too narrowly drawn, but more importantly, that ethics can be subject to rigid, righteous interpretations which place them at loggerheads with over-arching human rights concerns. (p. 113)

While participant consent and assurance of confidentiality are important aspects of ethical research practice—and something that we duly address in the chapter—we must also broaden ethical considerations to address the ways that power differentials affect the process of participatory research, as well as its outcomes and manner of dissemination. Dimensions of power include considerations of the ways that rapport and trust is built in the research process, the type of reciprocity accorded in the process with the communities and community members involved, and a recognition of power (im)balances inherent to matters of representation, to name a few.

Finally, we end by linking precursors of these methods—especially the theoretical and epistemological crisis in anthropology in the 1980s—to the development of participatory or collaborative research designs. In so doing, we review the differences between academic/social research and community organization goals and the uses of social research, both in terms of applied and basic research purposes. In particular, we discuss how these two sets of goals and purposes might be interwoven to "open up" the research design process through the use of participatory visual and digital methodologies.

Chapters 4 through 8 are each devoted to a particular visual and/or digital method that might be used in conducting participatory research: Photovoice, participatory film and videomaking, digital storytelling, PGIS, and participatory digital archives and exhibition. In each chapter we introduce the method and accompanying techniques involved. We then briefly provide a historical overview of the method, introducing the reader to pioneering scholars who helped to establish the method in the field. Finally, we present two to three "core methodology stories" of researcher/practitioners—all pioneering scholars in their own right—who have used the methods in their work. Such core stories cover the gamut of recent participatory visual/digital research projects, from those focusing on environmental and public health issues to youth activism and community development, and draw upon fieldwork conducted in communities in the United States, Canadian First Nations, eastern Europe, southern Africa, Oceania, and beyond.

Overwhelmingly, these core stories discuss potential ethical issues to be addressed when conducting projects using participatory visual and digital methods. Indeed, future scholars should heed the voices of the seasoned scholars presented in this book, as we believe their cases build a collective "how-to" guide for conducting ethically conscious social research. They present on-the-ground examples of ethical issues to be considered by social researchers when using participatory visual/digital methods, including: community building and decision-making when designing research projects; voice, representation, and power when producing digital/visual texts, and concomitant academic, community, and activist roles in the process; target audiences for dissemination of research products and modes of dissemination; and participants as knowledge producers and agents of change.

As scholar-activists using participatory visual/digital methods ourselves, we are particularly keen on exploring the nexus between the benefits provided by these methods for conducting ethnography and ethical and epistemological dilemmas elicited through their use. On the one hand, the methods grant researchers access to participants' emic categories, while offering participants more control in the creation of ethnographic representations. On the other hand, new ethical dilemmas arise as to who participates in the research process and who has the right to show or manage the products of research collaborations.

In addition, where PAR approaches are concerned, scholars using the methods need to incorporate some amount of reflexivity with regard to recent social science critiques of taken-for-granted concepts, such as the "community" (Creed, 2006) and "participation," and the ways these terms may be exploited in the name of getting research done. We are also interested in pursuing how social researchers using these methods reconcile the recent visual anthropology critique of the image-as-commodity or agent for reification of cultural identity. Responses to these quandaries hold ramifications for the production and consumption of visual representations, as well as for research participants. They also integrally affect the ways we might reconceptualize data analysis, and how we represent our data in research outputs or as "products."

In Chapter 9, we take a close look at traditional forms of ethnographic data analysis, as well as at the tenets of participatory research, which ask that we as researchers be self-reflexive when it comes to our process for conducting research and the ways we construct and represent research findings-outcomes. In particular, we describe more recent dialogic/participatory approaches to data analysis (Tedlock, 1995) that encourage shifting roles for the academic researcher and the research "subject" to those based on a more equitable relationship. We present several exemplars of a re-visioned analytical approach for participatory research that speak to the need for reciprocity when analyzing and producing research findings, as well as to reconsider our audiences when conducting social research in this now virtual age. We end the chapter by discussing how academic texts might be created based on a participatory approach that moves beyond written text, using new media to share our research with diverse audiences. Furthermore, we consider how emergent forms of knowledge production might affect scholarly publishing and what we might consider as venues for research in this new age.

We end the book perhaps with more questions asked than answers given. Several key questions apply to the emergence of participatory visual/digital methodologies, such as where are these methodologies leading the social sciences, and how do these methodologies respond to the call to recapture ethnography? We hope that this book will provoke future dialog on these questions, particularly in terms of the implications of the methodologies for the training of new social researchers, and of the goals we ultimately seek in social research knowledge production.

CHAPTER 2

Participatory Visual and Digital Research in Theory and Practice

INTRODUCTION

There is a growing interest in the social sciences in participatory and collaborative methods that use visual and digital media, which is reflected in an increasing number of publications and project websites each year. This rising tide is also demonstrated by the growing range and creativity of such research, from veteran visual anthropologist Jay Ruby's ethnographic multimedia suite, *Oak Park Stories* (Ruby, 2007), to the varied projects presented in sociologist Phillip Vannini's *Popularizing Research* (Vannini, 2012). Why are these approaches proliferating at this moment?

In this chapter, we present the theoretical context of the turn toward participatory visual and digital research in the social sciences, and maps out a process for translating theory into practice. The multipronged critique of traditional ethnography—articulated by postcolonial, feminist, and postmodern scholars since the 1970s and 1980s—has pressed qualitative social scientists to reconsider earlier positivist approaches and the power imbalance inherent in fieldwork on and academic writing about historically oppressed groups. Engaged scholars have turned to participatory visual and digital methods as a means of responding to these varied intellectual critiques in their research practice. Yet many of us have stumbled into these methods, learning as we go through trial and error. For those trying to move from critical theory to practice, we provide a roadmap for navigating participatory research design, selecting appropriate visual/digital methods, and documenting the research process.

Participatory Visual and Digital Methods by Aline Gubrium and Krista Harper, 27–43. ©2013 Left Coast Press Inc. All rights reserved.

Intellectual Foundations: Deconstructing and Decolonizing Ethnography

Many critical social scientists in the qualitative research tradition have embraced participatory and visual/multimedia approaches in response to the varied criticisms leveled at traditional ethnography. Ethnography developed as a social science methodology within the disciplinary contexts of colonial-era anthropology and the Chicago School of urban sociology. Both of these research traditions seek to study social and cultural settings holistically and to gain insight into participants' understandings through immersive participant observation and interviews. Ethnographers sought to produce rich, holistic descriptions of the groups they studied, but they also strove to retain a sense of detachment for fear of "going native" and thus making themselves vulnerable to the charge that ethnographic research was less "objective" than other social sciences based on quantitative and experimental methodologies.

In the "crisis of representation" beginning in the 1970s, postcolonial, feminist, and postmodern scholars criticized this traditional, objectivist stance. Postcolonial scholars drew attention to issues of power, trust, and ownership in ethnographic research as well as the ways in which literary tropes within academic writing reinforced the differences between "the West" and racially marked, colonized "Others" (Asad, 1973; Hymes, 1974; Said, 1979; Spivak, 1988). In *Time and the Other*, for example, Johannes Fabian accused traditional anthropological accounts of the "denial of coevalness . . . a persistent and systematic tendency to place the referent(s) of anthropology in a Time other than the present of the producer of anthropological discourse" (Fabian, 1983, p. 31). The ethnographic encounter itself is based on methods in which the researcher and research participants contemporaneously experience events and engage in dialogue, but ethnographers often downplayed this intersubjective quality to conform to norms of objectivity in scientific writing. This denial, rooted in colonial attitudes and class hegemony, creates distance between the ethnographer and research participants by rhetorically fixing colonized people and peasants in the past. Fabian proposed that ethnographers create further distance in their texts through a "visualism" that privileges the ethnographer's observations over fieldwork dialogs or participants' observations (Fabian, 1983, p. 107). Failure to recognize research participants as coevals, whether rooted in temporal or visual rhetorics, holds back the emancipatory and humanistic potential of ethnography for recognizing other people's lived understandings of the contemporary world.

Parallel to the postcolonial critique, feminist scholars noted how traditional ethnographies had neglected women's social worlds and drew attention to the gendered experiences of women ethnographers in the field (Bell & Caplan, 1993; Rosaldo & Lamphere, 1974). Black feminists and other feminists of color pioneered the theories of intersectionality, calling for scholars to analyze how race, along with gender- and class-based oppression (among other forms) cut across one another in a single participant's lived experience (Collins, 2000; Combahee River Collective, 1983; Davis, 1981). They also challenged all feminist scholars to acknowledge their subject position, between the elite world of the academy and the often-marginalized worlds of their research participants (Behar & Gordon, 1995). Still, the ethnographic method is well suited for feminist inquiry, with its close attention to daily experience and emphasis on empathy and interpersonal connection as a way of making knowledge (Stacey, 1988). These critiques emphasize that any feminist undertaking should take multiple perspectives, rather than a unified account of womanhood, as its starting assumption.

Like feminist scholars, postmodern critics pointed out that the objectivist stance of traditional ethnographers created its own blinders and biases by masking the power-laden, intersubjective qualities of the research encounter (Clifford & Marcus, 1986; Marcus & Fischer, 1986). They encouraged ethnographers to place themselves self-reflexively within their texts and to show the messy, dialogic quality of the fieldwork encounter. Donna Haraway characterized this self-reflexive stance as producing "situated knowledges," a corrective to the "view from nowhere" of positivist social science (Haraway, 1988).

Twenty-five years ago, ethnographers faced their critics and responded with an "experimental moment" of innovative, self-reflexive texts that used diverse writing styles to represent multiple voices within a single text (Behar, 2003; Tsing, 1993). This experimental moment focused mainly on the writing of social research for scholarly audiences, and much less on applying and communicating research outside the academy. Since then, postcolonial, feminist, and other activist scholars pushed the critique of ethnography beyond the production of academic texts into the practical work of decolonizing the research process (Castelden & Huuay-aht First Nation, 2008; Hale, 2008; Hemment, 2007; Smith, 1999). This moment marks a move from the "literary turn" of deconstruction to the "participatory turn" of collaborative research.

Intellectual Foundations: The Participatory Action Research Tradition

The participatory action research (PAR) tradition offers a well-developed framework for breaking down barriers between researchers and "subjects" and between analysis and praxis. PAR attempts to forge collaborative research relationships in which community partners take an active role in studying problems alongside a traditional researcher to develop strategies for change. Yvonne Wadsworth writes: "participatory action research is not just research which we hope will be followed by action. . . . It is action which is researched, changed and re-researched, within the research process by participants" (Wadsworth, 1998). Participatory action research begins from the following premises: 1) that all knowledge is socially constructed; 2) that the goal of social research is to inform practice and social change; and 3) that "cogenerative inquiry," in which local and professional knowledge interact, produces valid, context-centered knowledge (Greenwood & Levin, 2005). The basic model for PAR is the "research-action-reflection cycle" (McNiff, 1988).

PAR acknowledges and attempts to redress power inequalities inherent in knowledge production. The Mass Observation Project was a precursor of PAR and an example of systematic, collaborative social scientific documentation by laypeople. This popular literacy project was initiated in 1937 by Tom Harrison, a British social anthropologist, and Charles Madge, a journalist drawn to surrealism as an intellectual movement (Summerfield, 1985). Harrison and Madge developed this method of social documentation in response to media representations of British life that they felt obscured everyday people's perspectives on events. They invited ordinary people around the United Kingdom to contribute observations and reflections related to specific events and themes several times a year. The majority of participants were lower-middle-class civil servants, teachers, clerks, and housewives, as well as some educated industrial tradesmen. The Mass Observation Project was launched on May 12, 1937, the coronation day of George VI. Harrison and Madge asked one group of participants to write a subjective, daylong journal of their activities, placing them in the role of active research informants creating their own narratives. They instructed a second group of participants to record what they saw and heard throughout that day, using an objectivist mode of ethnographic writing and excluding the writers' own responses. When placed alongside one another, these observations elicited and presented what Harrison and Madge called "the social consciousness of the time" (Summerfield, 1985, p. 443). The Mass Observation Project prefigured the rise of British cultural studies and the postmodern critique of ethnography by several decades (MacClancy, 1995). The Project continues today: its archives have been used by journalists and historians to write about changing British views on sexuality, national identity, and health experiences (Sheridan, 1994; Sheridan, Street, & Bloome, 2000).

Continuing the tradition of engaging community members in social scientific research, PAR developed as a methodology between the Global North and South by scholars working in the fields of critical literacy pedagogy, social psychology, feminist inquiry, and grassroots community development. Social psychologist Kurt Lewin coined the term "action research" in his work on the social problems of minority communities in the United States after World War II (Lewin, 1946). Working during the same time period in northeastern Brazil, Paulo Freire led research and action in literacy pedagogy, working with impoverished rural people to develop practical skills and critical consciousness of oppressive social relationships (Freire, 2000[1970]). He influenced national education policy, leading to the development of thousands of popular cultural centers before being imprisoned and exiled during Brazil's military coup of 1964. Colombian sociologist Orlando Fals-Borda engaged peasants in PAR and studied the development of rural cooperatives. Meanwhile, Greenwood and Santos used PAR to study worker-managed factories in Spain (Greenwood & Santos, 1992). In East Africa, Dani Wadada Nabudere and his colleagues founded a network of institutes rooted in PAR traditions (Nabudere, 2008). And in the United States, Michelle Fine developed PAR working with low-income women (Fine, 1994), prisoners (Fine et al., 2004), and youth (Cammarota & Fine, 2008), and cofounded the Public Science Project, a PAR "science shop" (Torre, 2012).

PAR methods respond to a legacy of "extractive" social science, in which researchers descend upon a community, collect data for academic publications and policy reports, and then disappear without reciprocating the time and knowledge that participants have shared. Even when researchers share their final reports, participants may not recognize themselves in the academic language and theoretical questions. This unequal exchange has historically led to "research fatigue" in the marginalized communities and indigenous groups typically studied by social scientists, fueling a general distrust of academic researchers. "Nothing about us without us," the rallying cry of urban social movements, is relevant to social scientific research practice as well as to political processes. Similarly, indigenous communities are asserting more control over the research process and challenging scholars to develop projects collaboratively, and with clear benefits to the community studied (Castelden & Huu-ay-aht First Nation, 2008). PAR emerged with the development of applied social research, and its practitioners presented new ways of opening up the research process to collaboration with participants. And visual researchers moved from a naïve positivist stance focused on photographs and film as evidence to a critical reckoning with culturally constructed "ways of seeing" (Berger, 1972) and power relationships between photographer and subject. The growing popularity of PAR and other collaborative research methods reflects this shift away from the "extractive" model of social science toward a more "enriching" community-engaged model (Rhoades, 2006, p. 2).

Intellectual Foundations: Visual Research in the Social Sciences

Social scientists have used participatory visual research strategies in a number of ways, ranging from empirical to reflexive. Both visual research in the social sciences and documentary photography have developed over the course of the twentieth century. Early visual anthropologists countered the academic preference for text over visual media by emphasizing the technical advantages of using photos and film to systematically and unobtrusively record social practices (Mead & Bateson, 1977). The 1960s marked a shift toward collaborative work in visual anthropology, from ethnographic filmmaker Jean Rouch's call for a "shared anthropology" to Worth and Adair's participatory filmmaking project, *Navajo Film Themselves* (Ruby, 2000).

Around this time, Paulo Freire brought visual methods into the PAR field through his work on literacy and critical consciousness among the poorest urban communities of South America by introducing drawings and photos as elicitation tools for discussions. In his work in Peru, Freire and his colleague Augusto Boal invited impoverished children to produce their own images with inexpensive "Brownie" cameras for discussion of the forms of exploitation they experienced (Boal, 1979; Freire, 2000[1970]; Singhal et al., 2007). Freire and Boal gained a sense of the texture of the children's daily lives and early experiences of patron-client relationships, as well as a renewed appreciation of participatory photography and photo elicitation through this work.

Marcus Banks presents critical and collaborative approaches to visual anthropology as a response to the deconstruction of ethnographic objectivity: a way of recognizing the research participants' role in knowledge production (Banks, 2001, 2007). Banks recounts a moment in his fieldwork when, while taking photos of a feast in India, his research participants encouraged him to take a picture of a woman serving a special yogurt dish to male guests who were breaking a religious fast. By directing him to create this image, they communicated the social significance of the woman who had, unusually for a woman, hosted the feast, as well as drawing attention to the lavish, festive dessert. "Analytically, I 'knew' the social facts, but by being directed to capture them on film I was made aware of . . . the power of photography to legitimize them" (Banks, 2001, p. 47).

Contemporary "visual interventions" (Pink, 2007) are a hybrid offshoot of collaborative image-making and Freirean approaches to participatory action research. Visual interventions may include photography, film, or digital media. Collaborative methods of participatory filmmaking and photography arrived in the first wave of visual interventions, and more recently, researchers have modified these methods to highlight their usefulness for community organizing and policy interventions (Biella, 2008). The rise of digital and Internet communication technologies offers an even wider palette of visual tools for PAR and for communicating beyond the academy.

In practical terms, participatory visual researchers should be critically aware of the multiple facets and uses of photos, maps, and film: as documentary evidence; as a prompt for eliciting responses; and as a form of material culture, a source of power, and as social capital (Banks, 2007). We often use images and multimedia as a form of documentation: in other words, as evidence of events and conditions. Marcus Banks writes: "Euro-American society has constructed photography—and in due course, videotape—as a transparent medium, one that unequivocally renders a visual truth" (Banks, 2001, p. 42). While this sense of realism makes photography and film powerful forms of communication, it conceals how images are selected at the moment of focusing and picture-taking and further manipulated through basic aesthetic choices such as cropping. We can learn about the world from what a photograph or film captures, but as Banks warns, "[it] is not merely a neutral document or record of things that took place before the camera, but a *representation* of those things, persons, and events intended to explain society and its processes" (Banks, 2007, pp. 12–13).

Photos, films, and other visual representations can also serve as discussion prompts in social research. Visual elicitation is a major methodological component in Photovoice, digital storytelling, participatory filmmaking, and participatory archival research. Elicitation strategies include the use of interviews or focus groups for discussion of images generated by the researcher, by participants, from archives, or from popular media. Images may be used as a memory aid, jogging a participant's memory by illustrating past conditions or faces. They also "break the ice" in interview settings by offering a shared focus for the researcher and participant and relief from eye contact with an unfamiliar person (Banks, 2007; M. Collier, 1986).

Visual and digital images are also artifacts of material culture, a fact with consequences for knowledge production. Size, annotations, or other signs of use on photographs convey information about the intended audience or display practices. Very small photographs convey portability ("wallet-sized"), while standard snapshots are sized for storing in photo albums. Photographic subjects may feel comfortable seeing themselves in snapshots or videos but have stronger feelings—of pride or painful exposure—to seeing themselves portrayed "larger than life" in a poster print or on a projected screen.

The digitization of images allows wider access and helps to preserve film and photographs, but it poses new problems as well. Without careful curating, the context of visual material—the social processes leading to a group of photos being collected in one place—may be lost. A research participant who brings a box of family photos to digitize for a digital storytelling project or a participatory archive will select only a small subset of images to use, but unused images and the participant's selection process may provide important additional data. When conducting participatory visual research, researchers should attempt to record as much contextual information as possible.

Visual images can also act as a source of power and social capital. Indeed, researchers consciously choose participatory visual methods so that members of oppressed groups may challenge dominant representations and make themselves seen and heard. Learning to produce photographs, film, or digital media can be empowering. In Brazil during the 1980s, indigenous Kayapo people began taking their own films of themselves and assembling video equipment for their own productions with the help of academic anthropologists (Turner, 1992). The Kayapo not only used video as evidence of events, they also self-consciously presented images of themselves videotaping while wearing paint and feathers to draw attention to their political grievances. The group gained visibility and status in the international media by juxtaposing their use of high-tech media with physical markers of being indigenous (and therefore "primitive").

At the local level, individuals who gain access to digital technology or control over images may gain social capital within their communities. When Aboriginal Australians began making videos and producing television programs in the 1980s, new power dynamics emerged within the community between young, tech-savvy indigenous producers and their elders (Michaels, 1985). Visual observation may also act as a form of social control, or surveillance (Foucault, 1979). Photographers, even those from oppressed groups, must be sensitive to the power of being behind the camera.

Finally, if we see visual and digital media as socially constructed artifacts, we need to be self-reflexive about how these representations are made within our own participatory research projects. For Banks, being self-reflexive means examining the "external narrative" of images: "Researchers must ask themselves questions to elucidate the external narrative (why does this image exist? who created it? what is its biography?) as well as the internal narrative (what is this image of?)" (Banks, 2001, p. 114).

Banks cites photographer Victor Caldarola's principles for visual self-reflexivity: event specificity, context dependence, and social production.

"Event specificity" means that we should treat photographs as representations of particular moments, rather than the "typical scenes" used to illustrate traditional ethnography. "Context dependence" means that the meaning of visual representations comes not only from their content, but also from knowledge of the setting where the photo was taken. Context also includes paying attention to dominant visual tropes that photographers may replicate or disrupt. "Social production" means that visual social scientists must pay attention to the social relationships contributing to picture-taking: between the photographer, research collaborators, photographic subjects, and other people present.

In participatory visual and digital projects, it is not just the researcher who needs to be savvy about the basics of visual analysis and self-reflexivity: research participants also need to develop critical awareness of visual representations. In the next sections, we discuss how to include participants meaningfully in research design, how to use visual and digital media appropriately, and how to document the research process so that participants and researchers can consider their practice self-reflexively.

PUTTING IT ALL INTO PRACTICE: PARTICIPATORY VISUAL AND DIGITAL RESEARCH DESIGN

Participatory visual and digital research, like other methodologies originating in ethnography, demands that the fieldworker design a research project while remaining open and flexible to participants' interests and the realities of the field site. Van Maanen evokes jazz improvisation when he describes the work of the ethnographer as being "more akin to learning to play a musical instrument than to solving a puzzle. . . . [W]hat a fieldworker learns is how to appreciate the world in a different key" (Van Maanen, 1988, p. 118; see also Humphreys, Brown, & Hatch, 2003). It is hard to plan projects with any sensitivity without first knowing the local setting and consulting participants, but academics usually need to plan and design their research prior to fieldwork, given the demands of grant-writing and institutional review boards (Pink, 2007). The more a researcher knows about the community—whether learned from direct exchange with participants, previous fieldwork experience in the setting, or library research—the better they will be able to anticipate how to approach the collaboration.

The starting point of any PAR project is discussion between academic and community researchers to map out common goals and expectations for the project. Academics must be prepared to underscore the value of community co-researchers' insider knowledge and to "demystify" research by explaining methods in accessible language (Tang, 2008, p. 247).

The team should discuss the purpose, scope, methods, and desired audiences, products, or outcomes of the research. This is also a moment to develop clear expectations about what practical resources community members may expect to support their participation, such as snacks for an after-school youth project, childcare, transportation, and/or honoraria.

Collaborative research projects demand good communication and organization skills. It is important to find out collaborators' preferred ways to communicate (email, cell phone, home phone, face-to-face conversation, etc.) and to note this information in a project contacts file. The team should establish norms for group communication so that all members feel included and trust that their voices will be taken seriously. This is as important for email and phone communication as for holding face-to-face discussions. Academic researchers spend time checking email each day, but email may be difficult to access for some participants. Projects involving a very diverse set of participants, for example, youth and elderly members of a community, may require a plan for communicating by text messages (to the youth) and by telephone calls (to elders). Even if all collaborators use email, hashing out expectations ahead of time can improve communication later. When sending an email to plan an event, for example, knowing which people should be copied (cc'ed) prevents misunderstandings and hurt feelings.

It can take months to set up a community-based research project and to complete the university human subjects review process, but when the actual project is launched, the tempo of work is fast.

MATCHING METHODS TO QUESTIONS AND CONTEXTS

Once the project team is assembled, they must determine whether (or which) visual methodologies are appropriate, taking into consideration the research questions to be explored and compatibility of visual and digital technologies with local contexts and visual practices. Researchers must also anticipate ethical issues specific to visual methods such as potential harms and benefits to photographic subjects and control, maintenance, and ownership of images and research materials (Pink, 2007).

Teams should get a clear idea of the research questions they would like to explore before settling on a specific method, and then match methods to questions (see Table 2-1). Participatory visual research pursues the kinds of questions that are typical of other forms of applied and policy-oriented qualitative research. These include contextual, diagnostic, evaluative, and strategic questions (Ritchie & Spencer, 2002), as well as self-reflexive questions that explore the experiences of researchers and participants in knowledge production. Some visual media and

Table 2-1 Participatory visual and digital methods: Matching the method to the project

Method	Types of Questions	Types of Data Produced	Technology	Training Requirements	Benefits	Limitations
Photovoice	What are community concerns? What stories are told related to the project themes? What images and metaphors are salient among participants? How do participants negotiate conflicting interpretations? How are stories received by other audiences?	Photographs, photo-elicitation discussions, producer and audience texts	Film or digital cameras, photo-editing software, computer, audio recorder	LOW -Ethics -Basic or intermediate photography	Easy to use with participants varying in skills or literacy. Photos reusable in popular forms such as *fotonovelas*. Photo exhibition may be planned as a networking or discussion event.	Photos paired with captions may be less rich than filmed or multimedia narratives. Photo exhibitions require time and money for mounting photos.
Participatory video	What are community concerns? What are important cultural practices and how are these performed? How do people move or use space?	Narratives, documentation of events, video-elicitation discussions, producer and audience texts	Video cameras ranging from phone cameras to professional, editing software, computer	MEDIUM TO HIGH -Ethics -Video production -Digital editing using software	Excellent medium for showing performance, 360° context, movement. Accessibility to wider audiences.	Requires strong participant interest in developing media skills. Time-consuming.

(Continued)

Table 2-1 (Continued)

Method	Types of Questions	Types of Data Produced	Technology	Training Requirements	Benefits	Limitations
Digital storytelling	How is identity socially constructed? What types of stories are told about an event or experience? How are stories received by audiences? How does the workshop process affect participants?	Life histories, narratives, producer and audience texts	Computers, editing software, audio recorder, scanners, cameras	MEDIUM -Ethics -Digital multimedia software	Strongly focused on participant's story, builds technological capacities of participants.	Time-consuming, participant-intensive, workshop size prevents large samples.
Participatory GIS (PGIS)	How do participants' experience a place? What is left out of official maps? How are places associated with relationships, knowledge, or stories?	Multilayered GIS maps, map-elicitation discussions, producer and audience texts	GPS marking units, GIS software (ranging in user-friendliness), computer, audio recorder	LOW TO HIGH -Ethics -Use of GPS -GIS software	Shows spatial relationships and routes, GIS maps useful in policy and planning.	Presenting geospatial coordinates can be ethically sensitive.
Participatory digital archives and virtual exhibitions	How do participants understand the past? What stories are told? What meanings are attached to people, places, and artifacts? How do different participants negotiate conflicting meanings and stories? How are stories received by new audiences?	Primary collections, digital elicitation discussions (online or in-person), producer and audience texts	Camera, scanner, database or blog software (ranging in user-friendliness), computer, audio recorder	LOW TO HIGH -Ethics -Digital photography and scanning -Web or database design	Involves participants or descendants in curating a record of the community, makes archival materials available to broader public.	Not all artifacts or materials may be appropriately presented online when there are specific cultural prohibitions.

techniques are better than others for a given research task. Photovoice and participatory video are both good techniques for eliciting community concerns to be considered in designing research questions, particularly when used in combination with photo or video elicitation. Video is the best method for showing how actions or rituals are performed and how people move and express themselves in real time. Video and digital storytelling allow us to study the stories people tell about events or experiences. Participatory GIS is well suited for "where?" questions about the social use of spaces, the history of a place, or the distribution of resources or risks in a neighborhood. And participatory archives and exhibitions allow us to ask questions about the meaning of the past and the significance of artifacts to contemporary groups of people.

Matching methods to the social context and available technological resources is also crucially important. Researchers need to learn about the local meanings and cultural conventions around photos and other media. One practitioner working in rural El Salvador sent a group of indigenous women out with cameras, who were then ridiculed as pretentious for taking pictures (Prins, 2010). The researcher was embarrassed by this experience, but she learned about the power relationships affecting peasant women's daily lives, and the *campesina* women felt greater confidence and power from taking pictures and discussing their experiences. Prins' work using Photovoice is discussed in more depth in Chapter 4.

The age of the participants shapes the research design process as well. Doing participatory digital research with youth poses challenges for scholars who are accustomed to working with adults. Working with photography, video, and technology is especially attractive to youth participants, and given the opportunity, they can make powerful contributions to community-based needs assessments and evaluations (K. S. Flores, 2008). Youth may balk, however, at lecture-based training in ethics or research methods, particularly if they have already attended a full day of school.

A community's technological resources—in the form of equipment and skills—should also be taken into account. One PAR project involving GIS mapping of a New Orleans neighborhood hit by Hurricane Katrina failed because the GIS software required a level of technological skill that alienated many of the residents it aimed to include (West & Peterson, 2009). On the other hand, individuals and communities can benefit greatly from the equipment and training provided by academic partners. Digital storytelling trains participants in several software programs, building people's technological capacities and overall computer confidence as they create multimedia stories.

When the research team deliberates on using a specific visual method, it should consider potential ethical issues. As we discuss the ethics of participatory visual methods in detail in Chapter 3, here we just briefly mention ethical issues associated with specific techniques. Techniques based on participant-generated photography and video raise the likelihood of showing identifiable faces; so for projects where confidentiality is crucial, participants may need to frame pictures in ways that avoid showing faces. In other projects based on the model of community oral history, showing faces is less problematic. The use of GIS may expose contested land claims that bring up animosities within the community, for example, and in this case, research teams should weigh the benefits against the tensions caused by mapping. The team might design a GIS project that marks locations of cultural sites but consciously avoids representing property boundary lines, or they might choose instead to use Photovoice to gather images and stories about cultural sites without introducing maps at all. The research team must also consider the ethical implications of displaying and disseminating images and films. In the case of Harper's Photovoice project (detailed in Chapter 4), the team decided that exhibitions should ask the audience to engage in some way, whether in the form of direct dialog, a facilitated discussion, or at a minimum a guestbook addressed to the community team. These forms of engagement moved the exhibition away from a "human zoo" model the team wished to avoid. All participatory visual methods result in new visual data that, once produced, can be used in ways that no one can completely foresee. But researchers and research participants should nevertheless do their best to anticipate potential uses and ethical issues and address these as thoroughly as possible.

Ultimately, it may be the case that visual and digital methods are too problematic for use in a specific setting. If the technologies are so foreign to the site as to be deemed inappropriate by participants, if media poses insurmountable ethical issues, or if participants are not interested in these technologies, researchers may need to choose a different approach to carrying out PAR in the community. Visual and digital methods provide powerful tools for engaging participants and communicating to new audiences, but they are just the means, not the ends of the collaborative research process.

When the team has designed a workable plan, academic researchers can help community co-researchers envision the trajectory of the project by creating a timeline or other visual aids showing when research activities will take place and who will be involved at each stage. Participatory projects are not driven by a single person, so the group must discuss next steps and agree on specific individuals to complete each task. At the same time, even participatory research requires a point person—often the academic researcher—who keeps track of the "big picture" and who brings together the team to revisit the timeline throughout the project. These checkpoints remind the group of the original goals, what they have achieved so far, and what parts of the research need to be adjusted as the team learns more and assembles a body of data.

BEYOND FIELD NOTES: DOCUMENTING THE PARTICIPATORY VISUAL RESEARCH PROCESS

Once the team agrees on a research design, the exciting work of carrying out data collection and producing new images or media may begin. Very quickly, the team will generate a mountain of photos, video footage, and other media materials. Since visual elicitation techniques are usually part of the data collection process, researchers will also record interviews and focus group discussions in which participants comment on visual prompts. And researchers can expect to spend time writing traditional field notes as well (Emerson, Fretz, & Shaw, 2011; Schensul, Schensul, & LeCompte, 1999).

Researcher-produced data and participant productions are what we call "primary data." Primary data include forms of evidence documenting participants' perspectives on events and phenomena that are the main "topic" of research. Primary data also consist of our detailed descriptions and representations of what is happening in the field site on a day-to-day basis. Data in this category, taken on their own, are like the field notes, recordings, and transcriptions of traditional qualitative research, distinguished only by the special attention paid to visual images and media objects themselves.

Just as critical ethnography no longer views field notes and interviews as "transparent" (Briggs, 1986; Holstein & Gubrium, 1995) objective data, critical visual research has come to treat fieldwork images and media as socially produced representations. Jay Ruby writes of this shift:

> In a postpositivist and postmodern world, the camera is constrained by the culture of the person behind the apparatus; that is, films and photographs are always concerned with two things—the culture of those filmed and the culture of those who film. (Ruby, 1996, p. 345)

Participatory visual researchers should not only document the primary data of interviews and observations, but also "producer data": the producers' motivations and decisions in making visual representations. This

can be done by taking notes on and/or recording and transcribing production workshop discussions or team sessions to review participants'
images or video. If community producers are comfortable with journal
writing, they can keep diaries tracking the creative process. Later, in
the data analysis stage, these "producer texts" may be analyzed as self-
reflexive forms of data.

Audience response is a final category of data relevant to participatory
visual research. Audience data document how target audiences respond
to the media produced through the collaborative research process. Since
teams usually conduct participatory visual research with the goal of communicating to other community members, policymakers, or the general
public, they may want to know how those groups interpret the "finished
product," whether it is a photo exhibition, a video, or a multimedia
archive. Audience responses may be collected by holding visual elicitation interviews or focus groups, by collecting written feedback forms at
events and screenings, or by creating a Web 2.0 forum for comments on an
online multimedia project page. Audience data can help research teams
learn whether viewers understood the producers' intended messages or if
they developed alternative interpretations of images and narratives.

New technology and software programs can ease the burden of keeping track of three categories of data recorded in written text, image and
audio files, and other media. Digital cameras now provide time stamps
and geospatial markers automatically, and software such as iPhoto offers
face-recognition capabilities that, although imperfect, speed the process
of organizing collections. Qualitative data analysis (QDA) software programs such as Atlas.ti, NVivo, and MaxQDA allow us to apply many
categories or tags to the same piece of data: for example, one item can
simultaneously be labeled with a participant's name (or pseudonym), the
source "interview," and the data type (e.g., "producer data"), all prior to
analytic coding. Finally, the researcher must regularly back up the data
on external hard drives or a secure, password-protected online storage
drive.

Collecting and organizing three layers of data takes time and energy,
but it pays off in terms of greater critical consciousness and self-reflexivity
within the team and the knowledge of reaching an audience beyond the
academy. Researchers gain sharper focus and a new understanding of
shades of meaning when we bring together the three forms of data: primary, producer, and audience. By doing "research within research" on
the creation and reception of our knowledge, we make knowledge that,
starting from specific researchers' and participants' standpoints, moves
toward broader translation and application beyond the specific community studied (Nabudere, 2008).

CONCLUDING THOUGHTS

Every participatory visual/digital method we discuss has exciting possibilities, but no single method is appropriate for all projects. These methods map nicely to "classic" ethnographic methods, such as immersive participant observation and in-depth interviewing, which may serve as a first step in developing a participatory project. These "classics" allow the researcher to gain the contextual knowledge and develop the social relationships needed to design a participatory project that is contextually appropriate, logistically feasible, and ethically aware.

But participatory visual and digital methods are unusually effective in opening up the research process to collaboration. They link together PAR strategies and visual media in ways that change relationships in and after fieldwork. Participatory visual and digital research moves toward the goal of decolonizing knowledge in four important ways. First, it blurs the lines between researcher and research subject by involving participants during and after the fieldwork stage as co-creators of research products such as films, photo exhibitions, or multimedia websites. Second, it carefully documents and re-presents the collaborative research process, encouraging social scientists to write self-reflexively. Third, the research team may become conscious of and challenge visual stereotypes as they produce new images from within the community, avoiding the decontextualized "visualism" from above that Fabian criticizes (Fabian, 1983). Finally, the research itself may have more ongoing relevance to the group studied because it is communicated using accessible media that may be reaccessed and repurposed over time. Photos from a Photovoice exhibition, for example, may be reused for presentations to policymakers or may later become part of a community's online digital archive. By coming to see our research participants as co-designers, co-investigators, co-analysts, and co-producers of knowledge, we recognize that people once categorized as "research subjects" are our coevals, and translate this recognition into practice. In so doing, we respond to feminist, postcolonial, and postmodern critics who each in their own way have challenged us to change the way we do ethnography.

CHAPTER 3

Participatory Digital Research Ethics

FOUR "ETHICAL MOMENTS" IN PARTICIPATORY VISUAL AND DIGITAL RESEARCH

All participatory and digital research projects involve an "ethical sequence" that, while varying with individual projects, typically presents four distinct moments: 1) the decision to take the participatory action research (PAR) path, which positions participation itself as a research ethic rooted in dialog; 2) the development of a research plan that reconciles scholarly goals and formal norms of institutional ethics (such as confidentiality) with collaborators' goals and PAR ethical norms of collaboration and accountability; 3) the presentation of research findings to scholarly audiences and the public in a way that acknowledges and/or addresses power and the ethics of representation; and 4) the shared control and ownership of research output, which may include visual materials and policy interventions, as well as scholarly knowledge and plans for further collaboration.

ETHICAL MOMENT 1: CHOOSING PAR, OR PARTICIPATION AS AN ETHIC

Our first ethical moment takes account of power dynamics within research practice, including how we define participation. This includes a dialogic, iterative praxis of action, reflection, and experiential learning, to position "participatory communication" as "egalitarian dialogue and the action that results from it" (Peterson, Antony, & Thomas, 2012). Participation as an ethic regards dialog as "reciprocal, horizontal rather than vertical in nature, and encourages self-reliance and self-confidence of interlocutors" (White, Nair, & Ascroft, 1994, p. 16). This shift in power dynamics holds huge implications for the relationships we build with those engaged during the research process, as well as for developing

Participatory Visual and Digital Methods by Aline Gubrium and Krista Harper, 45–67. ©2013 Left Coast Press Inc. All rights reserved.

a mind's eye toward reciprocal research outcomes, including the ways that findings are represented within and outside communities.

Relationships, Reciprocity, and Representation

Participatory digital work is fraught with tension, as one can never predict whether its outcomes will be beneficial or, instead, potentially harm participants. Writing about collaborative ethnography—the claim of many a participatory digital project—and noting this tension as a distinct possibility, Luke Eric Lassiter accedes that this is a chance he is willing to take.

> Indeed, the negotiated ethical commitments around which collaborative ethnography revolve represent first and foremost a choice, a choice on the part of ethnographers and their consultants to engage in a very particularly bounded co-construction of knowledge that is responsive to local needs and interests—and again, we might hope, to more global needs and interests. (Lassiter, 2006, p. 21)

Participatory visual methods do offer the potential to disrupt commonly accepted hierarchies between "experts," audiences, and members of local communities, and present an alternative to standard methods of media circulation, as stories are shared in local, national, and global settings and online.

Like Lassiter, we note a similar choice being made by those conducting participatory visual and digital projects. The projects offer special opportunities for building a more ethical relationship between research institutions and the communities they study and serve to create forums where participants learn, interrogate, and ground the abstract principles of research ethics. In part, participants may receive formal training in the ethical conduct of research as defined by university- and, sometimes, community-based institutional review boards (IRBs). At the same time, community participants themselves contribute to more ethically grounded research practice by providing local insight on university/community relationships, power dynamics, and daily practices (Flicker et al., 2007).

While visual and digital technologies make research more accessible and able to reach a wider range of audiences, they also present an added dimension when considering social and ethical relationships. Indeed, the social practice of participatory visual research is more complex than the traditional model of a researcher studying "subjects" or participants. It includes participants who might be "engaged researchers" using photos to document social realities one day, but then "research participants" in a taped focus group discussion of those images the next. Furthermore, the subjects of digital media, such as those photographed, form another group of people involved in the project whose level of participation varies depending on the context, but whose rights and well-being as research subjects must be taken into consideration.

Research Relationships: Teamwork, Communication, and Organization

Photovoice and other participatory research projects are rewarding, but to be effective they also demand good communication and organization skills. It can take weeks, months, or even years to establish a community-based research project and to complete the IRB process. All the same, it may be difficult to keep pace with the tempo of the project once it is launched. Unlike many scholarly projects, applied and participatory research often has an external deadline timed to policy decisions. Researchers adopting a participatory or collaborative approach must have systems in place for organizing diverse sources of data, for communicating effectively with collaborators, and for working in teams. Participatory projects require coordination between collaborators, which can only succeed with clear expectations and open lines of communication. Explicitly discussing project expectations at the start of the research process is essential. These should be revisited as new tasks and collaborators are brought into the project. The idea of the "lone ethnographer" is one anathema to participatory projects. Instead, the collaborating group, or team, must be able to discuss next steps and specify particular individuals to complete each project task. At the same time, as noted in Chapter 2, even participatory research requires a "big-picture person," who tracks and openly communicates the progress of the project and is also able to specify the next tasks at hand.

Means and Ends: Process Intent versus Outcome

Gready's (2010) call for a responsibility to our research story evokes a core tension of participatory digital work. On the participatory end of things, we tell our participants that the research process is beneficial to them because it "gives them a voice" by encouraging reflective conversation, catharsis, and empowerment. However, as social researchers we are conducting this work for data collection and analysis purposes. The tension lies in negotiating means and ends. For example, how does one proceed with a workshop—such as the story circle process in digital storytelling—all the while figuring project activities as a forum for conducting ethnographic research, without destroying the original intent of the workshop by having data collection "get in the way" and potentially disengage participants in the process?

And then how do you then shift from a research purpose—such as analyzing participatory digital processes and outcomes as a means of research—to the creation and repurposing of these products for more liberatory ends, responsibly shared as tools for advocacy? Researcher-facilitators must be particularly vigilant about avoiding the commodification of ends, which might be positioned as objects simply "collected" and used to benefit researcher or organizational agendas around publishing, grant writing, marketing, and public relations. From the start, the researcher must ensure clear goals for supporting the production and sharing of products that benefit participants and their communities.

In terms of the potential for commodification of ends, it is easy for researchers to become fascinated by others' experiences and to forget that they are listening to and working with actual human beings, with concomitant feelings, reactions, and needs. Viewing audiences may also be tempted to reify research products, such that they may come to be seen as "authentic" community representations, without proper attention given to their socio-historical contexts of production. This includes acknowledgment of the ways that participants strategically perform identities through production (Butler, 1990; Hill, 2011), such that representation is seen as dynamic, and produced through dialog and reflection.

Above all, the participant must be happy with the end product, regardless of the amount of facilitator mediation. In this regard, it is also important for researcher-facilitators to be as transparent as possible about their agenda. In both research and advocacy settings, if there is a desire to create products that address particular themes, this must be made clear from the outset during participant recruitment and emphasized throughout the workshop. One way to run more "open" workshops, but to also eventually arrive at thematic concerns, is to create a discussion guide or curriculum surrounding products. This way, participants are allowed a certain narrative leeway, while researcher-facilitators are able to organize workshop activities such that means and ends (data collection, participatory analysis, resulting products, and audience responses) are more equitably balanced between community and academic priorities.

ETHICAL MOMENT 2: PAR MEETS THE IRB—RECONCILING GOALS AND INSTITUTIONAL PRACTICES

This brings us to our second ethical moment, toward the development of a research plan that reconciles scholarly goals and formal norms of institutional ethics, including confidentiality and informed consent, with collaborators' goals and norms of collaboration and accountability.

Consent to Participate and Release of Materials

One challenge for participatory digital researchers is how to approach an IRB about incorporating more participatory methods into the research process. The researcher may find it particularly difficult to remain within the constraints of preformatted IRB requests; and, in the case of participatory visual and digital research, the process of seeking IRB approval is often not yet codified. How does one respond to informed consent expectations of a university IRB, such as those expecting that that researchers maintain confidentiality of participants, while remaining transparent in acknowledging the multiple objectives of a participatory research project? For example, obtaining informed consent to air visual products in a public forum for advocacy (such as on a website or in a public exhibition) is a much different matter than obtaining consent for an individual to produce a story and air it within a workshop setting or use it as a relatively anonymous point of data collection presented in a peer-reviewed publication. Indeed, this question bears another question: how does one maintain participants' confidentiality if research outcomes are to be used in advocacy campaigns? Some have noted that IRBs tend toward "methodological myopia" when it comes to human subjects issues (Walther, 2002, p. 206), placing research in a monolithic context that may present extra hurdles for those doing participatory digital research.

As researchers, we must interrogate the notion of "participation" and be mindful of the limitations of "informed consent." We find Amy Hill's work to be especially useful when considering the nuances of participant consent and other ethical considerations surrounding participatory digital work. Hill, cofounder of Silence Speaks, an international digital storytelling initiative, casts a critical light on "participatory" research by noting, "few who have claimed to be doing 'participatory' video work in either the analog or digital era . . . are clear in their articulation of what that participation really means on the ground" (Hill, 2011, p. 128). Indeed, she questions the ways knowledge production is typically framed: as a "neutral activity rather than as a process through which economic structures and ideological meanings are reflected, reproduced, or transcended" (Hill, 2011, p. 128). Hill encourages researchers to thoughtfully reflect on the power dimensions inherent to the research process, as they affect whose voice(s) are privileged and whose may be silenced.

One starting point for thinking about informed consent is to consider personal and structural dimensions of participant consent. The researcher might "screen" participants, as Hill (2011) suggests, to be prepared for participants who might be still in the midst of "experiencing their stories," especially if their stories relate to traumatic experiences. Furthermore, in resource-poor settings where people have limited options, the notion of "informed consent" may be suspect; participants might agree to anything that they believe might give them assistance in meeting their basic needs (Pittaway, Bartolomei, & Hugman, 2010). In the case of externally funded work, when funders have expectations about the creation of "public" stories, the process becomes even more challenging. The researcher must carefully balance the wishes of the funder with the desires of participants themselves. Questions to ask of the informed consent and release-of-materials process include: When can participants be given an "out" if they decide later they do not want their stories to be circulated? And how can funders be educated about the importance of such an option? With these possibilities in mind, the researcher-facilitator should fully brief participants about the potentially public nature of their productions, and the risks and benefits of such public exposure, before project activities begin (Hill, 2011).

Timing also matters as to when participants are asked to sign consent and release-of-materials forms (see the Appendix for an example of a release-of-materials form). Consent should never be a one-time process in a participatory research project. Instead, it must be woven throughout. A discussion of consent to participate should take place before data collection or workshop activities (often one and the same) begin, and forms should be signed only after participants have been fully oriented to project activities.

Options for consent-to-release materials should be raised as project participants are recruited, discussed during project activities as participants make decisions about what to say/not say and what to show/not show, and revisited at the end of the project, when release forms may be signed. Participants are only really able to provide informed consent after participating in project activities and knowing the project outcomes. Asking participants to sign a release form before they have participated in project activities and know the final product they will have in hand, much less asking participants to decide upon options for dissemination up front, runs contrary to a participatory or collaborative spirit. Furthermore, in seeking consent to release materials from participants after production is complete, facilitators should review the various options of release, including: consent to release materials for educational, research, advocacy, therapeutic, and/or exhibition purposes; consent to release materials only within the confines of the workshop; or no consent to release materials.

(Re)Considering Confidentiality and the Right to Own Knowledge/Expertise

Confidentiality is not a cut-and-dried issue in participatory visual and digital research. Ethical issues may arise even when participants do not name names. They may live in a small community where the story they produce or the visuals they use are well known to community members or somehow expose experiences that another member of the community would rather keep hidden from public view. Researchers should acknowledge the possibility that local audiences might know, or might assume they know, who is referred to in the media produced (Reed & Hill, 2010).

It is also important to consider an alternative standpoint on the ethics of confidentiality. That is, we might also rethink who has the right to present themselves as experts in the research process, or to represent their expertise as knowledge validated in the public domain. Historically, human subjects boards were established as a way to directly address the heinous ethical compromises of past clinical research, most notably during the Tuskegee Syphilis Study, and as result of the Nuremberg Code. As participatory researchers, though, we might reconsider how cogent IRB protocols are surrounding confidentiality.

Participatory research is predicated on the idea that participants might stand on equal ground with academic researchers in terms of ownership of knowledge production. However, we ponder what happens to that footing when participants are given pseudonyms or their names are deleted in materials produced from a research project: what does this say about the ability of participants to reclaim an authorial role in knowledge production? We find Patricia Hill Collins' (1998) comments on knowledge versus wisdom as key to a reconceptualization of confidentiality in knowledge production, representation, and dissemination. Collins (1998) discusses the difference between "knowledge," which tends to be ascribed an academic role, and "wisdom," which lies with laypeople/the folk and is rooted in lived experience. Her Black feminist epistemology values people's stories as evidence of their experiences, with wisdom given equal (if not precedent) footing with knowledge as academically circumscribed.

Concomitantly, we might also question why it is that academics, policymakers, and the like (the "experts") are so keen to put their names and titles on knowledge productions, namely in peer-reviewed publications, as well as on documents that reach the lay public and are integral to the construction of dominant discourse, while the names and faces of research participants are expected to be shielded? How does this take away from their own ability to lay a public claim to and author their own experiences? How does this expectation continue to keep their voices hidden or silenced? Indeed, might this not contribute to a deficits-based model that positions participants as oppressed individuals with needs (to be answered by academic experts), rather than as those possessing agency and cultural capital? As "wise" experts (Collins, 1998) with their names affixed to their work, might not research participants better be able to lay claim to knowledge production, ownership, and dissemination?

As an added caveat: today we might also question the notion of confidentiality given the ever increasing tendency for people to publicly broadcast the nitty-gritty details of their lives—with names and visuals included—through social networking media such as Facebook and Twitter, or to publicly post their musings on blogs and email listservs. Nevertheless, this does not let us researchers off the hook!

Training Community Participants in Research Ethics

We often begin our own participatory visual and digital projects by holding an ethics training session with participants prior to commencing project activities. The difficulty in planning such a session, however, is in how to present and discuss something like "ethics" in a short amount of time. While one could hold a very basic session focusing on IRB protocol and related procedures, the topic of ethics is potentially rife with conflict. Various perspectives—including those of participants, other community members, field site organizations, funders, and researchers and their supporting institutions—must be considered. In this regard, perspectives may differ quite a bit as to what is considered as "ethical" conduct. Especially given the frequency with which virtual worlds are now a part of our projects, research ethics must also attend to and flexibly accommodate the shifting nature of field contexts.

For her work using Photovoice, Harper has adapted Carolyn Wang's ethical principles of conducting Photovoice research into a short training session, first presented through PowerPoint or a poster presentation. The presentation considers issues such as consent/assent to participate in the project, obtaining consent to have one's photo taken and when consent is needed, release of materials, and the ramifications of taking photos of people participating in certain activities, especially the potential dangers of doing so. Following this session, Harper divides participants into small groups to further discuss these principles and related ethical dilemmas. Discussion questions include the following:

1. What is an acceptable way to approach someone to take his/her picture?
2. Should you take pictures of other people (for research) without their knowledge? Why or why not?
3. To whom might you wish to show or give photos? What might happen?
4. When would you not want to have your picture taken?
5. When might it be dangerous for you to take a photo?
6. What images of your community bother you? Why? What images would you like to challenge?

Figure 3-1 Ethical issues of Web 2.0 (©2008, Joy of Tech)

While driven by the visual/digital media at hand, in this case photography, our discussion here can be used as a guide for constructing an ethics session for any of the participatory visual methods covered in this book.

Just as with other social research methods, participatory researchers must treat their subjects according to ethical principles of informed consent (see Figure 3-1). For example, when using a Photovoice approach, anyone who would be easily identifiable in a research photo must be consulted prior to taking a photo. Photographer/participants are requested to explain the purpose of the project and ask for the subject's permission prior to taking pictures, often using an oral script or a printed photo release form to do so. Obtaining consent can limit spontaneity in visual research projects. However, participants can develop strategies for getting good shots while looking out for the rights of their subjects. For example, with digital photography, some photographers offer photographic subjects the opportunity to review, discuss, and consent to using photographed images on the spot, using the camera's display screen.

Another option sometimes used by researchers is to blur or black out the facial features of identifiable individuals in the photo. Most of us have seen this done on the news or on reality crime shows. However, the researcher should question whether and how participants' perspectives are obscured if their photos are altered in this way. Given the participatory nature of the methods reviewed here, one might question the ethics of doing this for participants. By first seeking permission to use a photograph that is *not* altered in any way, the researcher respects the artistry of the participant and the privacy of the subject photographed. This positions the participant and subject as people with the same right to publicly depict their experiences and expertise as the researcher herself.

It is also important to recognize that the participant holds a certain representational power when taking photos of others for a research project. Thus, the participant is given representational leeway over the ways those photographed are depicted in the photo and, as a result, the way diverse audiences may interpret experiences depicted within. Ethical discussions should address the power of representation, and that it is not only driven by the *researcher's* agenda. The participant should consider the ways she represents her photo subjects, and be clear about her intentions to subjects when seeking their consent to be photographed. These points signal shades of gray in ethical protocols to be considered, and the flexibility needed for conducting ethical participatory visual and digital research.

ETHICAL MOMENT 3: PRESENTING PAR FINDINGS

Complex considerations of social and ethical relationships should be brought on board at all points of the project. For instance, during a digital storytelling workshop, one should think about both who is producing the story and whom the story is about, which are not always the same people. What happens when representation of the subject matter is not "nice" and, instead, reaffirms dominant discourses supporting negative stereotypes of particular social groups?

For example, through her work with young parenting women, Gubrium has witnessed participants in several digital storytelling workshops speak of "teen mothers" using a dominant discourse that depicts young women who are mothers as greedy recipients of welfare and "lazy, overreproducers." These themes have arisen when participating young women contrast their own experiences as young mothers with those of others, as well as when discussing their experiences being mothered. Stories taking up this narrative rubric are particularly difficult to navigate, especially when the goal of a workshop is to affirm participants' own experiences and subjectivities. Of course, context does matter and is largely dependent on purpose. For research purposes (for instance, a project using a narrative perspective to analyze the ways participants negotiate dominant and alternative discourses on young motherhood), the outcome of this type of digital story may not be nearly as caustic. On the other hand, if the story is to be used for advocacy or educational purposes, where the intent of storytelling is to compel others to action or to consider a particular topic, such as teen parenting, in a new way, then this type of outcome can run contrary to the original aims of the project.

In relation to contradictory outcomes resulting from intended liberatory projects, Gready (2010) writes that as researchers directing participatory digital projects, we have a "responsibility to the story." This entails the acknowledgment of the seamier side of participatory research: that "it can be used to spread 'uncivil' stories [and] create . . . its own forms of exclusion and risk . . ." (Gready, 2010, p. 180). New ethical challenges arise from this tension over the potential for both emancipatory and oppressive outcomes, with questions raised over ownership of knowledge and control over representation (Gready, 2010, p. 180).

ETHICAL MOMENT 4: THE ETHICS OF RESEARCH PRODUCTS AND OUTCOMES

Research projects that position participants as trustworthy researchers themselves must embrace new approaches to ethics (Berry, 2004). Nowadays, social scientists are adopting participatory methods to promote a research ethic of collaboration and accountability, in effect changing the face of scholarly dissemination practices. In virtual worlds, the rise of information technologies and Web 2.0 has posed new ethical dilemmas concerning knowledge production, the right to information, and access and control. At least three key ethical stances have emerged from these discussions, in virtual worlds and beyond: 1) intellectual property rights; 2) the "free culture" or "open source" stance; and 3) indigenous intellectual property rights and ethics emerging from indigenous media (Coleman, 2010).

In the "intellectual property rights" framework, intangible objects, such as inventions or artistic production, are seen as connected by law to an owner, usually an individual, who claims exclusive rights to use and exchange. This has been the past tradition in academia and is largely represented by copyright laws that place restrictions on the ways that intellectual property can be accessed, used, and reproduced, including by the author herself.

A "free culture" or "open source" ethical framework has emerged in response to the concern that intellectual property law and powerful media institutions can restrict public access to information, knowledge, and artistic works, inhibiting freedom of expression. In this alternative framework, intellectual production is viewed as part of the commons, and producers are encouraged to share their work for non-commercial and educational use under a range of designations. "Copyleft" and "Creative Commons," for example, allow authors and other creative producers to maintain a copyright while permitting a wider range of uses than traditional copyrights. "Open source software" is a programmers' movement that grants software users access to source code that they may use, modify, and redesign.

While the "intellectual property rights" ethic grants individual ownership rights to cultural products for which many people may plausibly claim rights—although these rights are notably restricted by publishers—the "free culture" ethic champions broad public access to knowledge and cultural production. The emergence of indigenous intellectual property rights and new indigenous media complicates this dichotomy even further (Bowrey & Anderson, 2009; Christen, 2008; Ginsburg, 1995; Smith, 1999). We explore these issues further in Chapter 8.

Participatory projects increasingly include Internet technologies, which are entering our everyday lives so rapidly that we are still figuring out what this means in terms of privacy, confidentiality, and representational control. In online discussions of "Facebook ethics," for example, users often propose that while it is acceptable (though unwise) to post pictures of oneself engaged in illicit behavior, it is ethically unacceptable to post photos of others doing so. In practice, it is increasingly difficult for individuals to maintain control over their personal information on the Internet (Zimmer, 2010). This means that social scientists now need to consider how a participant's personal use of the Internet outside of the research context affects privacy, confidentiality, and other ethical issues. While anthropologists used to give pseudonyms to the villages they studied, the Internet now makes it easy to identify people and places in a matter of seconds (May, 2010). Social researchers must take the ethical implications of the Internet into account, and this is doubly important for those of us doing participatory visual and digital research.

Research conducted through the Internet, such as analyzing blogs or websites, may be deemed "covert" research if it is done through forums that are said to be public in nature. Because of the nature of the medium—where people may anonymously contribute material to the site or even do so with their name attached (such as on Facebook)—consent to participate is not always obtained (Murthy, 2008). Indeed, much of the work published thus far on ethics and digital research focuses on "online" research conducted on the Internet (Berry, 2004; Bruckman, 2002; Scharf, 1999; Schrum, 1995). In this regard, Berry (2004) calls for an "open-source ethics" that takes "a more flexible approach to research ethics [that] contribute positively to the ongoing questions regarding the ontological status of the Internet" (p. 324). Specifically, he questions whether we should consider the Internet as "a space in which embodied human beings interact . . . [or as] a textual repository where authors deposit work . . .?" (p. 324).

A similar question can be posed of the other participatory visual and digital methods reviewed in this book and the ways we consider the producer/participants and the research process, as opposed to the products/outcomes of research. This speaks to our previously emphasized point that what makes these methods particularly suitable for social research is that they are rich sources for data in at least three contexts. Especially as new tools for ethnographic fieldwork, the participatory visual and digital research process serves just as much as a site for data collection and analysis as do the outcomes. Audience responses to research productions serve as a third site for data collection. This holds strong ethical implications: despite the fact that a research outcome may be a digital product, with a participant's intention to share it online, human subjects are involved in the process of construction. Thus, consideration of a project's ontological status—especially where human subjects and social interaction are concerned—is key to crafting appropriate methodological and ethical guidelines.

CORE STORY: BETWEEN A ROCK AND A HARD PLACE—ETHICAL TENSIONS EVOKED THROUGH PARTICIPATORY MULTISENSORY METHODOLOGIES IN THE WORK OF DARCY ALEXANDRA

Darcy Alexandra's photography, videomaking, and digital storytelling work serves as a case in point for consideration of ethical issues as they may arise when using participatory visual and digital methodologies in research and for advocacy purposes. Alexandra's initial interest in participatory digital visual methods was rooted in a passion for creating what she terms "intimate objects," which she positions in contradistinction to the way that visual anthropology has historically conceived of the visual object, such as ethnographic film. The tendency has been to hold visual objects "apart from": to politically position them as outside the experience of the storyteller, outside the experience of the researcher, and as visual supplements to anthropological texts (see MacDougall, 1997). Instead, she seeks to create a more transparent process in understanding that, as intimate objects, they were created by the storyteller, and through discussion and dialog with a community of practitioners.

Alexandra's position signals a shift in the way that participatory visual methodologies might be used to make meaning, to understand lived experience, to communicate, to evoke emotions, to create disruptions, and to explore uncertainties. She began to think about this potential in relation to the possibilities for telling stories in more intellectually nuanced and emotionally textured ways. Her experience with solidarity work was her first pathway for thinking about different contexts for visual methodologies. In the 1980s and 1990s she had actively participated in the international solidarity movement, organizing with local and national organizations like the Native American Student Union, ACT UP, and Queer Nation. In all of these contexts, activists were intensively engaging with storytelling to have previously marginalized voices heard.

Particularly in working with the movement as a Spanish–English interpreter, Alexandra became very concerned about the ways that stories and people's lived experiences were strategically used, such that the men and women who were disseminating the stories were not necessarily involved in the process of creating the stories. For example, within the Latin American context there is a long history of *testimonio* telling and the concept of the healing power of speaking out and witnessing. However, as an interpreter Alexandra began to have serious reservations about interpreting painful stories for audiences that had no connection to that tradition or to the storyteller.

In one specific example (for which she was not the interpreter), Alexandra witnessed a university-sponsored event that troubled her. The event began with two Euro-American women—a law student and an anthropologist specializing in Guatemala—framing the discussion about indigenous collaborations with legal responses to the ethnocide in Guatemala. The event was advertised as an opportunity to hear about the work of a Mayan participant in a key human rights case. However, the law student and the scholar dominated the discussion before introducing the Mayan woman, one of the few survivors of the massacre of her village, to publicly "tell her story." In this way, the Western experts were the ones who conceptualized and "made sense," while the Mayan woman was left to literally embody the evidence of her own lived story. The woman spoke in her second language, through an interpreter, and began to cry as she recalled the massacre of her village while the predominantly white, U.S. audience shifted uncomfortably in their chairs.

The traumatic spectacle prompted Alexandra to seriously consider representational strategies and methodologies that value the dignity of the storyteller, or interlocutor, thereby complicating the practice of representation by rigorously considering ethical ramifications. As a researcher she also began to develop a more critical gaze and to think about how her prior experiences could inform her work using visual methodologies.

Her experiences in an academic capacity—including storytelling work she had conducted with women and men on the U.S.–Mexico border as an adult educator, and her work as a research assistant on a project in which the researchers "gathered visual data"—led her to reconsider the visual more as a catalyst for thinking through concepts and experiences than as merely "visible evidence." As a result, over the past eight years she has shifted from an objective of gathering visual data to using the visual as an opportunity for creating pathways for richer understanding, particularly in circumstances where people are living in very tenuous and vulnerable circumstances.

In 2007, when Alexandra began research as part of her doctoral work with asylum seekers, refugees, and men and women who had fallen out of legality, she began to reconcile the differential understandings of process and outcomes resulting from visual narrative work. When project participants would talk about their stories, many were very conscious of the fact that there was not a "happy ending" to their stories, that the stories were not necessarily understandable or resolvable. However, participants also placed emphasis on the narrative process itself, that the process was a place of reconciliation with difficult experiences. As objects for thinking with and through lived experiences, Alexandra sees the process and practice of visual methodologies as allowing participants to "take back the tools," putting the tools of knowledge construction literally in the hands of storyteller/producer/participants themselves. All the same, Alexandra highlights the mediated aspect of visual methodologies, in which the researcher-facilitator has input in the process and outcomes. Acknowledging this up front allows for more transparency with regard to power dynamics. The end result is important, allowing us (researchers and participants) to complicate simplistic narratives and create possibilities for more nuanced understandings of peoples' experiences.

Alexandra described two projects that she has conducted using visual methodologies to highlight ethical issues that may arise in terms of process and outcomes. Both were longitudinal digital storytelling projects. The first, "Undocumented in Ireland: Our Stories" (Alexandra, 2012a), took place over the course of five months in 2007. The project was conducted in collaboration with the Migrant Rights Center, an Irish nongovernmental organization (NGO), in conjunction with their "Bridging Visa" Campaign. This was an advocacy campaign for workers who had fallen out of legality with the Irish state: people who would arrive legally in Ireland, and then because of circumstances beyond their control, would become undocumented. Alexandra spoke with members of the Bridging Visa Campaign, and invited them to participate in a digital storytelling workshop. Ultimately, four people self-selected to participate: two women and two men from Africa, Asia, and Eastern Europe.

Ethical issues that arose in this project had mostly to do with issues of confidentiality and protection of participant identity. This was something of an ongoing discussion, as participants had different ideas about how they wanted to represent themselves and their stories. For example, one participant was very clear that she did not want to use any self-identifying images in her story, while another participant whose legal status had been regularized wanted to use images of his children and his family. At times discussions also arose within the partnering NGO about whether or not it was okay for participants to make those decisions themselves. There was a very sensitive process between the NGOs, the storytellers, and Alexandra as facilitator regarding the narrative agency of participants and open discussion around what the outcomes might be and where the stories might be disseminated.

One concrete experience centered on the ethical issue of negotiating consent, and the need for its flexible application within particular circumstances or contexts. All of the storytellers had signed an agreement at the beginning of the process saying that the story was their story, that at the end of the workshop they could decide whether or not they wanted to publish the story, and that they had the right to deny publication at the end of the workshop if they chose to do so. In addition, at the end of the workshop participants were given another release form in which they were asked to think, once again, about under what circumstances they would like to share their stories. The project was funded by a public media organization and at times Alexandra felt a certain amount of tension in terms of negotiations with the organization's directors about the complexity of consent needed. The organization had invested considerable resources into the project and they wanted a fair return on this investment, which meant that they expected a return on all four stories. One participant produced a story that to Alexandra was incredibly evocative and very beautifully crafted. The organization's directors were quite disappointed when at the end of the workshop this participant did not grant release to her story. As a researcher and graduate student coordinating the project as part of her PhD work, Alexandra was placed in a tenuous position. She noted that as a researcher her first responsibility was to the storytellers and to the agreement of confidentiality that they had made and that they continued to make over the course of five months of story production. In the end, the leadership did honor the consent agreement.

In addition to inserting flexibility into the consent process, Alexandra also shifted the digital storytelling workshop process to accommodate the needs of participants. Because all of the workshop participants were new to media production and also because of their work schedules, it was more feasible to meet weekly for two to four hours than to meet intensively over the course of three days. She met with participants outside of the workshop space as well—at their homes, their workplaces, in a variety of settings—and together they created images for their digital stories.

Scripts for digital stories were developed mindfully over a longer period of time than is usually the case. Alexandra related that when she first began talking with potential participants for the project, one woman who eventually became a storyteller in the series said that she often found herself called upon by the NGO to speak out and "tell her story." The woman said that she always became very nervous with this suggestion, that she actually hated public speaking but felt a real responsibility to do so. She became interested in digital storytelling because she loved the idea of having the time and the space to actually think every word out, and to very mindfully consider how she was going to represent herself, what she wanted to say, how she would create images for her story, and which she would choose to use in relation to her script (Alexandra, 2008).

To initiate the script development, participants first informally interviewed each other. Although they knew each other somewhat before through working together on the Bridging Visa campaign, they came to know each other a little better through the interview process. They then began working on their scripts. When they felt that they were ready to do so, they shared their scripts with each other and with Alexandra, and they asked each other questions about their scripts in this regard. Though she did not proceed through more formal portions of the digital storytelling process—such as the story circle process or a presentation of the "Seven Elements of Storytelling"—Alexandra covered similar workshop components through more informal means.

One reason for not teaching about points of narrative development was that Alexandra was curious about the various ways that participants might enter the story (i.e., as culturally, socially, and politically nuanced) and she did not want to push for a particular narrative arc to the stories (such that stories had to resolve themselves or that there had to be a dramatic moment inherent to the stories). Instead, she sought a more reflexive and exploratory initial process that became more collaboratively honed as participants engaged with each other's scripts, asking questions of the story scripts and images, and dialogically editing their stories through the process.

Alexandra did not pursue a formal story circle process in response to informal discussions she held with one participant, who related that she was uncomfortable with telling her story in front of everyone in the group so early in the workshop. The workshop was thus collaboratively designed and implemented, as together the workshop participants and

Alexandra discussed the types of activities that they would do first, and slowly built up their level of trust and comfort with each other in the workshop. From there, participants decided when they felt their script and images were ready, and when they wanted to share their digital stories. Supporting the Freirean ideal of objectifying the problem instead of objectifying the person facing the problem, the process was about rooting the story to the objects produced, shifting objectification from the participants-as-subjects to the story itself.

Alexandra also spoke of the benefits of conducting a longitudinal workshop, which allowed participants the space to "breathe" after engaging in such intense narrative work. Participants expressed that they found it particularly helpful for them to be able to come together, work intensively, and then to go home, ruminate on the workshop activities, and then to continue anew. Participants all said that having the chance to work over a more extended period of time was very helpful, in terms of being able to process ideas, process emotions, and think about their stories in a very conscious and critical way. Participating in participatory visual processes, such as digital storytelling, can be exhausting physically, emotionally, and intellectually. Given the space to distance themselves from their experiences, so that they were able to turn the experience into an object in their own minds, rather than being objectified, allowed participants a sense of recovery and renewal in the narrative process, to ultimately enhance the multimodal media production process as a means for reflection.

Circumstances were quite different in Alexandra's second project, "Living in Direct Provision: Nine Stories" (Alexandra, 2012b), which was conducted with asylum seekers and refugees living in Ireland. Participants were people who had come to Ireland to make a claim for asylum and were living in asylum centers. Established more than 10 years ago in Ireland, the Direct Provision system maintains that asylum seekers be housed in asylum centers, receive a weekly sum of 19 euros and 10 cents, and not be allowed to work or study until their claim has been decided. Thus, asylum seekers are living in very uncertain circumstances, having very little idea when their case is going to be decided. The experience of these direct provision system centers is emotionally and physically difficult, with people living in cramped housing that is not their own to maintain, and who are uncertain how long they will be there.

The impact of these living conditions on men, women, and children living in the system, well documented by sociologists, has created a lot of fear and suspicion among asylum seekers: it was clear to Alexandra from the start that formal group activities—such as story circles in the context of digital storytelling—would not be appropriate in this setting, especially given that most participants did not know each other and many were fearful to tell their stories due to abounding rumors about what one should do or should not do as an asylum seeker. Within this context, the need for confidentiality and protection of identity became even more important. At the same time, this raised an ironic issue: a tension between telling one's story and having a "voice," literally hearing one's own voice, and not being able to have a face, not being able to physically connect one's body to one's voice through visual representation due to confidentiality concerns.

This tension surfaced the need to use multisensory ethnography and to consider various ways of telling stories within those circumstances. Even more so than with the "Undocumented in Ireland" project, Alexandra and workshop participants in the "Direct Provision" project developed a long-term, collaborative, visual ethnographic practice. Alexandra saw something qualitatively different in using a practice where participants become participant observers of their own lives, theorizing their own lives as they produce their stories (Gubrium, 2009a). Through the process they are afforded the time and space to engage with their stories on their own terms, to explore the process in a self-reflexive way, and to consider their own narrative performances or strategic narrative practice (Gubrium, 2006). Mindfully questioning the way they choose to represent themselves and their experiences, participants might ask themselves, other workshop members, or facilitators: "Is this clear?" "Is this really what I want to say?" as well as "What are the implications of representing myself in this way? What will it mean?"

The very end result of the digital storytelling workshop—the screening of stories—was extremely important to the storytellers, as they wanted policymakers and politicians who had decision-making power to listen to their stories. In this regard, Alexandra felt it very important that participants had access to professional-level media tools and that the end result, the digital story product, was as thoughtful and polished as possible so as to preclude viewers from dismissing the stories outright. For policymakers to want to make change, they must relate to the stories and feel a call to action. In this respect, Alexandra prefaces her use of the term "listening" with broad contours to consider the viewer's multiple engagements with a story. Digital stories are textured by the storyteller's voice, ambient sounds, and visual images, so that the viewer comes to "feel" the multi/con/textual digital story and develops a multisensory relationship to the story. However, as Alexandra pointed out, her experience has been that these senses are not on an even playing field when it comes to viewer response. A story can have terrible images, but if the sound quality is amazing, the listener/viewer will watch the piece. However, given the reverse, the viewer will likely not engage as well with the story. You can have incredible images, but if the sound is not good it is distracting, and concretely there is no voice. Thus, the ethical issues of aesthetics and technical know-how also come into play in participatory visual media making.

The "Direct Provision" project faced particularly difficult ethical terrain regarding an ongoing discussion about story ownership, especially in terms of dissemination: when and where the stories could be screened. Due to policy changes in Ireland and their impact on the organizations backing the workshop, the digital stories were never publicly launched as a DVD collection. Participants were placed in a particularly precarious position when the project's sponsoring organizations folded, leaving the project without organizational backing. However, the inaugural screening of the stories at the Irish Film Institute (IFI) was a groundbreaking moment, and the stories were selected for screening at the Guth Gafa International Documentary Film Festival in June 2009. Nevertheless, outside of these screenings, the DVD release of the stories was never publicly launched, as there was concern that two "particularly spiny" stories, as Alexandra put it, would not be well received and that they could potentially cause problems for the organizations involved. This was a disappointing outcome for many participants who had hoped to have their stories received by a broader, Irish audience.

Alexandra noted tensions of authorial control that played out in large and small ways in the project, and particularly so with these stories. One story about racism implicated an Irish business, which drew concern from one of the supporting organizations that this could potentially lead to legal problems. The other story was about the sexualization of female African asylum seekers. The participant's story spoke of her frustration with the ways in which she had been objectified as a female asylum seeker. The story also caused concern among some of the supporting organizations' stakeholders. In the end, aside from the inaugural and film festival screenings, the two storytellers chose to not publicly release their stories. Both of the storytellers were quite cognizant of concerns that the supporting organizations might have about their stories. For example, the participant who spoke of racism in his story asked Alexandra throughout the workshop, "Is it okay for me to tell this story? Do you think the NGO will be okay if I tell this story? Is this story going to bother them? Are they going to be okay with this?" He was very concerned about his position and conscious of being in a vulnerable position.

However, the whole series of digital stories (all nine) had been placed on a distribution DVD. Funding constraints have made it difficult to recreate the DVD to omit the two stories. Thus, all of the stories remain in curatorial limbo, despite seven of them being given full rights for distribution by their producers. This signals ethical tensions arising from dissemination and digital curation of participatory visual materials on the part of story producers and workshop facilitators, and the need to consider a clear curatorial policy among stakeholders (including the storytellers) from the get-go. For example, one of the storytellers in the series is a photographer and is very keen on having the series of digital stories screened in galleries and in diverse settings, including online. Addressing dissemination and curatorial issues also places an onus of responsibility on the workshop facilitator/director such that she must question her own authorial control in the workshop process. Where is the line drawn between making sure that the participant is ethically informed in providing consent to construct or air a story, and patronizing the participant by telling him that he should not produce a particular story?

Ethical issues arise when using participatory visual methodologies, especially in terms of participants' narrative agency: in this case, the agency to decide what their stories would be about. In the "Undocumented in Ireland" project, authorial control was also a source of tension in relation to the use of visual images. For example, one participant wanted to include images of his family in his digital story; some people from the sponsoring organization told him that he should not use the images because they shifted the story to being not so much about campaign issues as about his family experiences. However, the participant was as much crafting the digital story for his family as he was making it for advocacy purposes. It was very important for him to tell that particular story at that moment. In the end, he modified his story slightly to connect it to an overarching theme of immigration.

This sort of thing can often occur when a project is thematically driven. Either the participants do not think about their lives so concretely in relation to the topic at hand or they just do not tell a story that focuses on the theme as we might like, making a rigorous scientific analysis of the product difficult to achieve if this is the goal of a project. For example, a researcher might desire products that revolve around participants' experiences with reproductive and sexual health, but participants tell stories about all kinds of things. For some, this underscores the need for narrative and holistic approaches that see the world as multifaceted and not as discrete experiences that can be broken up into variables. In the case of the "Undocumented in Ireland" project, which was to consider the topic of living without documentation, the fact that one participant told a story about the loss of his father in a way that did not immediately resonate as an "immigration story" could remind researchers, policymakers, and advocates of the unexpected dimensions of the immigration experience and to consider these in addressing the issue.

Finally, ethical issues have also arisen for Alexandra in her position as a graduate student around ownership of knowledge and the respect paid to non-print material in academia. One tension arose surrounding her multiple roles on the project, as the project's workshop facilitator, researcher, and co-director (in collaboration with workshop participants). The "Direct Provision" project premiered at the IFI and was also invited to screen at an Irish documentary film festival, with all participants agreeing to both of these screenings. However, when the stories were presented to the panel that decided which films would be selected for the festival, Alexandra was originally credited only as "workshop facilitator." Several filmmaking colleagues told her that this would be a problem, since she would not receive proper credit at this festival or others if only listed as "workshop facilitator." In fact, most likely she would not be invited to the event since she was not credited as the director of the project. In the end, the participatory nature of the project became a sort of tyranny of collaboration: Alexandra was between a rock of conducting a project in collaboration with workshop participants, and a hard place of seeking credit for her work, both so she could be present for the story screenings and so she could be properly credited for her efforts. Of course, ongoing challenges also remain for ways to engage with non-print material in writing, which as always remains the bread and butter of academia.

Nevertheless, Alexandra remains committed to engaging with participatory visual methodologies in her own work as ethically responsive research practices. The methodologies respond to the need for a serious consideration of the ethical realities of participants and the circumstances of their everyday lives. It is her hope that the media produced from these projects are able to evoke concepts and emotions from those who see them, listen to them, and feel them in ways that simply does not happen when one reads an article or a research report. Alexandra presented two specific moments when she saw this happen with her own work. The "Undocumented in Ireland" series of stories was launched in collaboration with the release of a report from a sociological study on irregular migration into Ireland that made concrete recommendations on the issue. Those in attendance at the screening included high-level policymakers, such as former President Mary Robinson. The sociologist who conducted the study on irregular immigration commented after the screening that, in combination with the print material, the digital stories presented the material in such a nuanced and textured way. This well illustrated the affordances of using a mixed-method approach in research and policymaking. Then, for the internal/in-workshop screening of the "Direct Provision" project, supporting organization staff were invited to attend. At the end of the screening, one community organizer stood up and said "you know, in three minutes, you (talking to the storytellers) have said what we've struggled to say for years." To Alexandra, the comment spoke to the efficacy of participatory media making, with productions efficient at sharing complex experiences in complex ways.

CHAPTER 4

Photovoice Research

WHAT IS PHOTOVOICE?

The Photovoice methodology has dramatically gained popularity over the past decade. As articulated by public health scholars Carolyn Wang, Mary Ann Burris, and Xiang Yue Ping, Photovoice is a kind of participatory action research (PAR) method in which a group of community members uses cameras to take photos on a theme (Wang, Burris, & Ping, 1996). Photos are then selected by the photographers themselves and used to elicit comments in group discussions. Photovoice is aimed not only at raising awareness in a community but also at communicating with policymakers and representatives of institutions who are often inaccessible for members of disadvantaged groups. Throughout the Photovoice research process, participants discuss their ethical relationship with their photographic subjects, as well as changes the photographers and subjects would like to see in their lives, and strategies for collective action to address problems depicted in the photos.

Photovoice has roots in the work of visual anthropologists, sociologists, and education researchers who used photo elicitation in their data collection. Visual anthropologists have practiced "collaborative photography," in which participants guide the anthropologist's picture-taking in terms of determining content and cultural values of image-making (Pink, 2007). Some were attracted to photo elicitation because nonliterate research participants felt comfortable talking about pictures. Margaret Mead, for example, pioneered photo elicitation as a technique for interviewing young children (El Guindi, 1998). In the 1960s, critical literacy scholar and activist Paulo Freire used photographs as discussion prompts for workers and peasants in Peru and Brazil who could not read (Singhal et al., 2007). Others were motivated to use visual elicitation because of its effectiveness as a memory aid and as a tool to make the naturalistic, ethnographic research process more systematic. Anthropologist John Collier further developed the photo-elicitation interview method in his

Participatory Visual and Digital Methods by Aline Gubrium and Krista Harper, 69–89. ©2013 Left Coast Press Inc. All rights reserved.

fieldwork in Canada's Maritime Provinces in the 1950s. He compared verbal and photo-elicitation interviews with the same households, finding that looking at family photos improved participants' recall, generated longer statements, and prompted richer and more emotionally involved storytelling. Based on this study, Collier became a lifelong advocate for photo elicitation on the grounds that it provided better empirical data than interviews alone (Collier Jr., 1957; D. Harper, 2002).

Photovoice also draws from a tradition of participatory photography in the social sciences, and Freire's action research on literacy was again groundbreaking in its use of participant-produced images. Freire and his colleague Augusto Boal distributed cameras to residents of the poorest barrios of Lima, Peru, as an experiment in turning over the representational "means of production" (Boal, 1979). Freire and Boal became convinced of the value of participatory photography when they asked a group of children to take photos to represent the concept "exploitation." One child returned to the group with a photo of a nail on a wall, which Freire and Boal initially interpreted as an abstract metaphor of the hard lives of the children, who worked long hours as shoe shiners in the city and walked long distances uphill to their *barrios* above the city. Perplexed, Boal and Freire asked the children to explain the meaning of the image. In photo-elicitation discussions with the children, they learned that the image showed a specific wall where a storekeeper rented out nails where the children hung their heavy shoeshine kits at the end of each day before returning home. For the children, the nail symbolized their exploitation within the community (Boal, 1979; Singhal et al., 2007).

Influenced strongly by Freire and Boal's work, Wang and Burris introduced Photovoice as a systematic visual research method through a series of articles based on their 1990s research in the Yunnan Province of China (Wang & Burris, 1997; Wang, Burris, & Ping, 1996; Wang, Ling, & Ling, 1996). Distributing inexpensive Holga film cameras, they asked peasant women to each take a roll of pictures on themes related to their health, family, and work lives. The team had the film developed in the provincial capital, then returned to the villages to hold focus groups in which participants talked about the pictures they had taken. Adding the photo exhibition to the research process, Wang, Burris, and Ping (1996) articulated a new way of combining participatory photography, photo elicitation, and sharing research with policymakers and community members alike.

Since Wang and colleagues' original research project in China, the increased availability and affordability of small digital cameras has eliminated the high cost and inconvenience of photo processing, making Photovoice even more attractive. Other feminist scholars have used Photovoice in their work on women's experiences of urban space and violence in Belfast, Northern Ireland (McIntyre, 2003) and on indigenous Maya women's multifaceted accounts of civil war, discrimination, loss, and recovery (Lykes, 2010). The Education researchers have used the method to study El Salvadoran *campesino/as'* experiences with adult literacy education (Prins, 2010), and sociologists brought Photovoice to the study of street-children's living conditions in Accra, Ghana (Mizen & Ofosu-Kusi, 2010). Applied medical anthropologists and public health researchers have taken up the method enthusiastically (Hergenrather et al., 2009), using Photovoice to study the experiences of abdominal surgery patients recovering in the hospital (Radley, 2010), of long-term homeless men living on the street (Packard, 2008), of female-to-male transsexuals (Hussey, 2006), of children with asthma (Rich, Patashnick, & Chalfen, 2002), and of Latino youth perspectives on communication about sexuality (Gubrium & Torres, 2011).

Photovoice holds special promise as a path to participatory action research in political ecology. Building on Wang's work, Zackey (2007) conducted Photovoice research on deforestation with Yunnanese villagers as part of the Nature Conservancy's Photovoice initiative. By inviting peasants to document their conditions, Zackey integrated Himalayan peasants' concerns and interpretations of environmental problems into the research design. Zackey and his research participants compared mountain forest cover pictured in archival photos taken in the 1920s, 1980s, and 2000s. These images challenged dominant policy narratives by documenting that deforestation increased dramatically following waves of market reforms. Zackey's work demonstrates the potential of Photovoice for environmental research in bringing together participatory, interpretive approaches and empirical data on change over time. Other environmental anthropologists, geographers, and urbanists have turned to Photovoice to study rural Canadians' "senses of place" (Stedman et al., 2004), Los Angelenos' perceptions of urban environmental injustices (González et al., 2007), Colorado residents' interpretations of exurban development and transformation, and Indian peasants' views of nature and conservation in a biodiversity preserve (Bosak, 2008). This variation shows Photovoice's versatility and appeal as a means of not only collecting rich narrative data, but also going beyond a narrow focus on discourse into the realm of perception, experience, and spatial and embodied ways of knowing the world.

DOING PHOTOVOICE RESEARCH

Photovoice is a community-based participatory research (CBPR) method developed by public health scholar Carolyn Wang (Wang, 1999). Three signature elements of the Photovoice approach are community-generated photography, elicited narratives and participant voice, and work with community participants to reach a wider audience for their concerns.

The first element of the method, participant-generated photography, places emphasis on photos and seeing from multiple perspectives. After training in research ethics, cameras are distributed to a group of participants who then go out and take pictures on themes. Local participants take pictures representing community assets and concerns, generating "local knowledge" and varied perspectives according to individual photographers' lives and experiences. Participants then select the photos they see as the most important, or those that are simply their favorites, to share with the group.

The second element, "elicited narratives and participant voice," focuses on generating group discussion while viewing the photographs. During the viewing session, the research team uses the photos as an opportunity to discuss issues that emerge as people look at the images. Looking at images, people often bring up related stories that cannot be seen in the images themselves, or that are in the background of the image. To prompt discussion, Wang developed the "SHOWED" focus group interview schedule (Wang et al., 2004). SHOWED is an acronym of her discussion questions (Figure 4-1). These questions allow participants to discuss their relationships with photographic subjects, changes they would like to see in their lives, and strategies for collective action to address problems depicted in the photos. In practice, some Photovoice teams find the SHOWED questions repetitive or limiting and choose to develop their own questions (McIntyre, 2003). A review of public-health Photovoice projects found that only one-third of the studies used "SHOWED," whereas most used a simple photo-discussion prompt or facilitator-generated questions (Hergenrather et al., 2009).

Photovoice research is aimed not only at raising awareness within a community but also at communicating with policymakers and representatives of institutions that are often inaccessible for members of

1. What do you *See* here?

2. What is really *Happening* here?

3. How does this relate to *Our* lives?

4. *Why* does this concern, situation, or strength exist?

5. How can we become *Empowered* through our new understanding?

6. What can we *Do*?

Figure 4-1 "SHOWED" questions (Wang et al., 2004; our italics)

marginalized groups. "Being heard"—reaching a wider audience through the research process—is the third element of Photovoice. In some cases, the research team uses community-generated images to identify themes that can inform action and policy, as in the case of a Photovoice study conducted with people disabled by chronic pain who then developed a pain assessment protocol for doctors and nurses (Baker & Wang, 2006). Most Photovoice projects use photo exhibitions as a tool for bringing issues raised in the research process to the attention of a wider audience of community members and policymakers (Hergenrather et al., 2009). The research team mounts an exhibition or slideshow for an audience they have identified over the course of their project. The exhibition is not a passive event, but one in which viewers are invited to come and discuss the images informally with the photographers themselves or in a more formal facilitated discussion.

Photovoice and the Ethics of Participatory Photography

Photovoice and related participatory photography methods come with the same ethical benefits and risks shared by all participatory and digital research methods: 1) balancing institutional ethics of confidentiality with PAR ethics of collaboration and accountability; 2) identifying and addressing power disparities within the participatory research process; 3) negotiating how to share and communicate the knowledge we produce; and 4) considering the ethical implications of information and communication technologies (ICTs) for Photovoice.

Photovoice is popular because it requires less equipment and technical expertise than other participatory visual and digital methods, making it accessible to researchers and participants alike. Unfortunately, the "user-friendliness" of Photovoice can lead to its misuse as a "quick-and-easy" replacement for long-term ethnographic engagement and immersion in fieldwork contexts. When research teams rush headlong into "handing out cameras," bad things can happen (Nakamura, 2008). Without basic technical training, participants may make common technical mistakes like accidentally putting a thumb over the lens. Such gaffes not only reduce the usefulness of images, they also make participants feel ashamed or embarrassed and get in the way of developing good research relationships (Packard, 2008). Without careful consideration of potential ethical problems and protocols for protecting the rights of photographic subjects, researchers may encourage community photographers to take intrusive and unwanted pictures. At a minimum, Photovoice should be a technique embedded within a broader PAR framework for collaboration, and participants should receive basic training in how to use the cameras and be engaged in a discussion of visual research ethics.

Research teams should consider the specific context and conditions before launching into a Photovoice project. Esther Prins reflects on the ethical implications of Photovoice in postwar El Salvador, reminding us that the camera is not a culturally or politically neutral technology (Prins, 2010). A critical literacy researcher influenced by Freire, Prins integrated participatory photography into her research on *campesinos/as*' experiences in adult education. She was drawn to the method because of its growing use by PAR researchers and its potential to highlight connections between the night-school setting and other contexts of adult learners' everyday lives. Shortly after distributing disposable cameras to men and women in the literacy class, Prins learned that the cameras had aroused the suspicions of farm owners, school administrators, and other *campesinos*, leading to rumors about her intentions as a North American visitor to the community. Some objections were rooted in memories of surveillance by military and death squads during El Salvador's civil war. Prins (2010) writes: "Technologies that increase visibility are a means of social control; as such, taking pictures renders people vulnerable by making them and their possessions visible" (p. 435).

Participants in Prins' project found themselves rendered more visible and vulnerable, too, by their new role as photographers. Several participants were ridiculed for taking pictures, which was interpreted as "uppity" behavior, ill fitting to an indigenous *campesino/a*. When the act of taking pictures violates norms, photographers (who are also research subjects) face increased scrutiny in the "local reign of opinion" (Prins, 2010). Women photographers were especially derided for their departure from the norm of behaving like a "traditional Maya woman."

To address these concerns and difficulties, Prins recommends tailoring the method to the specific context. Before starting, researchers should find out about local norms and consider whether photography is appropriate. The team should have discussions aimed at sensitizing photographers to ethical issues, photographic subjects' feelings, and new power differentials that may come to light when they are taking pictures. The group may also seek to discuss means of informed consent that are appropriate and valued in the specific setting and to develop or revise institutional review board (IRB) consent forms accordingly. Finally, the team should talk about different ways to ask for permission, with photographers role-playing the social interactions involved.

Looking back on their project, both Prins and her participants felt that the benefits of the Photovoice project outweighed the risks. Many of the *campesinos* were proud of their photos and took pleasure in sharing the images. Photography afforded new ways to express creativity, and after looking at their own images of the landscape, some participants commented that they were seeing the beauty of their village with new eyes. Several photographers expressed a new sense of confidence because they had overcome their initial shyness. Some photographers stated that taking pictures caused them to start thinking more about their community's problems and needs. *Campesino* photography was controversial not only because it placed indigenous peasants behind the camera, but also because photos could expose local elites' abuse of power and recover subjugated knowledge.

CORE STORY 1: USING PHOTOVOICE TO BRIDGE THE RESEARCHER/PARTICIPANT DIVIDE—CLAUDIA MITCHELL'S WORK

Claudia Mitchell is the recent author of *Doing Visual Research* (2011) and coauthor of *Putting People in the Picture: Visual Methodologies for Social Change* (de Lange, Mitchell, & Stuart, 2007) and the *Handbook of Participatory Video* (Milne, Mitchell, & de Lange, 2012). She is also author of a number of additional books and articles on using participatory visual methodologies to address women and girls' health; gender-based violence; working with teachers, community health workers, and youth in the global fight against HIV/AIDS; and researching new literacies. While her work has spanned a range of participatory visual methods including photography, videomaking, and drawing, our case study here draws more specifically on her work with participatory photography.

Mitchell points to a project she conducted in Swaziland in 2003 in conjunction with the United Nations Children's Fund (UNICEF), which was focused on violence in and around schools, as the origins of her participatory photography work. Prior to this she had conducted research using archival and family photos and video work, but her interest in participatory visual methods began to grow as she read increasingly about participatory photography approaches in which researchers gave cameras to youth to capture their own experiences and perspectives on issues of concern. When UNICEF asked her to run the project on school violence, Mitchell suggested conducting a participatory project, giving cameras to school children and having them take pictures to document where they felt safe and strong, and where they did not. She began by working with one class of seventh-grade students. The photography project took place as a one-day event, where she worked with the students in the morning to take pictures, took the film to a one-hour photo studio to be developed, and then brought the developed photos back in the afternoon. In the afternoon, she and the students looked at and discussed the photos, sitting on the grass outside the school. As Mitchell explained, "the rest was history after that."

Mitchell found that the participatory photography approach was both extremely engaging for young people and that it produced rich data. As a result, she was able to publish extensively from the project: as Mitchell put it, her initial "toilet data" (focused on the unsafe conditions of school bathrooms) came from this project. She was also invited to present some of the youth-produced photos during a United Nations meeting. It was there that she was further convinced of the utility of the approach as a form of advocacy and to affect policy, as she realized the effect the photos had on the meeting participants.

After this experience, Mitchell continued to use a participatory photography approach, working with a research team in South Africa on projects surrounding HIV/AIDS. She continues to work with the same group, with many of her doctoral and master's students also participating in the projects. She has also worked with the Canadian International Development Agency (CIDA) on Photovoice projects in Ethiopia and has had CIDA and Social Sciences and Humanities funding to conduct projects in Rwanda, including a large Photovoice project with the Women's Council, a national organization that works with women in all parts of Rwanda.

Similar to several other participatory visual scholars presented here, Mitchell was not formally trained in photography. While she had worked before with photos, she had used them more as objects of elicitation in memory work studies and published a book (with coauthor Sandra Weber), *Reinventing Ourselves as Teachers: Beyond Nostalgia* (1999), that devoted a chapter to working with school photographs in this way. However, the work was clearly more archival and elicitation focused than it was participatory in nature.

Using an approach similar to the Photovoice method developed by Wang (1999), Mitchell begins participatory photography projects with a lead-in piece that focuses on the research topic at hand. Whether the project is focused on environmental issues, HIV/AIDS, or school violence, she begins her projects with participants discussing the specified topic. She then distributes cameras (now digital) to participants. The benefit of using digital cameras is that a photography project can be done in one day, with photos downloaded and printed on the spot. However, regardless whether cameras are digital or disposable, Mitchell prefers using hard copy (printed) photos during the group discussion. As she noted, "There's something about people pawing through those pictures, holding them up, and passing them along."

The project then continues with people working in small groups to visually document the research topic. Participants take anywhere between 20 and 200 photos, depending on the structure of the project. They then reconvene as a large group. One of two things happens next: participants may select photos to work with, directly on their cameras, and then download the photos to a computer. Or, if there is enough time, they might download the whole lot of photos to a computer. Select photos are then printed using a portable printer, as most of Mitchell's work is done in rural areas where printers are difficult to access. Yet another alternative is to use PowerPoint, such as in one project Mitchell conducted in Ethiopia where participants put photo captions right into the presentation.

The group then refers to the hard copy photos during follow-up discussion, with a resulting presentation or photo exhibition organized at the end of a project. For example, if the photos are printed out on the spot, there might be a photo exhibition directly at the end of a project, and then a more formal one might be organized afterwards. Another option is that participants might use their PowerPoint presentations to present their photos and discussion findings to a larger group.

In 2005, Mitchell conducted a project focused on South African youth perceptions of stigma surrounding HIV/AIDS. Eighth- and ninth-grade students were involved as participants. The teachers had already conducted a Photovoice project with the students on challenges and solutions to addressing HIV/AIDS. One of the challenges identified in the project was that young people tend to stigmatize each other. It was thus the teachers who identified the need for the stigma project. In this project, youth participants used disposable cameras and worked together in small, single-sex groups to take photos. From prior research experience in the area, Mitchell found that this format was the most effective way for participants to comfortably address the issue. The project was conducted in a controlled setting, with participants meeting at the school on a Saturday and then going out as groups for an hour and a half to take photos. They could go anywhere in the small village, but not beyond that. Each group took 24 pictures on stigma; a week later, they regrouped to review the printed photos. In small groups, participants chose photos that they felt exemplified challenges to addressing stigma, as well as photos that might represent possible solutions.

After reviewing and choosing photos, participants then worked on a "poster narrative." They were asked to pick representative photos and create captions for the photos, and then to affix the photos to large pieces of poster board using a glue stick and tape to create a story or presentation on stigma for the rest of the group. Using the poster narrative, similar in many ways to a digital story, participants told stories about stigma while also reviewing their photos and eliciting content themes for the research project. In one poster narrative example, the group first presented a photo depicting a boy sitting by himself, with the students remarking, "nobody likes him, he's HIV positive." They then described the next photo, showing his friends holding their hands up and shunning him. The group told a stigma story using eight to ten photos. Another group took a different approach, splitting the poster board into two halves, with four photos per half. One half had photos that represented the problem of stigma; the other half had photos that represented a solution to the problem. Since then, all of the work from this project has been digitized and continues to be used in health research, awareness, and promotion efforts.

Mitchell highlights the group approach as being especially important for participatory photography research. While Mitchell has run projects in which individuals take photos, her projects are more often group focused in photo-taking and discussion. While this is partially due to financial and time considerations, as group work can save time and requires investment in fewer cameras, Mitchell also sees the group process as absolutely critical. Participants' planning discussions for what they might photograph for the project and how they will do so highlights participant consciousness development surrounding the issue. However, she also warns against the "tyranny of the group" phenomenon: individually, someone might have taken really interesting pictures, but didn't because they didn't get the same opportunity to do so in the group setting.

In terms of benefits gained from conducting participatory photography research projects, Mitchell argues that the primary benefit is that the approach better enables the researcher to "look through the eyes" of participants. In addition to a richer perspective gained, she notes that participants also really enjoy doing the photography work and are sometimes surprised with what they come up with. Front and center is that the approach "levels the playing field," putting knowledge production in the hands of the participants. Then participants are also given the chance to analyze and interpret the data through their discussions surrounding the photos. While some participatory methodologies start out participatory, in that participants are integral to data construction or collection, their contributions may wane afterward. However, in a participatory photography project, the interpretive aspect does not just fall in the lap of the academic researcher. The process lends itself to positioning participants in a far more analytic mode as far as discussing representations and meanings surrounding the photos.

A further benefit of participatory photography is that it is also conducive to the longitudinal work so often missing in social research due to a lack of available funding and a range of other issues. The collection of photos and participatory archiving, something that Mitchell has been working on more recently, enables participants and academic researchers to collaborate in the development of metadata systems. For example, the South African project on stigma has turned into a longitudinal effort, with new participating students and teachers joining in. New poster narratives are created while old narratives are referred to in discussions to assess shifts in thinking and changing interpretations. In this sense, the project now serves as a participatory archive. Participants and researchers can look at how ninth-grade students represented stigma in 2005, and then have different students today look at those data, as well the photos they have produced, to compare these representations and identify shifting interpretations. In addition to the narrative data—a corpus of group discussion transcripts that can be analyzed over time—the digital photography technologies encourage a more participatory aspect of the metadata system, as they may be more accessible to participants than the transcripts.

In terms of challenges, ethical issues abound when doing participatory photography work. For example, Mitchell noted that within her participatory digital archive project, obtaining consent to release materials from participants remains a real challenge. While participants might understand what they are consenting to in the present moment of the project, six years down the road the same group of participants might think differently about their photos and their part in the archive. In addition, audiences, especially those from the same community, may question whether or not the archive violates participants' and other community members' rights to privacy or representational control. Mitchell thus spends a lot of time in projects focusing on ethical issues. She works with a standard collection of photos that might raise ethical concerns, showing the photos to participants and asking them to consider the ethical implications of taking and using photos such as these, and how they might negotiate these issues. Not only is this a challenge, but it is also a huge responsibility on the part of the researcher to ensure that these issues are considered and addressed. In this regard, as with all of the participatory methods covered in this book, participatory photography is not a guaranteed approach: it is not appropriate in all contexts and, in some settings, may raise more ethical concerns than other less participatory or visual methods. Ethical issues are also always changing: new ethical challenges arise all the time due to changing technologies and shifts in sociohistorical and political context. Thus, the number one consideration should be whether in using the approach you might be doing more harm than good.

While it is crucial to give full consideration to the ethics of a project, ethical protocols can also disrupt the project's intended creative and participatory process. For example, participants themselves sign consent forms to participate in a project and release materials. But they also must collect signed consent forms from any recognizable person depicted in a photo. Moreover, if something is written up or published from the project, if there is a photo exhibition, or if photos are presented in public settings (i.e., conferences, policymaking forums), then another round of consents are in order. While conceptually the consent process may seem to be cut and dried, in practice the consent process can become quite messy. Translation/language issues also come into play, especially in areas where multiple languages are used. In what language(s) is/are the forms printed? And with so many forms, will the participants just become completely overwhelmed with the whole consent process? One way this may be addressed is by having people consent to participate in the project at the beginning, distributing consent-to-be-photographed forms when participants are ready to begin taking pictures, and then asking participants to consent to release of materials after the photos are taken. Indeed, this allows for a more balanced distribution of forms, as well as for participants to know exactly what they are consenting to at each stage of the project.

Surveillance is also implicated in obtaining consent. For example, in some political contexts, and as Prins (2010) also notes, in areas of the world where communities are constantly under surveillance, might not participatory photography actually become a mechanism of surveillance? It is important not to work from the naïve perspective that participation is always liberatory. Mitchell gave the example of work done in Rwanda, where some participants were disinclined to sign consent forms, though they did want to participate in the project. Their signatures might implicate participants as oppositional, and in this way consent was actually creating a more ethically compromised and harmful situation. One way Mitchell has addressed these issues is by developing an oral consent process (permitted at some universities), whereby she obtains oral consent from the participant, writing down the date that consent was obtained.

While such a process represents one possible approach to the ethical dilemmas of consent, there is a distinct possibility that a university IRB may not have been previously exposed to this more flexible consideration of consent. Especially in settings where bench science is the norm, such as in medical schools, it is important that the participatory visual researcher be able to clearly describe their research protocol and educate the review board to be more attuned to a variety of ethical contexts. One way to accomplish this might be to have someone considered an "expert" in the field serve as an external reviewer for proposed participatory photography projects, something that Mitchell has done herself.

Despite the challenges, Mitchell's work demonstrates the possibilities afforded by a participatory photography approach. The participatory process allows people to produce on-the-ground knowledge, shifts the latitude of representation, and gives participants a tremendous role in the research process. As Mitchell notes, "I used to think that, 'well I'm the researcher, I'm going to try to get this information from these people as humanely as possible.' But now I feel much more that the participants themselves are gaining more awareness of what they're doing, and as a part of this 'doing' of research, they're also sharing part of what I wouldn't know as much about. In this regard, we all learn something in the process." The participatory approach thus supports social research as a much more socially engaged and responsible endeavor, shifting the process from being a one-way street of data collection to a more democratic landscape of knowledge production.

CORE STORY 2: USING PHOTOVOICE TO INVESTIGATE ENVIRONMENT AND HEALTH IN A HUNGARIAN ROMANI (GYPSY) COMMUNITY—KRISTA HARPER'S WORK

Klára: Everyone dumps their trash next to our neighborhood. The town government says that we're dumping it ourselves. That might be true in some cases, but if you look at these piles, there's packaging for brands that people in our neighborhood don't use.

Figure 4-2 Garbage with shadows, Sajószentpéter, Hungary (©2007, Judit Bari)

In the discussion above, Klára, a resident of a predominantly Roma (Gypsy) neighborhood in northern Hungary, is examining and commenting upon her neighbor's photograph of a nearby trash heap (Figure 4-2). As this brief exchange suggests, community-generated images can allow viewers to focus more consciously on mundane features of their daily environment, and residents' discussion can elicit stories taking place beyond the photo's frame. In the spring of 2007, Harper conducted a PAR project with members of the Sajó River Association for Environment and Community Development (*Sajómenti Környezet-és Közösségfejlesztök Egyesülete,* or SAKKF) in Sajószentpéter, Hungary (Harper, 2012; Harper, Steger, & Filčák, 2009). This collaborative project harnessed the power of visual images and critical discussion to examine the community's environmental and health issues using Photovoice methods. Working together, the team sought to assess and improve environmental and public health conditions for the community, to gain access to decision-making bodies, and to organize individual and collective actions toward a more livable, just, and sustainable future.

The largest ethnic minority in Hungary, Roma make up more than 5 percent of the population and face systematic discrimination and social exclusion (Szelényi & Ladányi, 2005). They have lived in Central and Eastern Europe for six centuries. Hungarian Roma are sedentary (not nomadic), having settled in towns and villages since the nineteenth century (Crowe, 1996). In Hungary, most Roma speak Hungarian as their primary language. Neighborhoods in which the majority of residents are Romani are more exposed to environmental harms and have less access to public infrastructure than non-Romani neighborhoods (Debrecen University School of Public Health, 2004), and on average, Romani life expectancy is 10 years lower than that of non-Roma (Doyle, 2004).

Despite the urgency of these issues, research on and policies targeting Romani populations in Central and Eastern Europe has traditionally not engaged the Roma themselves in problem generation or agenda setting. Even in the civil sector, many of the largest organizations promoting the human rights of Roma are led by non-Roma. In developing a collaboration with SAKKF, a small, grassroots Romani organization, Harper hoped to recognize and begin to redress the historical relegation of the Roma to the subordinated roles of "research subjects" and "target population" in relation to non-Roma professionals. This collaboration eventually led to the decision to use the Photovoice approach to investigate neighborhood residents' perceptions of environment and health.

Sajószentpéter (population 14,000) was a minor industrial center near Miskolc in northern Hungary for most of the twentieth century. During the state socialist period, there was 100 percent employment, and the factory's glass jars were used widely in Hungary's food-processing firms. The factory and a neighboring coalmine were privatized and closed down following the collapse of state socialism in the early 1990s. Managers and officials in charge of privatizing the firm sold it to a multinational corporation. The glass factory was closed, and its equipment was shipped to Slovakia. The population of the town lost its livelihood in the space of a few months, and no new employers have appeared in the subsequent decade and a half. Residents of the community where SAKKF is based were especially hard hit by the closing of the plant. Surrounded by fields and the Sajó River wetlands, the neighborhood has more than 2,000 residents, most of them Roma whose families have lived in the town since before World War II. Connected to the rest of town by a bridge, the community is a two-minute walk to the main square where the mayor's office is located.

Harper met Judit Bari, the president of SAKKF, in 2005. They were both interested in the connections between Roma communities and the environment and decided to work together on these themes. The founding members of SAKKF had included "environment" in the organization's name five years earlier, with the hope of involving community members in the restoration of nearby wetlands. The group set aside these initial plans to focus on youth, community development, and public health for its first projects. Nevertheless, several members of the organization remained interested in the theme and agreed to participate in collaborative research on environmental issues. Bari and Harper decided to develop a research plan involving young people from the community as researchers.

Bari and Harper were attracted to the Photovoice method because of its potential to attract the participation of young people and to rapidly generate visual data on environment and health issues. Bari also saw the project as a way of mentoring and developing skills in young people who had participated in the group since it was founded and bringing them into a more mature form of activism. Six young community-based researchers (ages 18–24) participated in training sessions on photography and ethics, leading to a discussion of critical themes: the politics of representation of Roma as a minority group, the young researchers' relationship to the rest of the community, and what it means to be on either side of the camera's lens. At the second official meeting of the team, Harper distributed small digital cameras to the photographers. Harper presented the first theme, "environment," and asked them to define the term broadly and to include both positive and negative aspects of environmental conditions and people's beliefs and practices related to the environment.

By the following week, the photographers had taken more than 400 photos related to the environment. Quickly running through the photos, the team noticed that almost half showed trash heaps and dumping sites in and near the neighborhood. Clearly, waste management and the problem of illegal dumps was an important theme. Other environmental problems appeared in fewer photos, but would emerge in discussions as key concerns for the community organization. Selecting a manageable number of photos for group discussion, the team quickly arranged them as a digital slideshow and gathered around the laptop computer to discuss the images.

Photographs drew attention to environmental problems experienced in the neighborhood: unequal access to household water, playgrounds, and sewerage infrastructure; inadequate waste management and illegal dumping by outsiders as well as residents; energy and heating insecurity; and lack of access to telecommunications infrastructure and information technologies that are available in other parts of town. Photographers also presented images related to health issues, including discrimination in healthcare settings, diet, tobacco use, and health threats posed by poor quality housing.

Photos also drew attention to positive aspects of environment and the health of the community, most of which had rarely been recognized by residents or outsiders. These included the sense of connection to surrounding wetlands through fishing and recreation along the riverside, as well as some residents' attachment to place expressed through gardening and animal husbandry. The use of environmentally friendly transportation such as bicycles, public transportation, horses, carpools, and walking appeared as a theme in many pictures. Photographers presented positive aspects of health in the neighborhood through images of participatory sports and performance such as football and dance. After conversing with her grandmother, who had just returned from a visit to a nearby thermal spa for rheumatism treatments, one participant took her portrait as a tribute to the importance of this older woman taking care of her own health. Portraying the central importance of family support networks in maintaining health, many photographers took photos of parents, grandparents, and other family members holding babies and small children with pride and love.

To prompt discussion, the team posed general questions about what each picture showed and did not show, and how the image related to everyday life or events in the neighborhood. Group discussions of individual images typically ranged from 10 to 30 minutes as photographers voiced the hidden stories and contexts behind images. Participants also talked about what the organization could do to seek remedy for environmental inequalities and to recognize and promote existing strengths and environmentally friendly practices.

Figure 4-3 Collecting firewood by bicycle, Sajószentpéter, Hungary (©2007, Sajó River Association)

Viewing images in groups opened up explorations of issues raised by the photos. Prompted by an image of a man collecting firewood on the back of his bicycle (Figure 4-3), the photographer explained that neighborhood men use the euphemism "going to the island" to refer to going to the wetlands to collect firewood. Gathering wood in the wetlands violates the civil code, but many residents take the risk of being caught, particularly in the late winter when they have run out of other fuel wood:

> Mária: Lots of families heat their houses with wood. Some people can afford to buy it, but otherwise you have to collect it along the river. If you get caught, they'll fine you, and if you can't pay, they'll take your bike away.

Participants went on to talk about how energy insecurity affects households in the neighborhood. Heating with electricity is too expensive, and there are no gas lines reaching the neighborhood; so most residents use woodstoves for heat. People who can afford to do so buy cords of wood from truck vendors in the fall. Families that cannot afford (or run out of) cordwood often cut branches from bushes in the wetlands. When residents do not have access to wood and cannot get to the wetlands, they burn trash in their household woodstoves. Participants were well aware of indoor air pollution caused by trash burning, and they presented this as a survival strategy of the neighborhood's poorest residents.

As the discussion moved on to the practice of collecting wood along the river, one participant noted that acacia branches are the preferred wood because they dry fast and burn hot, and others agreed with his assessment. Since acacia is considered an invasive species in Hungary, the practice of collecting firewood may not harm the wetlands, but in fact performs an ecological service. In this way, specific images elicited open-ended discussion of local practices, problems, and potential solutions.

After taking pictures on the themes of "environment" and "health," the photographers themselves generated a third theme for pictures, "individuality." This theme emerged as a direct response to discussions of stereotyped media images of Roma that they wished to counter. Discussions of these photos were less focused on generating narratives and context information for the research process. Instead, the team viewed these photos informally, sharing snapshots and portraits. These photos later fulfilled a very important organizing function, however—drawing a large audience to the local photo exhibition, as residents jostled to see pictures of friends and family members.

The group presented its work at photo exhibitions in Sajószentpéter and Budapest. The photographers took a lead role in organizing the local exhibition. They discussed a number of venues and decided to hold the local exhibition on the street at the entrance to the neighborhood. Although this venue posed logistical challenges, the team wanted to ensure that all of the community members who had participated as photographic subjects could see the pictures and be present. As an added benefit of holding the exhibition in the neighborhood, the organization would be able to see which policymakers and potential partners were willing to cross the bridge to attend an event on the *cigánysor* ("Gypsy Row"). Inspired by their choice of venue, the photographers decided to give the local exhibition the title "This is also Sajószentpéter" ("*Ez is Sajószentpéter*").

The photographers posted flyers around the town and invited the mayor and vice mayor, local council members, key public administrators, representatives of the Gypsy self-government, and doctors, nurses, and teachers serving the neighborhood. Bari and Harper invited members of environmental organizations from neighboring towns and human rights organizations from Budapest. The exhibition in Sájoszentpéter was supposed to be held on the street, but two hours before the exhibition was to open, a major thunderstorm rolled in, and the team had to quickly move all of the pictures on panels to the local general store's large, covered porch. Fortunately, none of the pictures were damaged, and the storm cleared before the beginning of the exhibition. The event was well attended, drawing an audience of more than 80 neighborhood residents, local officials and agency representatives, and activists from Miskolc and Budapest. The photographers assembled a large collage wall of smaller, four-by-six-inch photos from the "individuality" series to serve as "party favors" for neighborhood audience participants. The team took the exhibition as an opportunity to receive feedback from members of the community, to extend the organization's network of partners and supporters, and to open a broader discussion of environment and health issues with policymakers.

The team held the Budapest exhibition at the Central European University, hosted by the Center for Environmental Policy and Law. For several members of the team, it was the first time they had visited the capital city, less than three hours' travel from Sajószentpéter. The event included a 90-minute group discussion in English and Hungarian of the issues raised by the photos, facilitated by a nationally known Roma activist and a respected environmental lawyer. In addition to providing a broader audience for the photographers' work, the exhibition allowed SAKKF members to extend their social network beyond Sajószentpéter. Following the exhibitions, the organization received visitors from a human rights organization and made partnerships with non-Roma organizations that led to the submission of a successful grant application with an environmental organization in the capital city. This grant focused on environmental justice research and pilot programs in several communities around Hungary. Projects addressed concerns raised in the Photovoice project such as fuel security and energy efficiency, waste management, and water quality (Hajdu et al., 2010).

Through the Photovoice project in northern Hungary, the research team logged many achievements at different levels. On the individual level, the young photographers developed new skills and hidden talents, expressed themselves through documentary photography, gained the recognition of people in their hometown, and traveled to show their work in the capital city. Several of the people featured in photographs expressed excitement at appearing in portraits in the local photo exhibition and were pleased to see the neighborhood represented in ways that challenged stereotypes. As a community organization, SAKKF initiated a discussion of environmental inequalities and made linkages with potential allies on the town, regional, and national levels. Many of the images themselves were aesthetically striking as well as provocative; Harper and Bari were invited to present a slideshow of the images to members of the

United Nations Committee on Social, Economic, and Cultural Rights (UNCSECR) in Geneva as the committee evaluated official human rights reports. The research thus contributed visual and narrative data supporting a wider investigation of environmental and health inequalities in Hungary and the region.

The project provided a space for residents to discuss their enjoyment of fishing and relaxing in the wetlands, tending household gardens, and raising livestock, as well as to raise issues of limited access to public infrastructure, dumping, and community health problems. Inviting a range of activists and policymakers to the exhibitions allowed Harper and Bari to break out of the prevailing "Roma issues" frame, presenting residents' issues as part of energy policy, housing, waste management, and citizens' participation. Photovoice methodology enabled the team to collect visual documentation that supplements ethnographic data on the community and previous quantitative assessments of environmental and health inequalities among Hungarian Roma.

CONCLUSIONS

Despite its many benefits, Photovoice does have limitations as a research strategy. Although Photovoice combines activism and research in a PAR framework, the methodology alone is not sufficient to organize a community around the issues raised or to address all the data-collection needs of a research project. The Sájoszentpéter project allowed SAKKF to train young activists in PAR, to make new alliances with other organizations, and to raise awareness and discussion among community members, public officials, and others who viewed the pictures. Yet, in the process, Harper and Bari learned that policymakers at the national and international levels were more responsive than many local leaders: a daunting challenge for a grassroots neighborhood organization.

Certain problems or realities are also difficult for amateur photographers to portray in photographs. The emphasis on things that are photographable, such as waste dumps or housing conditions, may draw attention away from what is less easily visualized, such as mental health issues or air quality. In the case of the Sájoszentpéter project, because photographers consciously adopted a "first do no harm" ethic of picture-taking, they did not produce images of people engaged in illicit or illegal behaviors. While some of the more creative photographers attempted to portray intangible issues or illegal practices through abstract, metaphoric, or still-life compositions, others simply avoided attempting to represent these issues. All the same, Mitchell's Photovoice work with South African youth on the topic of stigma and shame surrounding

HIV/AIDS indicates the possibilities for using the approach, even when tackling issues that may evoke taboos or which may be difficult to represent through explicit representation.

Beyond aesthetic/visual limitations or ethical constraints, the experiences and social networks of the photographers may limit the kinds of images produced. In the Sájoszentpéter project, young adults were especially acute observers of the neighborhood's environmental concerns because they typically spent their spare time outdoors and had direct experiences of water and sewerage issues in their daily household life. Although they did produce many thought-provoking images of health issues, young adult photographers were inhibited by their fear of bothering the old and the sick and by their limited personal experience of illness. The health-themed photos would likely have produced richer data if Harper and Bari had distributed cameras to women between 25 and 45 years of age, who are often responsible for the care of young children and elderly relatives. As a research strategy, Photovoice very effectively elicits emic representations and narratives. The approach is best used in combination with other research methods to address the limitations of participants' experiences and inability to portray some issues visually.

Photographs possess special qualities as a medium that become apparent in group discussions, in public exhibitions, and throughout the research process. Unlike film, photos have no audio track, and so viewers may comment on what they are seeing. Unlike text, multiple people can view pictures simultaneously. This simultaneity may give rise to moments of accountability and negotiation, in which different viewers are provoked to acknowledge what they are seeing and to reconcile different interpretations of the issues portrayed. Photovoice holds the realist "documentary photography" impulse in tension with the idea of photographs as socially produced, context-dependent artifacts that challenge and invite response from viewers. The true potential of Photovoice as a new form of ethnographic inquiry lies in this productive tension.

CHAPTER 5

Participatory Film and Videomaking

For social research endeavors, participatory videomaker Claudia Mitchell (2011) notes a key strength of videomaking is its ability to contribute to deeper understandings of identity construction (p. 89). As Mitchell puts it, in participatory videomaking "nothing is accidental," and everything is up for grabs as a point of social construction and identity performance: "Digital production as creative construction . . . embodies the manipulation of gendered, racialized and sexualized identities. Visual evidence of this constructedness can be found in the video production itself" (Mitchell, 2011, p. 90). Videomaking can also be highly collaborative, reflecting social concerns and group effort. The fact that videomaking is a group effort "complements both the idea of constructedness . . . and the idea of negotiation. . . . [I]t is the capturing on film that adds to the identity-in-action process and the possibilities for social action" (Mitchell, 2011, p. 91).

Several books have been published on participatory or collaborative videomaking, which, indeed, cannot be boiled down to one approach, but rather embodies an array of approaches that are determined by the amount of time available for conducting a project, the "participatory" nature of the project, the population/community with which one is working, and also the equipment, materials, and funding available for conducting the project. It is also important to note that participatory videomaking is not just the stuff of academics. With the blurring of textual boundaries, especially through multimodal media production (Gubrium & Turner, 2011), community-based videomaking has become a part of the everyday experience of people (Mitchell, 2011). The Videovoice method is a great example of this blurring, with research, health advocacy, and health promotion goals intermingled using a community-based videomaking approach. For example, Catalani and colleagues (2012) implemented a Videovoice project in post-Katrina New Orleans. The approach builds on the Photovoice method; it is action oriented and

Participatory Visual and Digital Methods by Aline Gubrium and Krista Harper, 91–123. ©2013 Left Coast Press Inc. All rights reserved.

serves as a tool for advocacy while also incorporating participatory mediamaking/videomaking techniques that capture movement, audio, and sequential narrative (Catalani et al., 2012, p. 3; also see Catalani et al., 2009). In the case of the post-Katrina project, through Videovoice community members, academics, and filmmakers were engaged in a collaborative videomaking project that resulted in a 22-minute film, which was widely disseminated and viewed. The film was used to mobilize the community on three issues of concern after Katrina, while engaging community members in research efforts and the production of independent media.

Indeed, as can be seen from the protests and revolution in Tahrir Square in Egypt and other locations in the Middle East (i.e., the 2010–2011 "Arab Spring" protests), participatory videomaking is more than just an academic pursuit. Through the use of cellphone cameras and the ubiquitous nature of YouTube and the Internet, it has become fundamental to community organizing and social change movements (Rheingold, 2003).

PROJECT PLANNING

As Gregory and colleagues (2005) note in the introduction to their book on videomaking for advocacy and activism, one of the most critical stages for making an effective video (for research, advocacy, activism, or otherwise) is planning (and, as they put it, "followed by planning and more planning") (p. xiv). One of the first matters to address is why you are actually making the film and what audience you have in mind. Furthermore, before beginning to produce a video, researchers and those involved in participatory projects need to consider the ways that community members will be involved in the process of production and disseminating the final product/video.

The first step involves engaging community stakeholders in the project. Even before beginning production, researchers must make sure that community members support the project and then also consider the manner in which community members will be involved in the project. Will community members be actively involved in video production, or will they serve in a more advisory role? And if they are actively involved in production, in which parts of the process—project goals, audience, storyline, writing of articles, and so on—will they participate (Chavez et al., 2004, p. 398)?

Another question to consider before moving forward is how the "community" will be defined: who will be considered a "member" of said community, and which members of the community will be involved in production or represented in the video? Chavez and colleagues (2004) note that it is important to look internally at privilege conferred due to race, gender, class, education, sexual orientation, and institutional affiliation to see how privilege permeates everything done in the videomaking process (p. 400). Furthermore, in seeking approval to move ahead with a participatory video project, filmmaker/anthropologist Charles Menzies (2004) emphasizes the need to consult with multiple levels of authority —from the individual community member to the organizational level to community leadership—to adequately seek the "consent" of the community to participate. And these levels of authority may not always agree on participation or on the production process. This is the messy stuff of participatory action research (PAR) that may lengthen the timeline of a project, and also increase workload, but is critical to respecting the self-determination of the community involved.

Funding is also an issue. Chavez and colleagues (2004) note that budget items may include equipment such as video cameras; SD cards or other memory devices; accessories such as microphones, lighting, extension cords, and editing software; or professional expertise for editing. Also important to consider is the purpose of the video. Will the video be used for research purposes only, or are there also advocacy, education, or policy aims as well? If so, the budget will include lines for curriculum or materials development surrounding the videos, as well as money for the production of a composite video (see discussion below) to be used in public discussions focused on the videos. Budgets should also include lines for personnel, with paid and voluntary time for those involved in the project considered.

Furthermore, data ownership and dissemination should be considered in the planning process. Who will have access to video footage, the videos produced, and other materials resulting from the production process? Who will be involved in data analysis, write-up, and dissemination, including articles resulting from the process? Chavez and colleagues (2004) note that the foundation of community-based projects rests on the creation of shared ownership of data, whereas anthropologist and indigenous filmmaker Charles Menzies (2004) takes this a step farther. Working with Native fishing communities in the North Coast region of Canada, he advocates for communities maintaining ownership of materials produced. Thus, video footage, end-product videos, interview transcripts, and the like all remain a part of tribal property. This is one way that Menzies works against a history of outsider (including academic) colonialism that has continually taken from indigenous communities, exploited community resources, and has not often given back to the communities involved.

Gregory and colleagues (2005) outline four stages of videomaking: conceptualization and research, preproduction, production, and postproduction. Conceptualization and research includes identification of the reason for making the video, as well as the video's audience, and the elements of the video to be included. Another thing to consider in this stage is how your video differs from other videos or films that have been made on this or a similar topic. Finally, the videographer needs to consider background research that should be conducted to produce a fully informed video (Gregory et al., 2005, p. 108). The preproduction phase centers on coming up with an initial outline and shooting plan (i.e., a storyboard) for the video, as well as planning logistical details such as who will be a part of the video and how they will be involved, and how the video project will be funded (Gregory et al., 2005, p. 108).

Several sites of production should be considered in the planning phase, including the logistics of script writing, storyboarding, draft editing, and final editing. As Chavez and colleagues (2004) note, while community members might not have expertise on the technical end, they are experts in community life (Chavez et al., 2004, p. 400). Part of the project approval process should thus involve transparent discussions of who will be involved in which parts of production. A certain amount of narrative and editorial flexibility is needed in participatory video. Visual anthropologists—particularly those with a participatory bent—have long debated the "quality" versus "participatory" nature of videomaking and the best, most appropriate, or most "anthropological" ways to represent communities (see Ginsburg, 1995; Ruby, 1995; Turner, 1995). We see several responses to this quandary represented in the core stories presented in this chapter.

PARTICIPATORY FILM PRODUCTION: THE NO-EDITING-REQUIRED (NER) PARTICIPATORY VIDEOMAKING APPROACH

In writing about the "doing" of participatory video for research purposes, we are particularly indebted to Claudia Mitchell's excellent recent book, *Doing Visual Research* (2011), from which much of this section is drawn. Shirley White's (2003) commendable edited volume and Nick and Chris Lunch's (2006) book are also often cited as resources for researchers and advocates interested in using participatory videomaking in their work, particularly for those working in development contexts. As Mitchell points out, use of the word "participation" in connection with videomaking—or we would posit any of the methods reviewed in this book—is potentially contentious. Indeed, there exist a wide array of meanings for this word when applied to videomaking. This includes more "do-it-yourself" (DIY)–type projects, in which participants are the full producers of their videos, to those projects that might involve participants in a variety of ways, such as through script drafting, storyboarding, editing, and final production, to those projects that are claimed as participatory but limit participant involvement to the viewing, commentary, and critique of videos produced by researchers or professional filmmakers.

In this sense, Mitchell (2011) describes a spectrum of participation for videomaking projects and cautions against the orthodoxy of participatory videomaking that positions "participatory" as the only correct way to go about things. Diverse considerations of participation and/or collaboration are presented here in the core stories. In some projects, usually several days to several months in production length, participants may be heavily involved in the editing process, whereas in other "no-editing-required" (NER) projects, participants may conduct all filmmaking themselves but may do so in one day's time, with the video consisting of "first takes" and thus involving no video editing either during production or postproduction. In the middle of the spectrum are projects that take several sessions and involve participants in learning aspects of the videomaking process, but may include outside professional filmmakers or video editors who complete the final edits of the video or film.

Mitchell (2011) has developed useful guidelines for conducting a community-based videomaking project. In the following, we closely adhere to her instructions, which focus on a NER approach to video-making done in a day's time. Mitchell breaks the production process down chronologically, with before and after activities of filmmaking considered just as important as the actual filming of the video. She often begins the production process with warm-up activities to stimulate participant brainstorming, script writing, and practice with the more technical aspects of production. Similar to the digital storytelling idea-generation and script-writing process, if the project is "open" in terms of content, Mitchell will often work with small groups of participants, beginning with a brainstorming prompt such as "What are the issues that are important to you?" Other projects that are thematically focused may begin with a more specific prompt. Regardless, the warm-up session can be seen as an important site for data collection. Thus, during small-group brainstorming, the facilitator may want to take field notes of these discussions.

On the other hand, if the facilitator wishes to focus on the technical aspects of production, she might lead an activity that involves participants working closely with the video camera. Mitchell (2011) suggests introducing the camera to the group with a new train-the-trainer take on the old "telephone" game. One participant is provided with details on the workings and parts of the camera. She then teaches the next participant this information, so that each participant is responsible for teaching another about the video camera. The activity can also be combined with an actual filming, where the "trainer" participant also films the "student" participant, asking this person a discussion question that can be used as an icebreaker discussion or that focuses more directly on intended content.

Next, Mitchell (2011) discusses storyboarding. As with digital storytelling and other dynamic visual processes, a storyboard is used as a visual map or plan to guide the production process. In videomaking, the storyboard focuses on each shot of the video and the sequence they will follow. A low-tech version of a storyboard uses a sheet of paper with rectangles filled in with sketches of each shot, from shot to shot. Part of storyboarding involves the group considering the intent and type of film they are interested in producing. A consideration of genre—such as public service announcement, documentary style, or storied approach—is important here, as it can affect the way the film is perceived by audiences and, consequently, the ability of filmmakers' to achieve their stated intent. Indeed, Mitchell points out that the storyboard can also be used as a point of data collection, as the group uses it to determine the point of their story and the way they wish to tell their story. In this regard, the storyboarding process itself might be videotaped or audiorecorded.

In NER videomaking, Mitchell allows the group one hour to shoot a video. As often mentioned in digital storytelling with limits placed on the length of a story, giving participants a finite amount of time can help kickstart the filming process, often serves as a point of reference for the amount of time to spend on each shot, and in many ways reinforces participants' use of the storyboard as a guide for filmmaking.

After the shoot (and in a NER approach this means that the video recording is complete) participants view their videos. Mitchell (2011) suggests that the small group view their own video before showing it to the whole group on the big screen. Viewing within the small group offers participants a chance to discuss technical flaws and other problems that may have arisen in production before airing the story for the rest of the group. The large group airing is a time for videomakers to present the intent of the film and to discuss the video with the audience. Again, both small and large group airings are useful sites for data collection.

Even in NER approaches, after video production is complete, participants may wish to reconsider technical details of the video or to think about additional uses for their video. Indeed, as yet another site for data collection, reflective questions might be posed about the video postproduction to elicit further discussion. For some projects, the videomaking process ends there. For others, this might be just the beginning of a longer process focused on video or film screenings and reflective discussions with different audiences. As Mitchell notes, while this is an important part of the process—especially for outreach, education, advocacy, or policy purposes—it is often overlooked in social research projects.

Composite videos can serve as an important end product of participatory videomaking, as they take into consideration all of the material produced during the videomaking process (including that potentially produced by participants depending on their involvement in the film-ing process) and not just the outcome/produced film. Composite videos serve multiple purposes and as sources of data as a "researcher-produced data-driven video text . . . a research video, a research tool, a communi-cation tool that is more than simply video data . . . plus the contextual data in the form of video footage taken during the research process and often a musical soundtrack in some part of the video" (Mitchell, 2011, p. 161). Essentially, composite videos allow for both process and out-come layers of production to be represented in tangible form. They also highlight the narrative activity and agency of participants—researchers, community members, professional filmmakers, and others—involved in the production process.

As a "data generation tool," the composite video is different from a final "polished" video or film. Rather than serving as a final cut to be distributed as such, it often consists of compiled "snippets" of visual data that can serve as a reflective tool for the team to examine the cor-pus of data, and it can serve as a way for researchers to return the visual data to the community and to disseminate findings to other research-ers and audiences (Mitchell, 2011, pp. 161–162). Parts of a composite video that might fit into its "formula" include: the title of the video, the context of the issue presented (including statistical data on the issue at hand), footage of the videomaking process, exemplars or all of the short videos produced, the wrap-up, and the credits (Mitchell, 2011, p. 165). Composites may also include discussion questions or other curricular materials surrounding the produced film or video.

PARTICIPATORY VIDEO HISTORY AND PIONEERS

Jean Rouch's work in the late 1950s and early 1960s was one of anthro-pology's first experiments with applied visual/filmmaking (Biella, 2006; Ginsburg, 1995). Through films such as *Jaguar* (1967) and *Petit á Petit* (1969), Rouch was committed to the creation of film as a form of "shared anthropology," such that "knowledge about another culture [should] be produced in a way that [can] be shared with members of that culture" (Ginsburg, 1995, p. 65). Rouch is known for conceptu-alizing early participatory filmmaking in the form of *cinema verité*, in which the practice of filmmaking (the process) was positioned with equal importance to the produced film/outcome, serving as a site for reflexiv-ity and social engagement among those involved in the process, and as a site of *regards comparés*. The notion of *regards comparés* is similar to noted visual anthropologist Faye Ginsburg's (1995) concept of the "parallax effect," meaning that through the juxtaposition of a variety of cinematic perspectives on culture—"slightly different angles of vision"

(p. 65)—filmmakers (broadly conceived as the producers, those depicted or represented within a film, and audiences) can animate our idea of culture and media representations that engage with these visions.

Participatory filmmaker Peter Biella (2006) also writes of the importance of "collaborative visual anthropology," also known as "indigenous media," for the development of participatory videomaking. He refers to the 1972 *Through Navajo Eyes* film project by Sol Worth and John Adair as a key example: ". . . Worth and Adair hoped to use the films to show that the Navajo language and worldview determined an indigenous 'emic' style of shooting and editing" (Biella, 2006, p. 3). As Ginsburg (1995) notes, Worth and Adair "taught filmmaking to young Navajo students without the conventions of western production and editing, to see if their films would reflect a distinctively Navajo film worldview," which helped to disrupt the usual "us" filming "them" paradigm of classic ethnographic film (p. 67).

Participatory filmmaking in the early 1990s became increasingly imbued with the idea of filmmaking as a political or social action endeavor endemic to the videomaking *process* itself. Terence Turner's work with Kayapo videomakers served to promote a sense of group identification by using video production as a form of media making for self-determination. The films "promote collective self-definition and clarify political positions by using mass media to reach beyond the boundaries of face-to-face interaction" (Biella, 2006, pp. 3–4). In 1992, David MacDougall wrote of "intertextual cinema," signaling the acknowledgment of multiple voices and contributing producers in ethnographic film (Ginsburg, 1995, p. 97). Carlos Flores' work in 2004 with the Guatemalan Quiché Maya is exemplary as a form of intertextual cinema, as it used the indigenous filmmaking process as a cathartic practice for recovering the historical memory of civil war: ". . . the video documents produced provided a space within a wider practice of shared anthropology where each party could advance their own goals through hybrid products . . . [and] be simultaneously of use to the researcher and also to the communities studied" (Flores, 2007, p. 209). Central to indigenous media making, praxis-oriented notions of culture are used as a form of social action. As Ginsburg (1995) writes, this forces us to "move away from comfortable and taken for granted narrative conventions that reify 'culture' and 'cultural difference.' Instead, we—as producers, audiences, and ethnographers—are allowed to encounter the multiplicity of points of view through which culture is produced, contested, mediated, and reimagined" (p. 73).

Biella (2006) refers to more recent participatory/collaborative videomaking projects, whose purpose is to send indigenous messages to dominant powers (p. 4). One example is Richard Chalfen and Michael Rich's

(2004) work with Navajo children, in which asthmatic children were asked to film their experience with the illness to teach physicians about the children's experiences and increase patient-physician understanding (p. 5). Other recent projects center on collaborative community outreach and education. Biella refers to Kate Hennessy and Amber Ridington's work with the Doig River First Nation in British Columbia, such as in *Dane-ʒaa Stories and Songs*, as exemplary instances of videomaking based on long-term community collaboration and fieldwork preceding the filmmaking. We discuss this project in detail in the context of participatory digital archives and exhibitions in Chapter 8.

As discussed earlier in this chapter, the participatory or collaborative nature of video- and filmmaking projects spans a range of participation. The following case studies provide examples along this spectrum, with participation ranging along a continuum from process to product to dissemination and audiencing (White, 2003). Core Story 1 (Elder and Kamerling) presents an example of videomaking in which community members are positioned as key figures in the idea- and story-generation process and audiencing of the film, as well as in providing feedback on the film in the postproduction phase. Core Story 2 (Menzies) is an example of participatory videomaking largely driven by ethical considerations of research with Native communities, with participation also informed by multiple purposes, or uses, of the film. In this case, filmmaking is conducted with a team of academic and community-based researchers. Core Story 3 (Biella) is an example of participatory videomaking wherein the anthropologist/researcher has a large role in the production and direction of the filmmaking while collaborating with community-based organizations that serve the communities featured in the films. In this case, audience participation, engagement, and reception are seen as key to the success of the films. Each case demonstrates the benefits of participatory videomaking. However, they also draw out the difficulties that may arise in conducting participatory projects.

Core Story 1: Trusting the Process—Sarah Elder and Leonard Kamerling's Community-Collaborative Approach to Filmmaking

Sarah Elder, professor of Documentary Film in the Department of Media Study at the University at Buffalo, State University of New York, originally came to ethnographic filmmaking as an undergraduate anthropology student in 1968, viewing what she considered to be inadequate anthropological films in the classroom. The films were inadequate given their "distance, lack of intimacy, omissions and the lurking colonialism embedded in their construction" (Elder, 2001–2002, p. 94). Essentially, film subjects were erased by the filmmaker's own desires; the form and content of the films were subjugated by the filmmaker's own interests and did not represent the interests of the disempowered film subjects. Although not yet being able to theoretically pinpoint the source of her frustration, Elder remembers noting this sense of inadequacy and thinking that there must be a better way to make films.

As a graduate student from 1970 to 1972, Elder studied at Brandeis University with Timothy Asch, a leading visual anthropologist and ethnographic filmmaker. She also participated in a joint documentary film program at the Massachusetts Institute of Technology (MIT) with Richard (Ricky) Leacock, Ed Pincus, and John Terry, all filmmakers who were prominent in the American *cinema verité* movement. Elder also worked at the Center for Documentary Anthropology in Cambridge, Massachusetts, which later evolved into Documentary Educational Resources (DER), currently a major film distribution center for documentary and ethnographic film in North America. There she worked with well-known ethnographic filmmakers such as John Marshall, who cofounded DER with Timothy Asch, along with Asen Balikci, Roger Sandall, and others. At the time, ethnographic filmmaking was still very much a man's world, with feminist film concepts given very little credence, such as asking the film subjects to speak for themselves, giving subjects a role in filmmaking, or exploring the lives of women. With a strong feminist viewpoint, Elder cofounded and codirected the Alaska Native Heritage Film Project (ANHFP) in 1973 with Leonard Kamerling. The purpose of the project was to work collaboratively with Alaska Native communities to produce films that accurately represented the lives and concerns of Alaska Native people.

Elder's filmmaking partner for many years, Leonard Kamerling, currently curator of the Alaska Center for Documentary Film at the University of Alaska Museum of the North and associate professor of English at the University of Alaska, Fairbanks, did not start out as a filmmaker. Instead, his initial foray into participatory filmmaking grew out of his personal convictions living in Alaska Native villages as a college student in the 1960s. He spent a year living in a Yup'ik Eskimo village, which, as he notes, turned his worldview around rather dramatically. In particular, Kamerling began to look at ethnographic and cultural films about native/indigenous peoples and was struck by how wooden the films were and how superficial they were in their treatment of Alaska Native people, concerned more with what people did than with the emotional landscape of their lives.

In contrast, the world that he experienced living in northwest Alaska was quite different. He observed a kind of reciprocity that people had with the land and the landscape, and the interdependence that people exhibited as they worked together to survive. Kamerling began to question how this sort of observation might be captured and depicted, especially by a white person, an outsider, and arrived at the idea of doing filmmaking from the "inside out." This involved an ongoing collaboration between the filmmaker and the participating community in determining what a film should be about, who should be in it, and where it should go, in terms of both narrative and distribution.

Meeting in Cambridge, Massachusetts, Elder and Kamerling found that they had similar ideas about more accurately representing film subjects, and that they both wanted to film in Alaska. While they had not fully formed their methodology, their approach was rooted in many of Timothy Asch's tenets: that through the act of attentive seeing, ethnographic filmmaking might function more effectively as a medium related to field observation rather than as traditional autonomous documentary making, or quasi-illustrative lecture material viewed passively in anthropology classrooms (Elder, 2001–2002, p. 89). During the 1970s there was a worldwide renegotiation of what documentary was and what it could do, with directors reimagining both form and voice within their film, all of which was influential to Elder and Kamerling's approach.

While Elder finished her MFA degree at Brandeis, Kamerling completed his first film, *Tununeremiut: The People of Tununak* (DER, 35 minutes) in 1972 with Elder as consultant. Kamerling remembers: "it was sort of a miracle that [the first] film was actually made." While trying to produce the film, they realized a disconnection between their community-determined ideology and the actual practice of making a film, noting that because Kamerling was so very much wedded to the idea of community-determined, "coauthored" filmmaking, the film's first version did not have subtitles. Instead, he had figured, "if you *were there* you wouldn't have subtitles. You'd have to figure it out." While difficult to produce, the film was especially a success for Alaska Native audiences because it spoke to them in a way that other films had not: it was about them, by them, in their language, with a slower pace than most documentaries. The film was widely accepted, and Elder and Kamerling began to see the powerful possibilities of participatory filmmaking, eventually naming their approach "community-determined filmmaking."

In continued collaboration, Elder and Kamerling submitted a proposal to the Ford Foundation that set out their initial vision for collaborative filmmaking: a radical proposal to allow community members to decide the topic for the film. In 1973, with a large grant from the Ford Foundation, they cofounded the Alaska Native Heritage Film Project, where they continued to develop their collaborative process. The premise of the approach was that, as visual ethnographers, they would not determine the representation of their subjects, but also would not give up aesthetic or technical control or anthropological concerns in film production. Foregrounded in this approach was the idea of "shared authorship," a seemingly innocuous proposal that became increasingly "messy" over time (Elder, 1995). The filmmakers soon realized that rather than a relationship of "shared" authorship, one of collaboration was taking place instead. Thus, while the films were initiated and produced under the ethnographers' vision, through a dialogical process the communities involved were crucial collaborators that contributed to filmmaking.

Elder and Kamerling thus renamed their approach "community collaborative filmmaking." Two early films using the approach, *At the Time of Whaling* (DER, 1974, 20 minutes) and *On the Spring Ice* (DER, 1975, 45 minutes), were made on St. Lawrence Island in the Bering Sea. The filmmakers picked a conservative village, Gambell, where they had been warned by others not to go because villagers were deemed unfriendly to outsiders. Elder and Kamerling felt this might be good sign, signifying that the villagers were thinking about the health and continuity of their culture and that they might really value a collaborative filmmaking process.

Elder and Kamerling were initially insecure about their process. Kamerling visited the village and presented what they had in mind: to make a film with the villagers in control of the process. The filmmakers decided to give community members the space and time to make up their own mind about participation, even if this meant the two filmmakers leaving the village for a while. This strategy continues to be critical to the community-collaborative process, with community decision-making perceived as a cultural process that has to be made in its own time: it cannot be made according to the filmmaker's timeline (Elder, 1995). As Elder put it: "I like to present what we're going to do. Everything. Show our previous work. Have the questions asked. And then leave town."

Describing their first venture with this process, Elder spoke of feeling immense relief when they finally received a telegram from the Gambell Village Council that said, "We, the people of Gambell, want to make a film." To Elder, this was a significant turning point: the community had realized their role in the filmmaking and were committed to taking on full agency in the process. The filmmakers then proceeded with the process of going from house to house, visiting with people, attending village meetings, and asking community members what they would like to see in a film. They did not film anything at all for the first couple of weeks.

After eliciting community members' priorities for filmmaking, the filmmakers began to gather scene suggestions of what people found to be most important. This meant that the filmmakers had to give something up in the process. For instance, Elder noted that while she was intent on looking at women's lives and domestic life in the whaling film, she had to give up this goal because it was not shared by the villagers. This was tough for a filmmaker, particularly in the beginning when she had not yet learned and practiced these new participatory and community-determined methods enough to have complete faith in them.

The power of the community-collaborative approach lies in its informal and flexible nature, such that films produced rarely reflect their makers' original intentions. Kamerling elaborated:

> What *real* collaboration does, real sharing of authority; it thrusts you onto a roller coaster ride. And you lose control of the things that are part of your gyroscope; that give you your stability, your knowledge, and your direction. But this also creates the opportunity for opening something that's totally unexpected. That advances your work in a way that you could never have even thought of before. . . . For me, I always like . . . going to a new place and I like that feeling of being just thrust into a current and see where it takes me. . . . [I]t's usually the beginning of something that's very life changing. And *every* big film that I've worked on has really been life changing in some way. . . . What [begins as] a project to make a film [becomes] something much, much, much wider in this process of learning. . . . Possibilities for the film [open] up that I couldn't have dreamed of from the conceptual side of things at the beginning.

The process is challenging in that it reinvents itself relative to a film's context. Lessons learned from previous projects are not always applicable to working in a new community or culture.

The community-collaborative approach is not determined by any fast rules, but rather shifts according to the project at hand and the nature of the community involved. The approach is more about "putting [the filmmaker] and the film into the current of life, doing it for an extended period of time, and seeing what happens," according to Kamerling. However, several ethical parameters are used to guide the process. The first involves "relinquishing control," as opposed to traditional documentary practices that position the director/ethnographer as the driver in the filmmaking process, the decision-maker for choice of film topic, shooting choices, and editing decisions (Elder, 1995). Relinquishing control means letting those depicted in the film decide what footage will stay and what will be left out of the film, especially when the filmmaker is filming something unfamiliar. It also allows for community members to determine access to particular subjects or themes for the film.

For example, Kamerling spoke of a time when he filmed laundry flapping on a line, which he thought made for a beautiful image. However, the laundry's owner was embarrassed that everything on the line looked old and shabby and asked that the filmmakers not include the image. They agreed on the spot not to use it. This kind of community member control in determining representation supports the quality of the film-maker's everyday interaction with community members as well as the outcome of the film. Furthermore, by relinquishing control of the process to community members, the process "opens up" to allow those depicted in the film to feel safer about the material presented and be more receptive to being filmed.

A second guiding principle is that of community self-determination (Elder, 1995). Traditionally, anthropological documentaries were often made in and about communities that lacked any real political autonomy. A collaborative approach allows communities greater self-determination and empowerment in terms of the ways they are represented, both within the community and to outside audiences. At the same time, self-determination is a complex concept in relation to authorial power and representation. For example, while insider community perspectives, such as in media produced by indigenous community members, may allow a more "intimate" portrayal of community concerns than those produced by outsiders, such a result is not necessarily guaranteed and often depends on the filmmaker's social position. "Accountability" is key here (Elder, 1995). When the filmmaker and those filmed are accountable to each other—and hold horizontal relations of power in the filmmaking process—the potential for the film to be responsive to the community is thus heightened.

A third principle challenges Western notions of copyright and ownership of knowledge (Elder, 1995). In both the academy and the marketplace, copyright belongs to the image producer, the filmmaker, the researcher, or the author. A community-collaborative approach reworks this notion, taking the perspective that images produced are ultimately owned by those reflected in them. Often this involves a repositioning of the researcher/filmmaker in the production of knowledge, and a rethinking of notions of proprietary control. To many authors and filmmakers, this can be challenging. As Elder (1995) notes: "People can't believe that by giving up control, there is something greater to be gained" (p. 101). In addition, shared copyright can be quite complicated to implement. In Elder and Kamerling's first films, they attempted to share copyright and distribution of the film with the community filmed: the copyright was held between the village and the filmmakers, with an equal distribution split. However, the issue became tangled over questions surrounding who legally owned the copyright. Was it with the village? Some legal entity? Or a group of people? Eventually becoming too cumbersome and difficult to track, the filmmakers stopped this practice.

Elder and Kamerling produced and directed nine award-winning films together. Their final film, *Uksuum Cauyai: The Drums of Winter*

(DER, 90 minutes), was released in 1988. In 2006, the film was selected for inclusion in the National Film Registry of the Library of Congress, one of only 25 films named each year. *Drums of Winter* is filmed in Emmonak, a central Yup'ik village in western Alaska on the mouth of the Yukon River delta. Elder had previously served there as the only high school teacher in the village, at the first local high school established after the State of Alaska settled the Molly Hootch class action suit, in which a young Alaska Native woman sued to have local secondary education.

After living in Emmonak for a year in 1972 and 1973, knowing the community well, and having been involved in the dance world of the community, Elder wanted to make a film about dancing. She was quite familiar with the village dancers, having been encouraged to learn dancing by the local "dance boss" and Catholic deacon, Stanley Waska, to whom she eventually dedicated the film. As an active participant in dancing, Elder was positioned as a participant observer of the art she would come to film. Practically speaking, she also came to the film knowing whom the community deemed to be the best dancers, who attended dance practices frequently, and who might want to work with her. Her participation in dance also helped her edit the film. Elder relates that Stanley, the dance boss, often visited with her and taught her a lot about the music: singing songs, explaining the verses and choruses, diagramming and explicating the songs' structure, and explaining who sang which songs and who owned the songs. Thus, she was able to edit the film maintaining both musical and choreographic integrity.

Five years later, Elder returned to Emmonak in 1978 for a month, to request permission for Kamerling and herself to make a film on dancing and to set up the filming logistics. An important turning point for the community-collaborative process took place around the issue of allowing cameras and lighting into the *qusiaq* (dance house/men's house). As filmmakers, Elder and Kamerling could not have shot the film if they were not able to put up movie lights. Elder requested a village-wide meeting to present what she wanted to do, to ask for feedback, and to show some of their earlier films. As part of village consensus building, the process involved both formally and publically informing the whole village and asking for filming permission, with Elder saying that she wanted to do a film on dancing with the dance community.

The film process was slightly different from their preceding films in that Elder and Kamerling came with a topic in mind. The National Endowment for the Arts (NEA) had funded them to produce a film on Yup'ik music and dance, including elements of embedded reciprocity and spirituality. As Elder remembers, the meeting was tense and went on for a long time:

> There were a lot of eloquent people speaking in Yup'ik. I had no idea what they were saying. It was being translated . . . but not too much. And people spoke very adamantly about how there was a tradition that photographic lights were inappropriate for a spiritual place. And that this (film) was going to be breaking old traditions. . . . [T]here was some controversy about all this.

Elder sat in the back of the room and remained nervous, knowing that she had to trust the collaborative process and should not stand up and begin making an impassioned speech about the film's importance. She remembers the political leaders of the villages, who were in their forties and fifties, saying that they did not want lights in the dance house because it would break with tradition, and that this was a sacred place. The elders at the time, who were in their seventies and eighties, stood up and countered, "No, you're wrong! We want this. We've seen changes that no one could've ever imagined when we were your age . . . you young people. And we want this. As long as we can guide her and tell her what we want, we think this has value." And then the elders said, "We're going to let her bring the lights in." So they did, as Elder recounted with a laugh.

Kamerling arrived two months later and for the first month the two did not shoot anything other than exterior village scenes, so that villagers could get used to them and their film gear. They slowly worked their way into the filming process. Having previously participated in her own "first dance ceremony," in which she made and distributed gifts and other traditional foods such as *akutaq* ("Eskimo ice cream") to properly initiate and legitimize herself in the local dancing community, Elder was particularly interested in filming the preparation and reciprocal subsistence practices that families contribute to a first dancer's initiation ceremony. In fact, she and Kamerling went to Emmonak with the intention of filming the first dance process of a young person (commonly done between the ages of eight and thirteen). However, upon arrival they realized that there was to be no first dance that year: television had just arrived, everyone was watching it, and no one was hunting enough game to accumulate gifts for a large giveaway. Although Elder and Kamerling had proposed this topic to the NEA, they realized that they were not going to be able to film live footage of a first dance ceremony. Instead, through a previous connection Elder had established while teaching in the village, they were able to incorporate found footage from another film project. A tribal elder gave Elder some decaying 16mm footage stored in his cache that included a first dance ceremony. She edited this into her final cut of *Drums of Winter*.

Elder has continued making films in Alaska over the past 35 years. Her most recent film work, *Surviving Arctic Climate Change*, has her traveling back to Emmonak, this time to direct a film on the consequences of climate change on Alaska Native people. The collaborative process has paid off, such that 25 years later she is able to return to the village with community members still embracing *Drums of Winter* and ready to collaborate with her on the new film. With an all-woman crew, Elder has also directed the award-winning film *Every Day Choices*, about the abuses of alcohol in the Yup'ik town of Bethel, Alaska. The film was especially difficult to make because it touched on a topic both politically and personally sensitive, a topic more negative to portray than a culturally celebrated process such as dancing.

Regardless of topic, however, all of Elder's films are produced using a community-collaborative process. Key to the process, she notes, is that while she may be named as film director, she is *not in control of the process*; rather, she lets the process take its course, with the community sharing control. This point speaks to the most important aspect of the process—not just the film decision-making process, which is vital—but also the actual issue of control and power. For example, Elder has seen researchers/filmmakers pretend a type of collaborative approach, such that if push came to shove and a community member wanted something that was not furthering the success of the film (as deemed by the filmmaker), then the filmmaker would advocate for her own agenda. On the other hand, when communities understand that they have authority, control, and power, and that they can say no at any time without being pressured or convinced to do otherwise—and they exercise that right—it transforms into incredible support and action, according to Elder. This moment in filmmaking is key to community empowerment, when subjects realize their autonomy. Elder believes this is when filmmaking transforms out of its postcolonial past.

Elder put it succinctly:

> If you ask a person to be your equal they bring everything to the table and open doors for you that you would never know were even there to open. . . . And if they're as invested in something as you are then the material that you're dealing with is so much richer. I mean how can an outsider know memory, for instance, of a place? How can you access meaning of landscape when you haven't lived there before? Having people as your equal player is a thousand-fold richer (the kinds of material you get), because everybody brings everything to the table. So they start using you in the ways that they want to use you, openly. . . . And you're using them. Everybody knows everybody's using each other. . . . And so by bringing in other knowledge bases, whether it's a local person's or a biologist's, it just opens up the space that much more.

In addition to their rich filmmaking partnership, Kamerling, like Elder, has continued his own filmmaking work. *Heart of the Country* (Icarus Films, 1998, 58 minutes) is set in a small village in Japan and is one of four documentaries to be nominated internationally for the American Film Institute's prestigious Pare Lorenze Prize. He is also currently collaborating on a participatory videomaking project in Tanzania with visual anthropologist Peter Biella (see Core Story 3 on Biella). The community-collaborative filmmaking process has worked especially well for Kamerling while working with communities in which collective activity is central to their way of life.

Released in 1998, *Heart of the Country* tells the story of a small school in the rural village of Kanayama in Northern Japan. Kamerling began by working with an academic colleague (William Parrett) who specialized in small schools. Their broad aim was to investigate why small schools had been so successful in Japan. As part of a long-term collaboration with partners at a Japanese university, it took the team almost two years to find the right community with which to work. Eventually, Kamerling moved with his family to Japan for a year, with the intention of telling the story of what happens in small schools and why they worked. As part of the ethnographic filmmaking process, he saw an extended stay as important for establishing trusting relationships with community members: "Without those you have nothing. That's what the film is, a kind of a record of the quality of the trust that you are able to build," said Kamerling. In an online essay, Kamerling (2004) reflects on this experience.

The extended stay allows one's sense of place (akin to "emplacement"; Howes, 2005) to develop. One's visual understanding and sense of place tends to shift with time. Indeed, the types of things that might be visually attractive and filmed when first arriving at a place are usually different after a person has been there for a while. The place begins to be seen at a deeper level, as if the filmmaker is building visual literacy about the location. To Kamerling, this is an extremely important step in the process, such that he does not usually film a new place for the first month upon arrival, except for perhaps exterior scenery shots. In this way, the filmmaking process is a dialogical reflection of the filmmaker's own self-discovery in relation to a growing visual acuity of place.

The flexibility and organic nature of community-collaborative filmmaking lay at the heart of Kamerling's film. While he had planned an extended stay in Japan to film *Heart of the Country*, he also had little sense of how the film would be made or what it would be about. Instead, the process grew through collaboration with community members; namely, with nine school staff and parents involved in the school's Parent Teacher Association (PTA), and 30 students attending the school.

One of the first hurdles to overcome, Kamerling noted, was the Japanese tendency to value the expert. As the film's director he was seen as holding all of the chips; group members had difficulty grasping the concept that he was not going to tell them what the film would be about. Instead, he explained that as members of the school community they were the experts, and that if he were to make decisions about content, it would be a superficial film.

After meeting with the group a couple of times, Kamerling did not hear from them for a long time. After living in the village for a couple of months he still had not filmed much aside from exterior shots, and he began to worry about completing the project. Reflecting back on this time, Kamerling recalled a conversation with his wife: "I said to my wife, 'you know, this was a mistake, I don't know why I ever got involved in this.' She said, 'well you know, you say that about every project you get involved with. Just relax and trust your process.' . . . [A]nd suddenly there was an opening. A door opened and we went through and there it was."

Realizing that the community group was meeting without him, Kamerling became both nervous and excited. The collaborative story-telling process proved so effective "that they took it away from me and really kind of made it their own. And then invited me back into it when it was something that they had molded and they thought it was ready to go," he related. Finally summoned to a meeting with the group, they told him: "Okay, we've decided what this is about. It's about families. We've chosen the families and contacted them and gotten their permission. And now the rest is up to you." Eventually the film became a story about the school's principal and the ways he influenced the lives of different families, such that the school served as a form of family itself.

After a year of filming Kamerling returned home to Alaska, spending the next year and a half working with several native translators to translate all 60 hours of material into English, producing 1,600 pages of transcript as a result. Similar to what one might do in more textual forms of narrative analysis, he sought to discover the heart of the story through his editing work. This served as a process of discovery in itself, as he tried to elucidate a story while also producing a film that was interesting and dramatic. Editing was also collaborative, as Kamerling twice returned to Japan to receive input from the community group on his work-in-progress. He held community screenings where he aired the rough edit and then sought viewers' comments, then went back to Alaska to continue editing the material.

After some six years the film was almost completed. He and Parrett mailed copies to everyone who appeared in the film, with the instructions that it would not be publicly aired until the filmmakers were given approval to do so. The guideline of community self-determination held sway here, such that if anything were found by participants to be objectionable it would be omitted from the film without any question. In this way, community members had the right to determine the final cut. Nevertheless, although no objections were placed, Kamerling came away concerned about the social dynamic of informed consent, particularly because he was told personal and emotional things while filmmaking, due in part to the fact that he was a foreigner. He was thus able to skirt the boundaries of social expectations. He was also concerned about dynamics of time and social memory in relation to informed consent, such that while given consent to film a person in a particular moment in time, he became anxious about what might happen down the road when family members, employers, and others (to say nothing of the person filmed) viewed the film in the future. These issues, commonly faced in collaborative film- and videomaking, are not always able to be resolved or may be addressed according to circumstance. In 1999, Kamerling returned to the village after the final cut was ready, and a large event was held to publicly air the film.

The informal, uncodified approach taken in Elder and Kamerling's work illustrates the strengths of the community-collaborative process. As they both note, at the heart of collaboration is the ethnographer/filmmaker's willingness to allow the approach to develop from within, such that what you start with is a kind of openness, a willingness to be flexible, and a willingness to *not know* where you are, or where you are going. You must remain balanced in your imbalance.

CORE STORY 2: NO FINAL CUT—MULTIPURPOSING PARTICIPATORY FILMMAKING IN CHARLES MENZIES' WORK

The background story to Charles Menzies' work with participatory filmmaking is quite similar to that of other scholars presented in this book who did not initially intend to use visual methods in their work, but rather saw a visual approach as mapping nicely onto their already-in-use participatory approach. Menzies was not formally trained in filmmaking, nor does he come from a visual anthropology background. His foray into filmmaking was inspired while examining the techniques used in documentary film, such as the structure used in films in the National Film Bureau of Canada, and thinking about what could be done with this nonfiction form. Perhaps related to his dual aims of research and advocacy, Menzies notes the need to maintain what he calls "fidelity to reality" in anthropological filmmaking. For Menzies, this means that anthropologists have a responsibility to make films that have a connection to the real world, to what they are seeing, rather than being completely inventive or creative. In this way, Menzies invokes, as he put it, an old-fashioned sense of empiricism: that if somebody else was seeing the same thing they would come to a similar conclusion.

Menzies, an indigenous scholar, is an associate professor in the Department of Anthropology at the University of British Columbia (UBC). His filmmaking, conducted in collaboration with the Gitxaala Nation, fishing communities in the North Coast region of Canada, exemplifies work based on long-term community engagement and participation. His work is particularly important for considering the process and on-the-ground practice of negotiation and establishment of proper research protocol in collaborative projects. As director of the Ethnographic Film Unit at UBC, Menzies sees participatory filmmaking as having multiple purposes. As an "active research tool," the process can stimulate qualitative inquiry, while the film outcome or "product" can be used in a variety of ways and venues to stimulate deeper conversations.

Menzies' first film was produced as part of a project that included youth-oriented workshops, for which his project team intended to develop corresponding curricular material. The team figured that video might dovetail nicely with their youth focus. Filmmaking in this case served as a way to document youth participation, with youth interviewing people living in their community, the project team filming the youth during the interview process, and a film put together from the resulting footage. However, as Menzies put it, the resulting film, *Working in the Woods* (2002) has all possible filmmaking errors: headshot interviews, the color is wrong, the lighting is wrong, the sound is off, and the film quality is not good, as they were using a retail camera. He learned from this experience that applying a classic research model toward filmmaking, where filming is used as just another data collection technique, does not necessarily add anything to the process than the use of more standard techniques such as interviewing. Instead, the shiny new object of filmmaking may actually detract from the process and the intent of listening to what people have to say. After making the film, Menzies set off in a new direction in his filmmaking.

The Ethnographic Film Unit at UBC has since produced several award-winning films that take a community-based participatory research approach. Two such films, *View from Gitxaala* (2003, 16 minutes) and *Returning to Gitxaala* (2005, 16 minutes), focus on collaborative research and the dual relationship or responsibilities invoked in the participatory research process. In particular, the films highlight the collaborative relationship between UBC anthropologists and the Gitxaala Nation by documenting a research process that respects indigenous protocols, and provides the perspectives of both the anthropologists and community members involved.

View from Gitxaala deliberately focuses on the presentation and commentary on research ethics in Native communities by John Lewis, a Gitxaala Treaty Negotiator. Lewis's presentation was originally to be part of a Society for Applied Anthropology (SfAA) panel session. While Menzies and others had been working on another film with the community, there had been reluctance on the part of community members for the research team to use film, rather than interviewing, in their work. Based on Lewis's paper and this perceived tension, Menzies shifted the intent of filmmaking, using it in a way that offered an opportunity to do something safe, but that was also of value in the community. The film thus became about community-based methods and ethical research. Key points arose during conversations between Menzies and Lewis. The film then became *Lewis's* presentation, which was eventually shown at the SfAA annual meeting. In the case of the film, Lewis's written work led to the foundation of the structure for the film. Then, after transcribing Lewis's discussions with Menzies, they came up with the film's structure, the filmmaker went in, and they established a schedule for filming. Menzies deliberately chose to not be in the film, as this was Lewis's presentation and because the view was from Gitxaala.

Within the film the audience is presented with several "views" from Gitxaala. Viewers see John Lewis focusing on rights, title, and treaty issues, but they are also presented with the views of two key team members on the participatory videomaking process, including their initial impressions of the project and the ways their impressions have shifted. Sam Lewis, one of the community-based researchers, speaks mostly on youth and education issues. Another community researcher, a young woman, comes to exemplify the process of "learning our own word," as Sam puts it, through her participation in the research and filmmaking process. Native language is also sprinkled throughout the film to emphasize indigenous self-determination. At one point the film depicts Sam Lewis giving testimony in his own language. Similar to the approach taken by Elder and Kamerling in their first film, the testimony is not translated, with the absence of subtitles made meaningful in their own right, connoting power to this testimony by not having it "colonized" through English translation. On the other hand, toward the end of the film and referring to the stronger sustainability of resources in Native hands, John Lewis is shown speaking in his own language, with English subtitles appended at the bottom of the screen to transmit a political message to multiple audiences about Gitxaala Nation ownership of its natural resources.

With the public airing of the film, community members became much more invested in filmmaking as part of the knowledge construction process surrounding their community. This led to the filming of *Returning to Gitxaala*, a film Menzies said he had always wanted to make. In contrast to *View from Gitxaala*, in which Menzies is not depicted during the film, in this film he features prominently. The film's opening scene deliberately begins with Menzies speaking about the roles and responsibilities of the university and the university researcher, irrespective of a person's personal connections and commitments. As Menzies notes, despite his own connections to the community (his own family is in Gitxaala), as a filmmaker and researcher he takes on a different, more formal role, where he is seen as a part of UBC when he is conducting a research project.

Capturing project team member impressions of the filmmaking process, the film also documents the reflexive practice invoked in a community-based approach. In so doing, the film captures the strengths of participatory processes, while also serving as a political statement on the need for indigenous self-determination and knowledge/resource ownership. The film also pays tribute to community members who participated in the first film (*View*) by again presenting their perspective. The film features returning players: graduate students, community researchers, and community members alike.

In *Returning*, Menzies is filmed talking with community members about the collaborative filmmaking process, such as the need to seek community consent to begin a project, receive input on the project process from community members, and to acknowledge the knowledge-sharing process. Campus administrators, faculty members, and the filmmaking team speak to community members about the meaningfulness of the project. This responds to the multiple levels of respect that must be adhered to both within the community and the academy to properly establish and support campus-community partnerships.

Community-based researcher Sam Lewis is depicted giving public testimony to a group of community members, reminding them of the importance of public declarations of occurrences and events in Gitxaala life by saying: "If it's not stated publicly, it doesn't exist." The statement is a political one on behalf of the Gitxaala Nation, but also speaks to the strengths of the collaborative filmmaking process, which allows community members to determine their own representations on issues of import. All the same, collaboration with outside organizations is also seen as key to knowledge dissemination.

Menzies has produced a range of types of films, which indicates the multiple purposes to be realized when using digital technology in video production. For example, one type is the classic narrative film with a beginning, middle, and end. One recent film, *Bax Laansk: A Film about Gitxaala* (2009, 50 minutes), is of the classic narrative sort, serving as a directorial statement, a statement of picture and vantage point led by Menzies. However, the film has also been fragmented into vignettes (Forests and Oceans for the Future, 2012), to be used in a variety of ways. Referred to as community films, "equity filming," or "wedding videos" by Menzies, the vignettes serve as a form of "observational cinema" in that they reflect people in action and movement, to provide a deeper understanding of the process behind what people are doing. For instance, for one vignette he wanted to depict how the process of drying and smoking fish works. The vignette served to represent the action and talking around this process.

While the vignette might seem a "point of ephemera," as Menzies put it, it is also useful. The idea of creating vignettes initially arose when he began one film project, using a collaborative participatory model in which everyone gathered in the same room to hold a democratic dialog on the filmmaking. At one point in the discussion, one of his relatives pulled him aside and said, "you know, just *do the film*, we don't really care about this, all this other nonsense. What we want is the pieces, give me the pieces. Somebody smoking fish, preparing bark, picking berries. I'll put the commentary on it, you do the film, but make sure there's this." Whereas due to prior technical limitations earlier generations of filmmakers were more concerned with conveying a master narrative, with digital technology, filmmakers are no longer bound to one narrative structure; they are now able to segment, repackage, and restructure film in multiple ways. To paraphrase Marie Antoinette, said Menzies, he can now "have [his] film and eat it too," still creating the classic narrative film that represents his vision and voice while also fragmenting it into vignettes to fit other uses that may serve important purposes for the community, but not necessarily be viewed by those outside.

Menzies has also produced several short films with an advocacy angle. One film, *Naming the Harbour* (2009, 25 minutes) (see anthfilm.anth. ubc.ca/boat.html), is about a declaration of rights and title. The film was produced to serve as a point of advocacy in a legal struggle. In such a case, considerations must be made while filming such that the story follows a plausible line and is based on available empirical evidence. That is, if the film were to be presented in a court case, the filmmakers should be able to present the material from which the film was drawn. Again, the anthropologist filmmaker has an obligation to construct a credible film, especially when working with indigenous communities where so much is connected to issues of rights, title, and self-determination.

Menzies has also produced an archaeological film, with editing and some footage shot by his son. The purpose of the film was to document a community-directed archaeological field method project conducted with the Gitxaala Nation, with community members serving as more than half of the field workers in the project. The film also speaks to the other two films (*View* and *Returning*) that were filmed in the community. The film has been shown as a way for the anthropologists to talk about what they were doing and discuss the project process and implications with community members. In this way, the film serves as a sort of elicitation device for community-based conversations.

Continuous consultation with the community and ownership of the knowledge produced (including accompanying data collected) both serve as participatory elements in filmmaking for Menzies. On the other hand, filming and editing is more often than not conducted by the anthropologist/filmmaker rather than by community members. While going back and forth on the issue of who should actually produce the films, Menzies has eventually come down on the side of wanting a certain kind of technical precision and proficiency in the films, versus the argued-for "raw authenticity" of "real" ethnographic film achieved with the approach that he sees some visual anthropologists taking, of "throwing the film people out the back door." As the films' director, his part in filmmaking produces a certain kind of aesthetic that allows him to make particular political and ethnographic statements. On this perspective, he stated:

> I actually don't believe "the author's dead." I do think that there's a place for a directorial statement. And my way of making film with the community's interest in mind is to create film vignettes and dispersing the material in this usable form to the community. . . . [T]hat's the way in which I approach [filmmaking], just trying to shift it so that there is, in a sense, no *final cut* in the work that we produce. . . . [I]t's being democratized, [but] perhaps in a different direction, in a different way than people who are working with community members *directly* in the production of the film.

Participatory filmmaking in this respect is just as much about democratizing output and use as it is about input, or who is participating in the film's production.

Menzies is also clear about his directorial contributions to the films he makes. While the films are there as a form of documentation, they are still also structured in such a way so as to capture the story of the event. Menzies referred to the example of a film he recently directed about an all-Native basketball tournament. There are five parts to the film, including an opening and closing. While the film is anthropological and ethnographic, the filming is done in a very intentional way to depict the ethnographic knowledge that he has about the event, stemming from his work as an anthropologist and filmmaker, but also as a previous participant in the local high school basketball league. In this respect, he has certain things that he wants to say about the event, as well as an audience in mind for viewing the film.

Menzies sees ethical tensions in participatory filmmaking emanating not so much from the ways that community members are represented in film, or being met with confrontations by community members that he is appropriating cultural knowledge, or being asked to take things out of the films that community members came to regret saying or doing. Instead, Menzies takes a fairly "radical position" to community-based research ethics, which he and colleagues (Menzies, 2011; Menzies & Butler, 2011) touch on in relation to students conducting fieldwork with indigenous communities. Ethical tensions rest more with anthropologists and graduate students (the researchers), in asking what rights *they* themselves are willing to "give up" to participate in the filmmaking endeavor. Essentially, ethical relationships in ethnography and filmmaking exist in a sort of bartering system. Namely, by asking other people to give us ethnographers knowledge, we give up certain rights of refusal in terms of representation. If a researcher goes into an indigenous community that has been subjected to colonialism, oppression, and exploitation (materially as well as ethically speaking), and asks community members to give something to them—such as community-based knowledge—then the researcher should be willing to give something up in exchange. In the context of documentary filmmaking, what anthropologists give up when they enter a relationship with the community is a certain sense of privacy. As the instructor of service-learning courses focused on training students in collaborative approaches, including participatory filmmaking, one must be able to balance student safety and their navigation of new territory with the give and take of each person's contributions (i.e., knowledge, privacy, representation) to the process.

In this sense, burdens or costs are borne by the community in participatory research, albeit in a potentially different manner than in other, less collaborative work. As Menzies and Butler (2011) have noted, there's a reciprocal obligation embedded in participatory research, wherein community members are taking a risk by putting their trust in researchers and students engaged in the work. In exchange, there is an expectation that the researchers should also give something up in the process. All the same, across the board, anthropological practice involves this give and take, though it is not always recognized as such. Often instead, we think that we gain access to a community because of our own inner brilliance, when there are really other benefits that the community stands to gain from the research being conducted.

Menzies' participatory filmmaking approach exemplifies the need for anthropologists to take responsibility for their knowledge production, as well as to speak to multiple audiences and to produce knowledge that is *useful* for these audiences, and especially relevant for the communities with which one is working. Participatory filmmaking in particular accommodates such a multiplicity of purposes. While the films he has produced may not count as much in the academic measure of things, as Menzies noted, they do have a purpose in resonating with community audiences. The fragmented films, vignettes, are especially useful, highlighting the ways that new technologies can allow anthropologists to do better anthropology in that they free the anthropologist from the domineering and authorial voice of the master narrative, allowing a balance between the anthropologist's and other people's voices to take precedent.

Core Story 3: Filmmaking that Touches the Heart— The Applied Visual Anthropology Oeuvre of Peter Biella

In the late 1980s Peter Biella, now director of the Program in Visual Anthropology at San Francisco State University (SFSU) and former president of the Society for Visual Anthropology, produced his first AIDS education film, *AIDS in the Barrio: Eso no me pasa a mi [This can never happen to me]*. Partially funded and partnered by the Philadelphia Department of Public Health, the film focused specifically on the Puerto Rican community. After making the film, Biella took a decade off from film production to work on a large multimedia project. Eventually, he came back to collaborative video production through a yearlong class he began teaching on anthropological filmmaking, in which a number of his students were from SFSU's Cinema Department.

To encourage student involvement in anthropology, Biella designed the class so that students would be required to work with an existing community organization. The students were required to adopt a target group identified by the partnering community organization as their film's primary audience, and to do fieldwork, both concerning the needs of the organization and the media viewing practices of the target group. The film was then produced to respond to these needs. Biella became increasingly interested in a participatory approach to filmmaking through the process of teaching this course, and even more so after collaborating with Kate Hennessy on the Virtual Museum of Canada project (see the core story on Hennessy's work in Chapter 8), working with Hennessy, other UBC collaborators, and Dane-zaa elders for 10 days. This experience confirmed his belief in the usefulness of a collaborative mission for visual anthropology.

Around the same time, Biella returned to Tanzania after a long hiatus, having conducted dissertation fieldwork there in the early 1980s. With the intention of producing films now using a Freirean collaborative model, his plan was to find local organizations to work with, which would determine the sort of film to be made. All the while Biella also knew that he was still very much interested in AIDS education. He began working (and still works) with a Kisongo Maasai, Simon Meigaro, who knew of a Maasai-led nongovernmental organization (NGO) called *Emburis-Engai* (Blessings of God), which was led by a Maasai board of directors and was proposed as the contact organization.

The two (Biella and Meigaro) had made plans the year prior to produce a series of five films on various Maasai predicaments. However, they were still unsure where to begin. Together in conversation with the organization's board members they determined that the board would have authorial control over the basic content of the film, as a group they would negotiate with Biella over scenes to be shot, and they would have a say during the editing process. The *Maasai Migrants Series* project thus emerged, giving people a chance to view the original film, as well as recordings of the Tanzanian screenings and audience responses to the film screenings.

The first films were shot in 2008. Meigaro and Biella worked closely with Rosie Tureto, the chair of *Emburis'* board of directors, and with graduate student Shamia Sandles, who produced a reflexive master's thesis film about the collaborative project called *Subject to Change* (this and the other *Series* films are to be distributed by DER on DVD). The group discussed what film subject they should first tackle as a pilot to work out the kinks of a collaboration they anticipated would last for at least five years. While Biella's first preference was to do a film on AIDS and sexual practices, the group ultimately decided that they would have trouble with such an intimate topic because the filmmakers would not have time in their five weeks in Tanzania to develop the trusting relationships necessary to produce such a film. Instead, and as Biella puts it, naïvely, they believed they were doing themselves a favor by taking on a "simpler" topic: the challenges of Maasai migration.

Needless to say, related Biella, it turned out that the topic of migration was nearly as difficult to film as would have been sexual practices and HIV/AIDS. In five weeks during the summer of 2008, the film team produced a 22-minute film called *Maasai Migrants*: scripting, shooting, and editing the film, and then screening it three times in Tanzania. According to Biella, Sandles' *Subject to Change* is a "no-holds-barred, warts-and-all" vision of the team's mistakes and successes during the first year of the collaborative filmmaking process.

Two particular conflicts arose during the collaborative editing process, centering on inclusion of content. The first concerned a scene shot of four or five Maasai men who were playing pool and joking together in Ma'a. At one point, one man, who presented himself as being particularly acculturated, insulted another man with a racially derogatory slur. Biella and Sandles were both intent on keeping this footage in the film, as a way of depicting the complexities of racism invoked in the context of migration. Yet the board of directors disagreed, insisting that the filmmakers cut the footage. In another case, the filmmakers felt that other footage should be cut from the film, while the board of directors felt it was fine to keep. To Biella and Sandles, the footage in question presented the Maasai in a bad light to outside audiences. However, board members were surprised with this perception; to them the footage merely captured the realities of Maasai migrants. Both cases spoke to the issue of audiencing, with the board members focusing more on Maasai audiences, and the filmmakers giving more consideration to outside audiences. In this respect, audiencing determinations inevitably affected what came out in the final cut of the movie.

The *Maasai Migrants Series* also includes two additional films about film screenings with Maasai in another part of Tanzania, shot by Biella in collaboration with documentary filmmaker Leonard Kamerling (see Core Story 1 in this chapter). Student films were also produced as a part of the project. In 2009, Biella returned to Tanzania with three students and Kamerling. There they worked with the families of two Ilparakuyo Maasai brothers Biella had met during his dissertation fieldwork. Biella's students produced two short films, one about young warriors, and one about women and children. As discussed elsewhere (Biella, In press), the student filmmakers had many collaborators in the project. Codirected with Meigaro, Biella, and Kamerling also produced a feature-length documentary about elders during this stay.

Then in 2010, Biella again worked with Meigaro, Tureto, and a number of other Maasai. They took Sandles' film, the film completed by two of Biella's students, and clips from the film that he and Kamerling had produced about elders. They aired the films 200 miles away, in the northern Kisongo region. As Biella noted, the Maasai are enormously vulnerable to HIV. Their exposure was slowed because they were late to migrate to the cities, with ecological change, new laws, and land loss only recently prompting their migration. Now that the Maasai are migrating to urban areas, the virus is beginning to spread rapidly in their communities. His theory was that the location where they had filmed for the first several years, near Dar es Salaam, was where the effects of migration would be felt the most, including the transmission of HIV. Biella's idea was to take these films documenting poor conditions and show them in areas where migration was not so common and HIV had not yet penetrated as deeply, as a warning of sorts for what could be coming.

However, the filmmakers did not get the screening results hoped for. According to Biella there were several reasons behind this. One was due to the inexperience of the facilitator hired to guide audience discussions. Another was that the HIV catastrophe seemed relatively minor in comparison to more immediate problems, such as water shortages and land degradation. Finally, AIDS education and health promotion in the Maasai context is rife with gender, age, and ethnic discrimination. For example, the northern Kisongo men who viewed one of the films, *Longido Waterhole*, had virtually no response to depictions of HIV.

Instead, disagreeing along age lines, they argued about what encroachment of the cities, as opposed to migration *to* the cities, meant to them. Thus, the issue was not that men were migrating to the cities; rather, it was the disastrous movement of cities and highways arriving on their doorstep. As a result, the men spoke of losing their land and stressors placed on their water system. Discussion also centered on the Maasai men's lack of connection with the Chinese immigrants who were living nearby, who held contracts to build highways in Tanzania and for whom a new town had been constructed to house them. The immigrants served as a locus of blame for rationalizing the degradation of the land and water system. Thus, among Maasai men in the northern region, the films did not succeed in generating discussion of HIV.

On the other hand, Biella relayed, when the same films were shown separately to Maasai women in the region (as he noted a distinct gender segregation among the Maasai), they grasped the intention of the film very well. Indeed, the younger women took the opportunity of the screening to inform older women about HIV, information that the elders did not yet seem to know. In this case, the screening was extremely successful and made it clear that the filmmakers' messages in Ma'a resonated with a group in which few of the women spoke Swahili, especially when faced with Tanzanian health education resources that are all conducted in this official language of Tanzania.

Biella considers audience response as key to his collaborative/participatory filmmaking approach. The approach follows the Freirean tradition of conscientization. Through conscientization, filmmakers and audiences learn from people depicted in the film. The process is clearly depicted in *Longido Homestead*, a film about Kisongo women conversing about the other HIV and migration films that were part of the *Migrant Maasai Series*. The film shows the women remembering and articulating the AIDS education messages of the other films, while also educating one another and audiences using this information. The film was ultimately successful because it brought young and older women together, as depicted on film and as viewing audiences, to stimulate conversation. On the other hand, if the films do not work, as *Longido Waterhole* did not seem to be working with the northern Kisongo men, then that is a message for the filmmakers that something is wrong with their strategy; collaborative, participatory, or otherwise.

In this sense, Biella positions viewers as key to the collaborative process and sees his films as "triggers" (see Ber & Alroy, 2002; Fisch, 1972), with audiences positioned as collaborators in the project of knowledge production and transmission. In trigger films, a series of provocative but ambiguous stimuli are put before the audience, with viewers given the choice as to how to direct their conversation. The idea is that you are creating an opportunity for dialog, or *codification* (Freire, 2000[1970]). Codification serves two purposes here. As a noun, the term refers to stimuli or "triggers," in this case the films. As a verb, or an activity, the term refers to the deconstruction of narrative to examine social contradictions contained within.

A significant influence on Biella's thinking about the importance of audience in collaboration was *Steps for the Future*, an HIV/AIDS intervention project that ultimately produced 38 films in southern Africa. In 2003, Biella was inspired to edit an issue of *Visual Anthropology Review* dedicated to the project, with articles in the issue focused on issues of audience impact and postscreening discussion. His essay in the issue (Biella, Hennessy, & Orth, 2003) centers on AIDS education media making, audience response, and postscreening discussions as integral to the collaborative intervention process and very much linked to Freire's notion of codification.

In addition to audience response, Biella sees facilitator participation as crucial for the resonance of films with particular audiences. In the case of the difficulties faced with the Kisongo men in terms of picking up on the HIV prevention messages of the films they were shown, it was also important to examine the way that local politics came into play. At the time of screening, the postdiscussion facilitator for the films was running for political office and did not want to push the buttons of any male voter, so he remained silent during discussions. Biella notes that the same person had no such scruples when facilitating discussions with Kisongo women, who he did not see as potentially detrimental to his future success as a politician.

Both in terms of viewer attitudes and facilitator preoccupations, Biella also questioned the value of "local sensitivity" for audience resonance and successful messaging. Anthropological and increasingly more often public health wisdom holds that AIDS education must be culturally "competent" to resonate with the local values of recipients. However, despite the filmmakers' efforts at producing media in the Ma'a language and in response to local sensibilities, their goals were partially stymied by the fact that Maasai living only 200 miles north of those filmed were distracted from grasping intended messages by their prejudice against southerners and others.

Asked Biella, does this mean that to be "locally resonant" and "culturally appropriate" AIDS media must be produced within 80 miles of the intended viewers? Pragmatically speaking, how does this affect one's ability to get funding for such a film? Biella elaborated: "If you're investing $25,000 and 500 hours into making one of these and you learn that you need to make a different one each time you move 80 miles away, wow! That's not something you can convince funders to help with." He has thus concluded that generic messages can be more strategic, as they do not tend to prompt audience dismissal of the intended message through ethnic, gender, or age prejudices. In this respect, Biella is convinced that the use of ambiguous, unresolved trigger film plots is needed, allowing his film to communicate with both men and women and to people in different locations.

Yet another group identified by Biella as critical participators in the collaborative filmmaking process is the community of applied visual anthropologists. In assembling a DVD that depicts the applied collaboration process (the *Maasai Migrants Series*), his aim is to provide a self-critical model of each of the steps of such a process from inception to screening, with the goal of inspiring this group to include interventionist films in their repertoire of legitimate anthropological filmmaking.

For example, noted Biella, applied anthropologists often look for cost-effective approaches, how they can get the most benefit for the least amount of money. While film production used to be a costly endeavor, the digital and computer revolution has changed all that. Now, for $10,000 or less one can buy the tools of professional-grade filmmaking, not only the camera and audio gear, but also the editing suite. Nevertheless, although the expenses are profoundly minimized, the labor time required is—as was also true in the past—about 40 hours of work per minute of finished film. In this respect, film production is still a costly undertaking.

The question for applied visual anthropology, then, is what do films do that cannot be done better with a flipbook or a nurse in a white suit walking around from village to village? Does visual anthropology do something that an article in *American Anthropologist* or *Human Organization* cannot accomplish? For Biella, there is a two-part answer to this question. First, many of the people who are drawn to visual anthropology are artists as well as academics. The fact that they have both local–global knowledge and artistic expertise gives them unique, unmatchable ability. The second part of the answer is that films do something that you really cannot readily do with a flipbook, chart, or nurse. Biella put it this way:

> Films touch the heart. And when they touch the heart they become memorable and they transform people's thoughts and actions. So, [as applied visual anthropologists, we] have the courage of our convictions. We acknowledge the power of artistic communication. We acknowledge that fieldwork allows anthropologists to create strong human bonds, the depiction of which touches the heart. Then there is a place for applied visual anthropology, a place that cannot be filled in any other way. That's the benefit.

To this effect, film is still the major means by which anthropology can communicate and "touch the heart" of the public. This was clearly recognized in a 2002 unanimous declaration of the American Anthropological

Association Board of Directors (Biella et al., 2002), in which visual anthropology publications, such as films, photographs, and multimedia, were acknowledged as holding equivalent value to publications in print media, especially due to their important outreach purposes for the discipline.

Concluding Thoughts

In this chapter, we have described the way participatory videomaking is increasingly making strides in the social sciences, as a method of research, intervention, and advocacy. As a PAR strategy combining research endeavors with advocacy efforts, a videomaking approach is particularly viable because it can engage community partners in ethnographic inquiry. As reviewed in these three core stories, participatory videomaking is particularly amenable for political engagement work, especially work focused on cultural revitalization, community self-determination, and allowing communities and community members to have a role in representing themselves and their communities. As noted by Chavez and colleagues (2004), it is also fun to do!

Elder and Kamerling's work exemplifies a participatory videomaking project that has grappled with, and seems to have come to terms with, notions of "multiple authorship" and "collaboration." The collaborative production of knowledge can serve as a platform for the diverse representation of images and voices, and can work to rebalance power differentials inherent to the research process (Chavez et al., 2004, p. 397). Menzies' work offers up an in-depth discussion of ethical protocols when conducting community-based research. While this chapter addresses his videomaking work more directly, Menzies' suggestions should carry weight across all of the methods we review in this book, indeed for the entire field of anthropology and other social sciences. Finally, as reviewed in Biella's story, the process and outcomes afford multiple opportunities to diverse audiences: community members and researchers alike. As Mitchell (2011) points out, it is important not to hold "participatory" videomaking as orthodox. The three cases speak to the need for flexibility in this regard, in terms of approach, production, outcome, and dissemination.

The future of participatory videomaking lies in the affordances it offers—both in *process* and outcome—for documenting community assets and concerns, documenting findings, and disseminating results and produced videos for research, educational, policy, and advocacy purposes.

CHAPTER 6

Digital Storytelling

What Is Digital Storytelling?

Digital stories are three- to five-minute visual narratives that synthesize images, video, audio recordings of voice and music, and text to create compelling stories (Lambert, 2006). Digital storytelling originated in the San Francisco Bay Area at the Center for Digital Storytelling (CDS; www.storycenter.org). Digital storytelling has been used in conjunction with oral and local history projects (Meadows, 2003; Tucker, 2006), K–12 and higher education programs (Hull, 2003), public health and youth services programs and courses (Dupain & Maguire, 2007; Gubrium, 2009a), domestic healthcare and international health and development programs (www.silencespeaks.org), Spanish language projects in the United States (Contando Nuestras Historias, n.d.), and research and advocacy projects conducted in countries such as Norway, India, and Brazil (Aguilera and Peterson, 2002; Hartley, 2009; Hull, Zacher, & Hibbert, 2009; Lundby, 2008).

Digital stories are constructed from participants' own subject positions and told as personal narratives. The aim of a digital storytelling workshop is for participants to tell a story that speaks to their own experiences. The workshop process, outcome of the workshop (a produced digital story), and audience reflections on the digital stories can be used by researchers to investigate sociocultural understandings of experience while also providing a venue for participant input on these matters. As artifacts of the process, digital stories can be viewed as sites for the production and transformation of identities of the individuals and groups that produce them.

Daniel Meadows (2003), director of *BBC Wales—Capture Wales*, describes the shifts of representational power played out through digital storytelling:

> No longer must the public tolerate being "done" by media—that is, no longer must we tolerate media being done to us. No longer must we put up

with professional documentarists recording us for hours and then throwing away most of what we tell them, keeping only those bits that tell our stories their own way and, more than likely, at our expense. If we will only learn the skills of Digital Storytelling then we can, quite literally, "take the power back" (Meadows, 2003, p. 192).

Indeed, digital storytelling plays with the notion of empirical reality in terms of who is in control of producing and interpreting reality. For example, de Leeuw and Rydin (2007) use digital storytelling to investigate the ways that youth represent and express their experiences of migration. In particular, they use digital stories as sites for analysis, to explore youth social constructions of cultural identities in relation to these experiences. Echoing Meadows' claim, they situate youth participants as media producers, with their media productions serving as sites to analyze the social construction of identity. Thus, digital storytelling seemingly invites "the natives" to "talk back" (Clifford & Marcus, 1986).

In this chapter, we begin by describing the digital storytelling process. We then discuss the potential for digital storytelling to be used as a participatory ethnographic method and present two case studies, focusing both on the digital storytelling process and artifact produced. The first case focuses on a U.S. context, in which Aline Gubrium has used digital storytelling as an applied research method for humanizing the social "problems" often delineated as statistics in a public health context. The second case centers on Amy Hill's work with Silence Speaks, an international digital storytelling initiative facilitating workshops that blend oral history, popular education, and participatory media production methods to enable people to tell and witness stories of experiences with violence (www.silencespeaks.org).

THE DIGITAL STORYTELLING PROCESS

The digital storytelling workshop process itself can serve as much a site data collection and analysis as the artifact, the digital story, produced. Workshop trainers ("facilitators") guide participants through the process that results in a digital story (Figure 6-1). A train-the-trainer model is followed in workshops, in which facilitators work with participants to construct their own digital stories. Participants "learn by doing," producing a digital story over the course of 24 hours. Three-day workshops are the norm, as a concentrated period of time allows for less disruption of the process.

The workshop is commonly organized into three phases. In the first phase of the workshop, facilitators orient participants to the process by presenting several examples to the group, as participants may come to

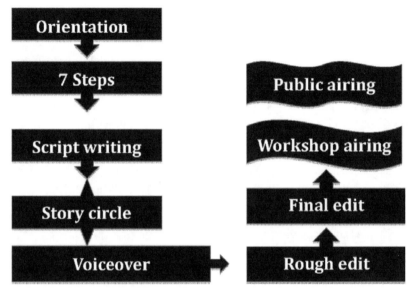

Figure 6-1 Digital storytelling process (©2012, www.silencespeak.org)

a workshop not having previously seen a digital story. Facilitators may then present a brief lecture on the seven "steps" of digital storytelling as conceptualized by the CDS. These steps relate to core elements of storytelling that contribute to the whole and include "owning your insights," "owning your emotions," "finding the moment," "seeing your story," "hearing your story," "assembling your story," and "sharing your story" (Lambert, 2010, pp. 9–29). Participants are asked to consider these steps when writing and revising their stories, as well as when listening to and commenting on other participants' stories during collaborative story circle sessions.

The second phase of the workshop focuses on crafting a script for the digital story. Participants are asked to arrive at the first day's session with a one- to one-and-a-half-page draft of their story, or at least an idea for a story in mind. In addition, they are asked to bring along personal digital photos or print photos to be scanned, and/or video clips to incorporate into their stories. However, the decision to include personal photos may be affected by the topic matter at hand. For example, in workshops conducted about highly sensitive matters, participants may be reluctant to include personal photos that could publicly "implicate" themselves or others. Instead, they may choose to visually represent their experiences through implicit images collected from open-access sources, such as Creative Commons. In this regard, depending on the way that the digital story is constructed, the ability to ensure the confidentiality of data and protect participants' anonymity may vary. This should be emphasized to participants during all workshop activities.

After the orientation, participants and facilitators take part in short written or spoken activities that serve as icebreakers. In addition to serving as a forum for group members to get to know each other better, the activities are also used to stimulate story ideas and to encourage participants to think about their stories in a concise manner. Participants are then given an hour or two to refine a story draft or to write down a story that may have been elicited during the icebreaker activities. They then participate in a story circle activity. The purpose of a story circle is to create a safe and comfortable space for participants to present a draft or idea for a story and to allow for group collaboration in story construction. It may also provide a first outlet for participants to acknowledge and discuss potentially difficult experiences presented in their stories.

Participants are given the same amount of time, usually between 10 to 15 minutes, to discuss their draft and ideas in the story circle. Participants are also encouraged to consider the seven steps of storytelling when reflecting on and discussing each other's stories. The story circle thus provides a shared format for feedback and story construction.

After completing the story circle, facilitators present a tutorial on editing digital images and video in a program such as Adobe Photoshop Elements. Participants are taught to scan printed photos into their computers and to visually modify their digital photos and video clips for use in their stories. Participants then revise their story scripts in collaboration with facilitators, record a voiceover of their scripts, and then create a storyboard to map out their digital stories in terms of the ways that story components—visual, oral, and textual—mesh with each other.

In the third phase of the workshop, facilitators provide a tutorial on working with a nonlinear video editing application, such as iMovie, Movie Maker, Final Cut Express, or Adobe Premier, used to create rough and final edits of the digital story. During the tutorial, participants learn how to import and work with their source materials (such as digital images, video, and voiceover) in the application, eventually producing a rough edit of their stories. Participants then learn how to incorporate a background soundtrack, story title, and credits (as well as subtitles or other textual elements if desired) to produce a final edit of their stories.

By the end of the workshop, each participant has produced a digital story. As part of this collaborative effort, workshop closure is important in the digital storytelling process. Screening each digital story at the end of the workshop is a way of celebrating the group's collective accomplishments (Lambert, 2010). The first showing of a digital story is usually restricted to workshop participants and facilitators, helping to sustain a safe space and group cohesion built over the course of the workshop.

Digital Storytelling as a Participatory Ethnographic Method

The digital storytelling process and outcome offer an array of visual, oral, and textual empirical material for participatory ethnography. The method is participatory in that digital stories are based on the telling of storytellers' own sociocultural worlds, with the story largely directed by the participant. We conceptualize digital stories as identity performances. They are crafted with an audience in mind and integrally connected to the wider conditions and circumstances in which they are situated (Riessman, 2008, p. 177). Essentially, digital storytelling can serve as a participatory approach for investigating participant subjectivities. In this way, the workshop process is just as important a site for data collection and analysis as the digital story artifact produced.

Digital storytelling meshes well with other ethnographic methods. In fact, the workshop itself can serve as a microethnography of sorts, used to document participant identity construction and sociocultural worlds. The digital storytelling workshop opens up several sites for data collection. Researchers who participate as facilitators in the workshop have the advantage of gaining a firsthand perspective on participant narrative agency. The workshop thus offers a distinct vantage point for participant observation. The epistemological basis for digital storytelling is actually quite similar to that of the Mass Observation Movement, which foregrounds micro, local understandings as empirical data for ethnographic research (Fyfe, 2007). However, as a method of social research, digital storytelling moves beyond the observational qualities of Mass Observation. Rather, it allows participants, themselves, to construct and represent their own experiences, as well as to consciously observe the way they move through the production process.

As a facilitator, the researcher can observe and take field notes of workshop activities and participant interactions. In contrast to the academic researcher role taken during interviews, in a workshop setting, the researcher-as-facilitator is able to interact with participants through a different power dynamic. While the researcher may not obtain conventional data from participants during the digital storytelling process, she may arrive at a more complex understanding of their lives and the ways they chose to represent themselves and their experiences. The workshop places the multiple dimensions of participants' experiences on center stage instead of backgrounding them to the presentation of the "real" data at hand.

Core Story 1: Humanizing Public Health Concerns through Digital Storytelling—Aline Gubrium's Work

Aline Gubrium takes a narrative approach in much of her work, which focuses on sexual and reproductive health and the wellbeing of marginalized women and youth. In one project, focused on women's experiences with Depo-Provera (a long-term, provider-controlled method of contraception), Gubrium used digital storytelling as an ethnographic method to complement interviews she had conducted with participants. While conducting interviews with the women, she described the digital storytelling process and asked each participant if she would be interested in participating in a workshop. Many of the women were interested in the workshop. However, time constraints and childcare issues, as well as the transitory housing situation of a number of the participants, precluded many of them from participating.

In the end, three women participated in the workshop, which took place over the course of three days. Gubrium cofacilitated the workshop while also taking field notes on the workshop process and outcomes. Over the course of the workshop, she was struck with new perspectives on participant concerns that were different from those presented in the interviews she had conducted. Whether it was through discussions she held with participants as they worked on their story scripts, assistance she provided as they chose photos and a background soundtrack, or decisions they made about weaving together elements of their stories, Gubrium saw more clearly the ways they actively situated themselves and their sexual and reproductive health in light of digital storytelling production choices.

For example, while working one-on-one with one young woman whose interview had focused largely on the dashed dreams of being a young mother, Gubrium asked her about the intent of her story (one of the seven steps of storytelling being to "find the moment"). Through workshop conversation, she gained a deeper grasp of the ways that the participant thought of herself as a woman and young mother. During her interview the young woman cast herself largely in static, one might say even stereotypical terms: as a regretful young mother who wished she had made better decisions in life. Admittedly, her self-presentation was somewhat circumscribed by Gubrium's interview questions. It was also constituted through a dominant public health discourse that assesses and measures sexuality and attendant "risk" behaviors through health beliefs and behavior models based on individual decision-making (Buchanan, 2000) and along a continuum of rationality (Krause, 2012).

In contrast with the interview, throughout the digital storytelling workshop the young woman cast herself with a decidedly less-fixed identity set. Instead, she portrayed herself in variety of ways, according to the shifting activities of the workshop. Similar to traditional participant observation, Aline witnessed the many facets of "I's," "me's," "we's," and "them's" that the digital storytelling process evokes, many of which would seem to be contradictory or confusing if the context of construction was unknown.

In a way, the young woman was situated as an autoethnographer of sorts in the workshop, both observing and activating narrative agency. As a participant observer of her own life, she chose from among a variety of ways to frame her lived experiences while participating in workshop activities. For example, she made decisions about ways to portray herself and her experiences in crafting her story script drafts, describing and explaining her experiences during the story circle, modifying her tone of voice while recording multiple voiceovers, selecting images to represent her experiences and to create a certain mood in the story, and choosing a background soundtrack, also to create a particular mood in the story. Then, as she brought these story elements together in a more technical way using the editing software, she became even more conscious of the ways she could represent her experiences and the choices she made to do so. The outcome of the workshop—the digital story produced—was thus a result of a set of interpretive choices made by the young woman as she represented herself as a certain kind of woman in her story.

In addition to the potential for participant observation, Aline noted several other avenues for data collection in the digital storytelling workshop. Given consent, the researcher-facilitator could record discussions taking place over the course of the workshop. If interested in exploring the ways that story content develops from the very start, the researcher could record the orientation session, participants' discussions with facilitators as they work on their story drafts, group discussion during the story circle, and then group discussion during the in-workshop screening of the stories. Recordings of story circle proceedings may be especially useful because the activity can serve as a focus group of sorts, in which participants share and discuss their stories with the group and receive feedback from others. Each participant has a chance to be heard, with group dialog focused on emergent themes as well as questions and comments arising from the stories and discussion.

Aline also found that individual interviewing could mesh well with the digital storytelling workshop process. Pre-, during-, and post-workshop interviews could be conducted with participants to gain perspective and evaluate the production process and the development of stories. Ongoing and more informal "briefing" interviews could also be conducted with participants and workshop cofacilitators as a way to gauge movement through the process and to gain a more on-the-spot assessment of participant understandings of their stories. Furthermore, digital stories could serve as elicitation devices in interviews held outside the workshop to prompt individual or group discussion about a topic of concern.

Finally, Aline found that a wealth of data could be gleaned from audience feedback during semiprivate, in-workshop and public airings of the stories. Indeed, she noted during a final in-workshop airing of the digital stories during which family and friends had been invited to view the stories, that part of the follow-up discussion entailed audience members and digital storytellers conducting their own content analysis and interpretation of the stories. The dialog between audience members and storytellers was also ripe for an analysis of performativity, with the performance of identity highlighted through storytellers' conversations with audience members when describing and explaining why and how they made their stories, and how the workshop process had personally affected them.

Aline has also incorporated digital storytelling in her teaching, using the approach one semester in her public health and social justice course. She found that the method was especially suitable for introducing students to working with narrative approaches in a community-based participatory health research context (Gubrium, 2009b). Digital storytelling was situated in the course as a method for advocacy, in particular for conducting more sensitized community health assessments, crafting culturally specific health promotion programs, and initiating community participation in health research and promotion.

For the first half of the course, 14 students were trained in the digital storytelling process during in-class meetings. By the middle of the semester, each student had produced a digital story related to his or her own experiences. The students were not asked to construct digital stories based on a particular topic. Rather, they were asked to construct a story that was meaningful to them, written in their own voice, and about themselves. Despite the "open" nature of the workshop, meaning that topic matter was not directed, thematic analysis of the stories indicated three main, and overlapping, themes of stories: family issues, the interrogation of identity, and health matters.

In terms of family issues, one student produced a story about shifting conceptions of her relationship with her mother as an adopted daughter. Another student told a story about her last name and how this name related to the way she thought about her personal relationship with her family. Related to identity, one student told a story about her experience as a former "teenage mother," now seeking a graduate education. Another told a story about his shifting conceptualization of self while living abroad in France. Finally, in relation to health matters, one student told a story about her relationship with her dying father and how her own perspective on parenting and parenthood had shifted as a result. Another told a story about her experience volunteering in a health development program and examined her preconceived notions of what it meant to be "healthy." Due to the fact that students were participating in a course centering on health and social justice, with readings focused largely on these themes, it made sense that students' stories contained at least one of the three themes.

For the second half of the semester, students partnered with a range of other youth, both on and off campus, to facilitate digital storytelling workshops. Again, students were asked to conduct "open" workshops. Students registered for the course met weekly with partnering students to provide cohesive and consistent training sessions in digital storytelling. As part of this "engaged scholarship" component, a group of seven students provided a digital storytelling workshop to students at a school for pregnant and parenting young women, in a city located about 30 miles from the university. The graduate students met with five young women at the school on a weekly basis to facilitate the production of digital stories.

In the end, all five young women produced digital stories, with most centering on their experiences of parenting and being parented. Again, it made sense that the young women's stories centered on mothering experiences, given the situated context of production. The workshop took place at a school where students received services—including GED prep, daycare for their children, and extracurricular activities—that were meant to assist them in pursuing a "better life" for themselves and their children.

One participant, Luz, produced a story that was particularly evocative of what it might mean to be a young Latina mother living in a disenfranchised community. In particular, through observations of the digital storytelling process and the story she produced, Aline gained a rich sense of the circumstances behind what Luz firmly situated as a *choice* to become a young mother. Luz told a story of having a difficult relationship with her mother while growing up, to the extent that her mother eventually turned her over to the Department of Social Services and foster care. Luz described moving from "house to house" and having a difficult time in the process. In turn, she contrastively spoke of her own parenting outlook, comparing her own experience of neglect from her mother with the way she thought about her own daughter as a "miracle," who had changed her life prospects for the better. Now that she had a daughter, she had a new lease on life.

Luz directed her story to multiple audiences. In a sense, she made the story for her boyfriend, who she situated in the story as another "miracle" in her life, as he had "changed her life" when she met him. He had supported her through her pregnancy and continued to serve as a source of support for her and their daughter. The digital story was also directed at her daughter, to whom she dedicated her story. Finally, the story was made for other young mothers. This was evident through the poignant credits she wrote at the end of the story, in which she told other young women to live their lives fully and to not accept difficult circumstances as determinant of life outcomes.

While Aline had previously conducted interviews with several young women at the school about their experiences as young mothers, the digital storytelling workshop process and the stories produced stood out as being particularly incisive as they highlighted issues of import to the participants. Precisely because the story topic, script, and editing choices were driven by Luz, with Aline observing the process as teacher, cofacilitator, and researcher, Aline was allowed to see the veritable construction of a "young mother's" identity and to interrogate the uneasy notion of pregnancy and intentionality that is so commonly used as a measure when assessing birth outcomes, especially among social groups (such as young Latinas) often targeted for teen pregnancy prevention programming.

At the end of the semester, youth participating in the digital storytelling workshop and graduate students registered for the course presented their work in a gallery exhibition. The exhibition, held at a local museum, afforded a public venue for screening the digital stories and for digital storytelling participants to discuss the workshop process and produced stories with family members, friends, teachers, and other interested audience members. Indeed, the in-workshop and public exhibitions could serve as sites for conducting a dialogic/performance analysis of the digital story artifact and the spectacle of production. Especially in terms of the location of the gallery (as a site where the young women's artwork is often exhibited), the young mothers had the largest attending crowd. The gallery exhibition provided the young women with an opportunity to articulate their "choices" using an artifact that documented their own experiences.

From the perspective of a researcher, the workshop and public screenings allowed Aline to observe differences in the ways that the young women situated themselves over the course of the workshop and in the ways that they presented themselves, mostly as proud mothers, during the public exhibition. In addition, while most of the graduate students had been duly exposed to dominant discourses and some critical perspectives on teenage pregnancy, welfare policy, and the notion of meritocracy in the past, the digital storytelling workshop shed new light on what it might mean to be a young mother in this context. This served to humanize what is usually positioned as a social problem and indicated a need for more salient public health programming and policies.

CORE STORY 2: AMY HILL AND SILENCE SPEAKS

Amy Hill, founder and director of Silence Speaks at CDS, came to digital storytelling from a public health background, where she was doing family and community-based violence prevention work focused on provider training, policy advocacy, and community mobilization endeavors. Hill told us that she "kind of stumbled across the Center for Digital Storytelling (CDS) through research that [she] was doing as a consultant for a technology capacity-building initiative for domestic violence shelter agencies." Digital storytelling seemed to be a really good fit for the initiative, both in terms of its technology skills-building aspects and in terms of its user-friendliness. Perhaps most important, digital stories could serve as short-form, narrative pieces that people could use in their work. To Hill, digital storytelling served as a significant *process* for people involved in making the stories, as well as an *outcome* (the produced digital story) that could be shared in many useful ways.

The first five years of the work Hill did with Silence Speaks were based in the United States. However, she said that she became frustrated with the "balkanization of issues related to violence in terms of how child abuse, versus sexual assault, versus domestic violence, versus community violence are often segmented and addressed as distinct issues and not addressed holistically." She also became frustrated with the polarization of the "therapizing" of gender-based violence on the one hand—where people are sent to support groups and therapy as a cure-all—and on the other hand, the really punitive aspects of criminal justice remedies. In 2005, she ran her first digital storytelling project in South Africa, and since then much of her focus has been on trying to develop Silence Speaks as an international human rights initiative. This has involved broadening the focus of the organization beyond digital storytelling to look at participatory media in a variety of ways, as a tool to advance human rights agendas and protections.

In this respect, said Hill, while Silence Speaks uses a lot of digital storytelling in its work, the emphasis is not "just on creating digital stories, but developing interesting venues and ways and approaches for them to be seen." This involves strategic thinking about appropriate audiences for the stories, in terms of linking them to policy issues and developing curricular materials surrounding the stories. It has also included developing radio campaigns to air stories as radio spots with public service announcements. Because a lot of the overseas environments she's worked in have been fairly resource-poor in terms of access to technology, and there are often literacy issues—both in terms of technology and language literacy —Hill said that they have had to adapt and integrate different kinds of methods to stay true to the participatory media approach, without necessarily sticking exactly to the CDS workshop approach described earlier in this chapter.

We asked Hill to describe some of the adaptations she has incorporated into the workshop process at Silence Speaks. Hill referred to a digital storytelling project that she had conducted in Uganda, working with women who have experienced obstetric fistula (Hill, 2010). The workshop included visual, textual/literacy, editing, and participatory adaptations to fit participant needs, particularly in the context of work conducted on such a personal and sensitive topic. In terms of visual imagery, adaptations include how to work with a lack of Internet access and, thus, access to online open-access visual images, and working with individuals who do not possess collections of their own print photos. Hill spoke of using a Photovoice-style approach that adds a photography component to the workshop. In this adaptation, facilitators train people in how to use disposable cameras and give them the chance to take photos of their lives and communities to bring into the workshop, where they are developed and included in stories.

In terms of adaptations focused on story development, Hill noted that when workshop participants are not literate or might not even have a written version of their language, facilitators might take more of an oral history approach. This entails recording participants telling their stories line-by-line, facilitators then working with participants to adapt, interpret, and develop their scripts, and finally feeding the lines back to the participants for voiceover purposes. This means that participants are not dependent on reading and writing to complete production of a digital story.

In terms of digital editing, instead of participants doing much of their own editing—as might be the case in a typical CDS workshop—facilitators might instead conduct storyboarding sessions where a participant cuts up pieces of her script and then pastes the pieces together in the order desired, with thumbnail versions of photos or visual images printed in color and affixed to the script, so as to create a hard copy, paper storyboard. A trained facilitator would then use the storyboard as a map for assembling and editing the digital story. Another option is to conduct a less-formal storyboarding session, in which participants sit in small groups or with a facilitator one-on-one to "interact with the editing piece" by reviewing the way they would like their stories (including visual and voiceover aspects) to be assembled on the computer.

Finally, Hill reviewed adaptations used by Silence Speaks facilitators to ensure a more "participatory" experience for workshop participants. In this way, the digital storytelling workshop structure need not be carved in stone, with workshop activities mostly focused on story production. Instead, pedagogical, planning, and advocacy activities can be incorporated, with the digital storytelling process foregrounded to create multiple purposes for the workshop. For instance, while Hill might be editing digital stories, another facilitator might lead a discussion session in which story voiceovers or rough drafts are shared in the group. Participants might subsequently partake in planning sessions where they put forward ideas for what people can learn from the stories and where the stories might be shown—at the community, regional, or national level, depending on the country—and what impact they hope the stories will have. Silence Speaks has also integrated health-education, gender-related, and antioppression types of training activities into their workshops so that workshop participants are "not just sitting around" while their stories are being edited. In this way the digital storytelling workshop becomes more like other forms of participatory video production. As Hill put it, rather than just "making stories for the sake of making stories," from the outset Silence Speaks' work entails clear and deliberate thinking about the goal(s) of a project, in terms of why the stories are being made and how they are going to be shared.

When asked to describe a project conducted through Silence Speaks in more depth, Hill spoke of her work with a large-scale organizational capacity-building project for Sonke Gender Justice (Sonke Gender Justice Network, 2012), begun in 2006 and based in South Africa. To date, this is the most comprehensive project conducted through Silence Speaks and the basis for their thinking about multiple-level and strategic ways to share stories. Silence Speaks has conducted two facilitator trainings, and in coordination with Sonke staff, have conducted a total of eight digital storytelling workshops. The workshops took place in a variety of settings ranging from the very urban, such as those in Johannesburg and Cape Town, to the very rural, such as those conducted in the Eastern Cape and KwaZulu-Natal.

Related to the sharing of stories, Hill said, "We've basically done every sort of possible spin on sharing the stories." For example, through the project they have produced three curriculum/discussion-based guides built around the stories that review how people can plan screenings, what types of questions they might ask related to different stories, and what kind of key themes, or learning themes, they would want to pull out of the stories. These materials are available to the public on the Sonke website (www.genderjustice.org.za/digital-stories/tools/digital-stories).

As another example, Hill and her collaborators at Sonke wrote and pilot-tested a formal training curriculum related to South Africa's Sexual Offenses Act. The objective of the training was to train male allies in ways to support women survivors of sexual assault, in particular in seeking justice under the provisions of the act. The curriculum repurposed digital stories as case studies to teach the men basic education about

sexual assault and how they could support survivors both emotionally
on a personal level, and in making decisions about pursuing police or
criminal justice intervention. The curriculum was then linked to shorter
versions of the same digital stories, in which the digital stories were re-
edited and made into 30-second (audio) radio public service announcements (PSAs). The end of each PSA stated: "if you or someone you know
has been sexually assaulted, the Sexual Offenses Act can help. Call this
number."

Finally, Sonke is currently rolling out a large radio program to collaborate with specific community radio stations in different provinces
across the country. Hill has developed a series of call-in radio shows, in
which each show features a different issue and story, with a corresponding script for the host of the show to use in talking about the story. To
the extent that the station has the resources and ability to do so, they
may include a segment during which listeners can call in. They also bring
in a Sonke staff person to serve as a kind of "expert-on-the-issues" to
field questions. Importantly, the radio stations are linking the program
locally to other community mobilization activities.

Hill is currently working on a second Silence Speaks DVD (the first
DVD focused on digital stories produced through the first five years of
work in the United States), which focuses on international women's
human rights stories. The curriculum guide accompanying the DVD was
written by Lucy Harding, a student who wrote her master's thesis on
digital storytelling as a method for participatory education in human
rights and who served as an intern on the Sexual Offenses Act project.
As a result of their collaboration, Hill and Harding have written a set
of ethical guidelines for digital storytelling. One is a longer set of guidelines that pertains to relationships with project partners and the ways
that projects are carried out. The other is a short, one-page document, a
Digital Storyteller's Bill of Rights (Figure 6-2).

Hill uses the guidelines and the bill of rights with specific people with
whom she plans to work or is currently working so they can agree on
guiding principles for how to approach a given project. The impetus for
crafting these documents came out of challenges that have arisen in previous projects. The biggest issue has been requesting that some sense of
focus on the storyteller's process and role in a larger project be preserved
so that the project does not become completely subsumed by the agenda
of a funder or a partner agency.

Hill gave the example of a project that she conducted in the context
of international development work, in which the collaborating organization wanted to collect the stories of participating women. The organization used a top-down approach, precipitating class issues between
project facilitators and participants, and demonstrating little concern for

Digital Storytelling for Healing, Transformation, and Justice

Digital Storyteller's Bill of Rights

In relation to a workshop, you have ...

- The right to know from the outset *why* a workshop is being carried out.
- The right to assistance in deciding whether you are ready to produce a digital story.
- The right to understand what is involved in the process of producing a digital story.
- The right to know who might view your finished story, after the digital storytelling workshop.
- The right to decide for yourself whether or not to participate in a workshop.
- The right to ask questions at any stage of the workshop, before, during, or after.
- The right to ask for teaching instructions to be repeated or made clearer.
- The right to skilled emotional support, if your experience of making a story is emotionally challenging.
- The right to tell your story in the way you want, within the limits of the workshop.
- The right to decide whether or not to reveal private or personal information to fellow participants and instructors, at the workshop.
- The right to advice about whether revealing your identity or other personal details about your life, in your story, may place you at risk of harm.
- The right to leave information and/or photographs that identify you or others, out of your final story.
- The right to reject story feedback (about words and images) if it is not useful or offered in a spirit of respect/support.
- The right to decide what language to use in telling/creating your story.
- The right to be respected and supported by capable workshop facilitators.
- The right to a written consent form, if your story will be shared publicly, including a signed copy for your records.
- The right to know what contact and support you can expect after the workshop.

In relation to sharing your digital story after a workshop, you have ...

- The right to decide with project partners how your story will be shared.
- The right to view and retain a copy of your story before it is shared publicly in any way.
- The right to know who is likely to screen your story and for what purposes.
- The right to know who is likely to watch or read your story and when (e.g., rough timeframe).
- The right to advice about how the process of publically sharing your story may be difficult.
- The right to emotional support if you are present when your story is shown in public.
- The right to demand that no one should be able to sell your story for profit.
- The right to know if any money will be made from your story being shared (e.g., to support not-for-profit human rights work).
- The right to withdraw your consent for the use of your story at any time.
- The right to information about the limits of withdrawing consent for your story to be shared, if it has already been circulated online or on CD, DVD, etc.

An international project of the Center for Digital Storytelling
www.silencespeaks.org

Figure 6-2 Digital storytellers' Bill of Rights (©2012, Amy Hill)

the aesthetic aspects of the project or how storytellers could continue to be involved after the workshop was completed. Essentially, the organization was not focused on community-based applications for the work, in terms of how the stories could benefit the local community. Instead, they ran the workshops so they could have some "splashy stories" to put on their website to demonstrate what great work they were doing.

Hill noted that this is a common issue in the digital storytelling world, with people coming to the work with really different values. Sometimes people just want to make stories that are going to make their organization look good, or to raise money, and not much consideration is given to the impact the workshop has on its participants or on wanting to make the workshop process and outcomes be about creating a solidarity-building and healing experience, or on wanting to figure out how storytellers can be involved in deciding how the stories will be used.

Hill emphasized that much of the ethical tension invoked in digital storytelling is based in the tension between the process and outcomes of digital storytelling, two commonly confused aspects. Digital story*telling* as an activity is a process of making stories, encapsulated by the digital storytelling workshop however it is conceived and adapted, and can be the process of making a final product: the digital story. The produced digital story is only one of many possible outcomes of a digital storytelling workshop. Framed as a participatory research method, digital storytelling is problematic unless the researcher is committed to having a hands-off approach in the process. Hill put it this way: "If you are doing [digital storytelling] strictly as a way for people to organize their own narratives and take pictures, you're going to have to stand back and refrain from inserting your own suggestions about content, wording, or images."

Hill noted that in her experience, this is a very difficult thing for researchers to accomplish. Indeed, people do not write or talk enough about the ways that workshop facilitators (including researchers) mediate the content of the final stories produced. In this sense, it is extremely important to be transparent about a project's goals and objectives. Silence Speaks frames the process as being a joint effort between participant and facilitator. In other words, while the participant creates the story and the story is from events in her life, the facilitator provides support throughout, with ways this is done clearly specified throughout the workshop. Facilitators also make clear the reason for the workshop and the ways that stories will be used, in particular how they are meant to inform a particular project goal or activity. Thus, rather than framing digital storytelling as "this is your chance to tell your story, in your own words," Silence Speaks facilitators are really clear with participants that they are empowered as *coproducers* of media pieces that will be shared as concrete tools for research, education, community building, and/or advocacy, with the specifics determined by the goals of a given project.

According to Hill, another major obstacle to using digital storytelling in a research setting has to do with privacy, confidentiality, and safety concerns. To assure confidentiality, researchers must be able to assure participants that the words or images they disclose in their stories can remain private if the participant wishes. The only way to guarantee this is that the researcher cannot have an agenda around publishing story scripts, or putting digital stories up online or showing them publicly. Of course, this guarantee can conflict with the priorities of funding agencies or sponsoring organizations, as well as with academic career advancement. As a practiced digital storytelling facilitator, Hill noted, "unless you've been working with digital storytelling for a while, I think it would be difficult for a beginning-level social researcher to really grasp all the implications of some of those ethical considerations and really see through how an IRB process should be handled." Indeed, she also spoke of a "learning curve" that institutions need to be able to negotiate and ended by relaying that these ethical concerns apply to work with any type of visual- or narrative-based methods.

To Hill, the bottom line for incorporating digital storytelling into research projects is that the endeavors are based on larger community-building or self-determination processes and that researchers take these processes to heart. On the other hand, if digital storytelling merely serves as an end in itself—with the central aim being to produce digital stories—then there exists a conflict between the obvious benefits to the researcher and the benefits to the participant.

Finally, Hill ended by provided a warning-of-sorts to those who are interested in using digital storytelling in their work:

> People tend to get really enamored with digital stories, the object—in the same way that people are enamored with YouTube videos or visual media in general. And so I think there's a bit of a danger to being excessively focused on the fancy technology and the media pieces that can be created with that technology and losing focus on the lives of the people and the struggles that they may have experienced. Social change and movement are not going to happen by just making a bunch of little movies.

In this regard, people (including researchers) involved in social change work need to bring a critical eye to the ways in which new media may or may not be useful. As Hill mentioned, this means being able to link new media projects with existing strategies, much in the vein of Larry Wallack and colleagues' (1993) media advocacy work and the work of Sam Gregory and colleagues (2005) at WITNESS, where they intentionally link advocacy by media sources to very specific policy agendas.

CORE STORY 3: BENDING GENRES, BLENDING PURPOSES THROUGH DIGITAL STORYTELLING—MARTY OTAÑEZ'S WORK

Marty Otañez's digital storytelling work exemplifies the connections between research, pedagogy, advocacy, and practice (see www.side-walkradio.net for examples of his visual work). Otañez, an assistant professor of anthropology at the University of Colorado, Denver (UC Denver), has a strong background in participatory visual methodologies, stemming from his dissertation fieldwork on tobacco workers in Malawi in 2000. He relates that it all began when he bought a video camera before leaving to conduct his fieldwork and then took 25 hours of video footage in the field. Returning from Malawi, he enrolled in an introduction to documentary filmmaking course as a graduate student at the University of California, Irvine. The course provided him with insight into a nonanthropological approach to image-making, in particular the aesthetic considerations of imagery and other artistic aspects, as well as a critical lens on ethnographic filmmaking as it represents social issues affecting "the other." At the same time, Otañez spent this first year back from the field learning how to edit his footage. As an anthropological project, he realized that the editing process moved beyond a matter of technical know-how. Rather, he needed to deeply consider the representational choices, and implications of power, that came through in the work.

With guidance from tobacco control advocates in Southern California, Otañez produced a 15-minute film about his dissertation work (Otañez, 2012). Eight years and a few films later, he arrived as a new faculty member at UC Denver and learned about digital storytelling from cinematographer Brad Johnson (now creative director at Second Story Interactive Studio; www.secondstory.com), with whom he had collaborated to produce a documentary on men in the nursing profession in California. Johnson had previously worked with Daniel Weinshenker, Rocky Mountain/Midwest region director for CDS. Working with Johnson, Otañez learned more about the nuts and bolts of digital storytelling and his interest was piqued. Funded by the Colorado Clinical and Translational Sciences Institute (CCTSI), he began a digital storytelling-based project focused on health disparities and tobacco issues, in particular looking at smoking and cancer issues among Latinos living in Colorado. He ran three digital storytelling workshops, working with people who were experiencing cancer-related issues as a result of tobacco use. Over the course of the next three years he conducted two more research-oriented workshops with support from CDS. Now a longitudinal project, Otañez uses digital storytelling as part of a larger three-pronged process: 1) to understand how digital stories can be used to influence community wellness; 2) to enhance different ways of doing anthropology; and 3) to explore the ways that this new media can be used to influence policymaking.

Otañez was also quite keen on digital storytelling due to its potential for forging new collaborations with local organizations. New to Denver, he wanted to develop a foundation of trust with local community groups. Through his digital storytelling work, he was able to cultivate relationships with folks in the community and to develop a longer term, community-based participatory research project based on the approach. Through their participation in workshops, Otañez has developed relationships with two local groups, Sisters of Color United for Education and Community Research Education Awareness (CREA) Results, both of which focus on Latino health issues.

In 2010 Otañez established the Coalition for Excellence in Digital Storytelling (www.dscoalition.org), an organization that works to build university–community relationships through digital storytelling. While universities may have a rich history of partnership with community groups, publications resulting from the partnership that are so vital to academic career advancement are often not such stimulating reading for community members. Digital media production skills and a DVD with a number of digital stories on it, collaboratively crafted by community members and academics, may be much more interesting and relevant. The digital story product/DVD serves as bridge-building mechanism between the university and community groups, who see these as tangible outputs resulting from the relationship.

Based in Colorado, the coalition is focused on community, state, and international levels and oriented to three areas of interest. One is curricular development: the coalition is working to figure out how to get more people in a learning environment, such as the university, to recognize the value of digital storytelling as a process in the classroom. The second focus is on partnership building, in particular centering on incorporating digital storytelling into ongoing partnerships between the university and community groups. And third, the coalition is interested in moving beyond a Digital Storytelling 101 approach to incorporate different theoretical perspectives, and to explore and tinker with different analytic and conceptual frameworks that can be used to really critique and further enhance the existing digital storytelling model.

As a social researcher, Otañez sees himself as having multiple roles during research-oriented digital storytelling workshops. First, he serves as principal investigator on the project. He also cofacilitates workshops; however, his role is secondary in this regard, as he works with CDS staff or students who have been trained in the process to cofacilitate the workshops. Another role is to document the process through camera work, both video and still photography. In addition, due to the range of skills among workshop participants, Otañez does a fair amount of software training, script development, and image work with participants who are new to the technologies involved in producing a digital story. Finally, as an anthropologist, and as a member of a community in the Denver area, he strives to create connections between the university and various local community groups, particularly to better understand local priorities.

Otañez takes a flexible approach in thematically driven workshops, such as those he has run on cancer, health disparities, and tobacco use (see www.fairtradetobacco.org). While he might have parameters established to guide the thematic development of stories, when people come to the workshops they may realize that they have a more compelling story to tell that does not necessarily fit within the established boundaries of the project. Otañez allows participants the space to develop these stories, as opposed to saying, "No, I need a cigarette story, I need a cancer story." His more holistic approach to storytelling and narrative inspiration reflects an anthropological understanding that has allowed him to cultivate relationships with people, demonstrating that he is more interested in listening to the stories they want to tell, in hearing participants' voices, than he is in "collecting data," or stories guided by a prescriptive theme.

A recent research-oriented digital storytelling project conducted by Otañez focused on exploring understandings of prevention and treatment issues surrounding viral hepatitis (Hepatitis C) as they circulate among people who are affected or infected by the virus (see vimeo.com/album/1623476 to view the digital stories). Using critical discourse analysis, his aim was to analyze the qualitative data as framed through a Visual Political Ecology of Health approach. Developed by Otañez, this approach seeks to understand, in an exploratory fashion, various ways that digital storytelling could be used as an intervention to address wellness issues among Colorado Latinos and other disenfranchised groups. In collaboration with the Colorado Department of Public Health and Environment, Otañez encouraged participants to produce a set of digital stories that could be used to educate the public about issues surrounding the virus that are currently being discussed, such as whether to be tested for the virus or concerns over intravenous drug use. Produced digital stories served as one data set. The researchers also conducted pre- and post-tests with each digital storyteller to measure if participants actually benefited from the digital storytelling process, in terms of increased knowledge or an expanded network. This served as a second data set. The research team also implemented a public screening of the stories, which was open to the public and advertised through different venues. Forty people watched ten of the digital stories, with 30 audience members completing pre- and postsurveys. This served as a third data set. In addition, a few of the digital storytellers were also present to discuss their stories, with the dialogic interchange between the storytellers and the audience members, as well as the team's presentation of the process (i.e., what worked and what didn't work) and findings, audiorecorded and serving as a fourth data set. Finally, the research team also put the digital stories online, with viewers encouraged to complete accompanying online pre- and postsurveys. Twenty-three viewers completed surveys. Otañez noted that in another project he paid a web-based service to collect surveys from viewers watching digital stories posted online; the number of responses was much higher. However, 80 percent of these respondents were white, so the digital divide might have affected the diversity of responses in this venue.

Otañez notes that at times, procedural issues involved with digital storytelling overwhelm a research project. In this respect, it is important to be flexible in designing workshops. They may be more accessibly designed than the workshop process as described in this chapter (the three-day workshop model). The three-day workshop model requires a significant time commitment: not only 24 hours, but 24 hours where all participants can be together for the allotted time. Along with the time commitment involved, other barriers faced by potential participants include access to transportation, childcare, time off from work, and good health. In response, during the Viral Hepatitis Project, Otañez conducted one standard group workshop with three of the participants and then worked one-on-one with seven other participants in a "miniworkshop" to produce their stories. Thus, while all of the participants were recruited using a standard recruitment approach, the workshop process varied to meet participant needs. This served as an advantage in that participants who normally may have been inhibited from taking part were able to participate in a workshop. On the other hand, a disadvantage, notes Otañez, was that the project also became much more time consuming for him as a researcher-facilitator who was responsible for running multiple workshops to get the same amount of data output that he might have gotten in one workshop under different circumstances. In addition, the one-on-one participants did not take part in the story circle process, which is key to the collaborative spirit of digital storytelling, a collaboration that tends to be forged when participants work through a longer group process.

In addition to access issues, other ethical issues abound, especially when using the digital storytelling as part of a research project. For example, as Otañez put it, "How do you get people to feel that they're in a good place to tell a story, that they're okay disseminating widely?" One way that he has addressed this issue is that he gives participants four different options of consent forms to opt out of different components of the process and to select venues (i.e., research/journal publication, conference exhibition, community exhibition, and so on) for releasing their stories. However, as Otañez noted, "If so many folks get to a point where they tell a story that they've never told before and they feel they don't want to go public, then for me as a researcher, I can write about that, it's exciting. But it doesn't necessarily help with the overall goal to get people to understand the process."

The Viral Hepatitis Project was particularly challenging for Otañez because there was a range of participants in the project from different socioeconomic and ethnic backgrounds. For a number of participants, they were not used to having access to a creative space; this was a new area for them. Furthermore, given their inexperience with this sort of work, Otañez found he had to negotiate and at times relinquish control of his aesthetic expectations, as participants' ideas sometimes differed from his own. Being able to relinquish some creative control is a challenge faced by many participatory visual researchers, as they must be able to carefully balance the give-and-take aspects of production. In other words, how does one negotiate the impulse to suggest ideas or assist participants with the technical aspects of their stories with the idea that participants should produce what they want to produce, the idea that participants are empowered through their own creative efforts? This challenge is compounded by the fact that participants often seek advice and at times really want to give up technical and/or narrative control to the facilitator, who they see as the "expert"; someone who is more technologically proficient and might know better than they how to produce their story.

For example, Otañez notes that in the Viral Hepatitis Project, several of the participants in the one-on-one sessions told him to "go for it" when he made editorial suggestions, in effect turning him into a coauthor (or perhaps first author) of the story. Providing participants with access to the construction of knowledge is a multifaceted issue. For example, the intent behind using digital storytelling as a method may be to provide participants a "voice" in (re)presenting the research topic. However, some participants may not have access to this voice, even in the workshop setting. In the Viral Hepatitis Project, not all participants were able to access this voice, either due to a history of drug use which has affected their ability to clearly articulate themselves by written or oral means, or due to digital illiteracy, by having virtually no experience in working with computers, which has left them unable to manipulate computer hardware, such as a mouse, or to piece together a story in the editing software. The facilitator's role is key here, in working with participants to produce the kind of stories they would like to represent their experiences. Clearly, voice and access are flexible concepts that shift according to context.

In this way, Otañez's receptiveness to adjusting the digital storytelling workshop process to accommodate participants' needs truly exemplifies the collaborative spirit of digital storytelling. As has been frequently noted, researchers inform the knowledge production process, such as with knowledge produced through active dialog between the interviewer and interviewee (Holstein & Gubrium, 1995). Similarly, digital storytelling facilitators play an active role in the story production process. Otañez is quite open about his "aesthetic imprint" on participants' stories, noting that his videomaking background is quite apparent in participants' stories: they tend to integrate video excerpts into their stories, as opposed to only still photographs. For example, in one story, a participant from the Viral Hepatitis Project speaks of using heroin in a public park. As a facilitator, Otañez went to the park to film the location of use, a women's bathroom. Aesthetically speaking, incorporating this video clip lent the story a much more dynamic feel than had they panned across a still photograph of the building, which is a technique commonly used in digital stories to convey movement.

Describing his collaborative work with participants to construct their digital stories and provide them with access to depict their own perspectives on issues of concern, Otañez emphasized a key benefit of digital storytelling: it affords more participatory and multisensory modes for the representation of ethnographic data. The increased participation of the "researched" as subjects rather than objects, and the use of visual representations to draw participants and audiences into the data, are central to anthropology projects, especially public anthropology projects predicated on a dual agenda of research and advocacy (i.e., Bergan & Schuller, 2009; Biehl & Eskerod, 2005; Bourgois & Schonberg, 2009; Vannini, 2012). Professionally speaking, one of the benefits of digital storytelling is that ethnographic data, culture-based information, is presented in a visual format.

As Otañez noted, the practice of digital storytelling as a form of social research can serve as a disciplinary intervention in and of itself, encouraging anthropologists who are traditionally wedded to written text to see the value of knowledge in a visual form. At the same time, participatory visual anthropologists must also constantly advocate for their work to be regarded as valid in a field where, like many others, written text still predominates. In this respect, Otañez strives to modify disciplinary rules so that his and others' visual-based work is properly rewarded, especially in a contemporary society dominated by the visual. Furthermore, the old standard of a "proven track record" must be shaken to consider more than just text-based, peer-reviewed publications, whether it's publishing using visual critique methods, where you not only produce things but you unpack and critically analyze images, or tangible productions (i.e., DVD, film, and Internet broadcasts). Finally, as Otañez suggested, we need to figure out ways to measure the effect of these visual publications on communities outside the university, and to break the myopic way of thinking about traditional publication standards that prioritize the written text over the visual text. This includes the recognition of e-publishing or open access publications (Anthropologies, 2012), particularly how academia might better create parity between these venues and traditional print publications, especially if visual material are intended for publication.

Another academic intervention to be implemented by participatory visual anthropologists (also noted by Claudia Mitchell in discussing her participatory photography work and Sarah Elder in discussing participatory videomaking for research purposes) is to negotiate the institutional review board (IRB) process. Ethically speaking, how, as researchers who embrace a participatory process, do we more effectively educate human subjects boards on our methodologies and research practices? Otañez elaborated:

> I think our role is to educate [IRB committee members] and to share the innovative strategies we deploy as anthropologists. How we are experimenting and exploring new methods, whether visual or traditional texts, and how we can do projects that *don't* harm subjects and that *don't* make the university vulnerable. And that we have a good set of tools where we can make people know what could happen with their digital story if they agree to participate in the project.

In working with the IRB, Otañez suggests open communication: explaining in a very transparent way what happens during the digital storytelling process. This includes elucidating the fundamental activities of project recruitment, ensuring that there are multiple options in the consent process to allow for participants to opt out: in terms of the research process in general, in terms of storymaking details such as the types of images or audio to be included if the digital story is to be publicly disseminated, and finally also in terms of seeking release-of-materials from participants in relation to permissible contexts for airing the stories. In this vein, negotiations might also include appearing before a full committee board, hashing out the details, and providing remedies in cases where an unanticipated ethical issue might arise. For example, Otañez mentioned the need for a media release form in addition to the standard consent-to-participate form as a way to cover multimodal dimensions that are new to most IRB committee members.

Beyond working with the IRB, another basic challenge to conducting a digital storytelling-come-research project is covering the financial expenses of doing so. Receipt of research funding to support this kind of work can be difficult, as the approach is now an incipient form of participatory visual data collection, really running on the heels of more accepted approaches such as Photovoice. Otañez notes that, logistically speaking, he has also faced challenges with conducting workshops on a long-term basis. This is both because of the usual challenge related to maintaining contact with research participants over a long period of time, but also due to the substantial time commitment required from them.

However, while the approach may face challenges on the research front, it holds the potential to affect many different levels, including policymaking. In this regard, another challenge might be to encourage researchers to broaden their perspective on the approach, to see it as something that can be repurposed to fit multiple agendas. In this regard, one avenue that is opening up is to use digital stories to influence the policy-crafting landscape, which can ultimately improve the wellness of different communities. As Otañez sees it, this has the potential to elevate digital storytelling to a level beyond that of individual transformation, to having an effect on the macroenvironment in which digital stories circulate and how they can be used as a mechanism of influence, whether regarding health inequities, policymaking, legislative change, or human rights.

Furthermore, on another level, digital storytelling also holds immense appeal for participatory pedagogy, especially in anthropology and related fields. Historically speaking, participant observation and long-term fieldwork abroad, or even in one's own community, were seen as rites of passage for anthropologists. According to Otañez, this is changing. One reason is that with emergent multimedia approaches, such as digital storytelling, Photovoice, or GIS technologies, we are now able to collect a huge amount of ethnographic data in a relatively short period of time. Moreover, the purpose of visual ethnographic data is shifting. While in the past it may have served as a record, something to visually document ways of life, nowadays it is seen as something to be analyzed. A digital story allows us to put data in a form that condenses the theoretical points and the methodological steps taken to collect the data, and then to represent this data in an accessible way to nonanthropologists. In this sense, participatory visual approaches like digital storytelling are pulling anthropology in a direction, one in which we see the visual text as crucial to understanding different cultures, and to how we prepare students to anthropologically engage with cultures.

In Otañez's courses on political ecology, current theory in ethnography, and video and social change, students learn about the power of digital storytelling to express anthropological knowledge (see www.sidewalkradio.net/?cat=8 for examples of student produced stories and course assignment materials). Video-based assignments are integrated into the courses to allow students multiple ways of expressing their understanding of culture and social change. For example, in his video and social change course, students create digital stories about their engagement with stereotypes, resistance strategies, and other social practices. The course is conducted in a computer lab, and students are provided instruction on basic video editing. Otañez provides students with a grading rubric that details how their projects will be assessed. Assigned readings and class discussion relate directly to student projects and stimulate critical thinking about representation, image-based knowledge, and audience analysis. He also requires students to use survey research techniques to identify and analyze perspectives on their work from peer audiences outside the university. Finally, students screen their digital story projects in a public venue at the end of the semester. The screenings generate lively discussion and debate about the process of producing anthropological knowledge through digital storytelling.

Digital storytelling also works to interrupt the duality between theory and methods in the anthropology classroom. The method can be used to critically assess how one theorizes or analytically understands knowledge produced from visual material, while it is simultaneously used as a collaborative process between anthropologists and communities engaged in research. For example, Otañez's current theory in ethnography course is designed to increase students' knowledge of and ability to incorporate theory-driven approaches into engaged and collaborative approaches to anthropology. As part of his interest in traditional and alternative forms of scholarship, he integrates digital storytelling and other media-related activities into the course to augment traditional writing assignments and to increase students' expertise in synthesizing and representing anthropological knowledge through new media.

Otañez strives to integrate research into teaching, and digital storytelling facilitates this process. One of the challenges for students is that, since kindergarten, they are wired to write using a traditional text method. As anthropologists, and as digital storytellers in the university, it is important that we are able to demonstrate to students and faculty the value of media literacy, as well as the value of theoretically rigorous digital stories that demonstrate the knowledge that we *have* about anthropology, but are also valuable in their *use* for drawing more people to the discipline of anthropology as a tool for social justice. To Otañez, using digital storytelling in the classroom is a natural next step to accomplishing these goals. In this regard, digital stories do not replace the written word or the written research paper, but rather are used to augment traditional writing with a visual format. Digital storytelling opens the potential for the discipline to play a greater role in community change and to understand cultures differently while providing the space for people outside the academy to contribute to the knowledge production process.

CHAPTER 7

Participatory GIS

Introduction

A transboundary coalition in Nogales, a city straddling the U.S.–Mexico border, was working to improve air quality. Applied anthropologists from the University of Arizona assisted the coalition with household surveys in neighborhoods believed to have a high rate of household wood and garbage burning, and the research team created maps representing the results. Using geographic information systems (GIS) mapping software, they overlaid these maps with official maps of city services and census tracts. These composite maps showed that neighborhoods had grown beyond the official boundaries represented on the city maps, and that residents in new settlements often lacked municipal garbage service and were thus more likely to burn their trash. The city used the information to update its garbage collection routes, and the environmental health coalition gained a better understanding of people's motivations for small-scale burning (McMahan & Burke, 2007).

As this example demonstrates, maps help us to visualize and solve problems. Since the 1990s, researchers in the fields of geography, anthropology, public health, and urban planning have increasingly taken interest in participatory methodologies using GIS. Geographers have contributed their expertise in cartographic techniques and sophisticated spatial analysis, and now other social scientists are turning to GIS as a tool for studying how maps and space matter in their projects. Because GIS is used in urban planning, public health, and environmental and land use policy settings, it is rapidly becoming part of the participatory action research (PAR) toolkit.

GIS Technology and Its Critics

GIS takes advantage of the processing speed and flexibility of computers to generate sophisticated maps and spatial visualizations. GIS uses

Participatory Visual and Digital Methods by Aline Gubrium and Krista Harper, 151–168. ©2013 Left Coast Press Inc. All rights reserved.

georeferences to depict different layers of spatial data derived from published official data such as census or topographical surveys or from participants. As Burrough and McDonnell (1998) explain, "GIS is a powerful set of tools for collecting, storing, retrieving at will, transforming and displaying spatial data from the real world for a particular set of purposes" (p. 11). GIS maps allow users to visualize key spatial concepts such as point location, distance, neighborhood and region, networks and routes, overlays, scale, and spatial dependency (Janelle & Goodchild, 2011). GIS provides ways of visually representing data that highlight the spatial dimensions of phenomena, making it possible to identify patterns. GIS acts as a form of "visual shorthand" that can be used to create a composite of ethnographic and quantitative data (McMahan & Burke, 2007).

GIS critics are concerned that the spread of this technology widens the "digital divide" between the technological haves and have-nots. Members of marginalized groups are less likely to have access to sophisticated maps and the technological skills to design and use them. GIS requires time, money, and technical expertise, placing it out of the reach of many grassroots community organizations. GIS critics also voice the concern that the technology inherently facilitates "top-down" planning and policies by offering an authoritative, official representation of the "view from above." Dunn characterizes two main limitations of traditional GIS: "[T]raditional GIS represent an overly simple world-view in terms of two interrelated aspects: the type of information that is fed in and on which spatial decision-making is based, and the limited sources of that information" (Dunn, 2007, p. 619). Traditional GIS representations are not the "view from nowhere" but are socially produced and are likely to reflect the dominant group's perspectives and priorities (Nyerges, McMaster, & Couclelis, 2011). Because of these limitations, critics believe that GIS can reinforce dominant and official perspectives while placing mapping technologies out of reach of many members of society.

In response to these concerns, critical GIS practitioners have proposed "counter-mapping" and alternative ways of visualizing space that challenge the representational norms of GIS as it was first developed. As feminist geographer Mei-Po Kwan elaborates, "the purpose of these alternative cartographic practices . . . is to re-present the world in ways that question or destabilize dominant representations, which are often imbued with various silences (especially on subaltern groups) and insensitive to the effects of oppression and violence" (Kwan, 2006, p. 139). One way of producing "counter-maps" is to use GIS as a community-based participatory research tool. In these projects, researchers share their technical knowledge of GIS with local partners to create maps that reflect the community members' priorities and corresponding narratives. Different practitioners have named this approach participatory GIS (PGIS), public participation GIS (PPGIS), and community-integrated GIS (CIGIS); we use "participatory GIS" here because it is the most inclusive term.

A list of principles for PGIS takes an ethical framework of social justice, democratic deliberation and participation, and ecological sustainability as its starting point (Table 7-1). PGIS, according to these principles, should attempt to involve marginalized social groups in decision-making processes and promote capacity building and learning. The approach should build partnerships between academic institutions, communities, nonprofit organizations, and policymakers. It is committed to promoting citizens' "right to know" and access to public data. PPGIS advances social science through its use of applied qualitative research to build

Table 7-1 Principles of public participation GIS (Aberley & Sieber, 2002)

1	Is an interdisciplinary research, community development and environmental stewardship tool grounded in value and ethical frameworks that promote social justice, ecological sustainability, improvement of quality of life, redistributive justice, nurturing of civil society, etc;
2	Is validly practiced in streams relating to place (urban, rural), organizational context (community-based organization, grassroots group, non-governmental organization, local government, regional government, state/provincial government), or sector (transportation, watershed restoration, food security, housing, public health, etc.);
3	Endeavors to involve youth, elders, women, First Nations and other segments of society that are traditionally marginalized from decision-making processes;
4	Is both functionally and holistically based, that is, can be applied to help solve problems in specific sectors of society, and/or to provide broader integrated assessments of place-based or bioregional identity;
5	Is best applied via partnerships developed between individuals, communities, non-governmental organizations, academic institutions, religious or faith-based institutions, governments, and the private sector;
6	Endeavors to always include a strong capacity-building dimension in its application;
7	Is linked to social theories and methods originating in planning, anthropology, geography, social work, and other social sciences;
8	Is linked to applied qualitative research tools including participatory action research, grounded research, participatory rural appraisal, etc;
9	Is a tool that is best applied in a wide variety of manual, digital, 2- and 3-dimensional formats and data types (digital, oral, image);
10	Enables public access to cultural, economic, and biophysical data generated by governments, private sector organizations, and academic institutions;
11	Supports a range of interactive approaches from face-to-face contact to web-based applications;
12	Promotes development of software that is accessible to broad acquisition and ease of use;
13	Supports lifelong learning of its practitioners in a manner that helps to bridge the divides that exist between cultures, academic disciplines, gender and class; and
14	Is about sharing the challenges and opportunities of place and situation in a transparent and celebratory manner.

theory, and it promotes the development of new, user-friendly software applications.

DOING PGIS RESEARCH: TEAMWORK

Any participatory GIS project involves two interrelated components: the social production of geographic knowledge and the use of cartographic tools to make maps. Because it requires more resources than other kinds of participatory digital research, project teams should first consider whether GIS is necessary and appropriate for answering their questions and achieving their goals. GIS is best used when a project requires mapping and spatial analysis. Maps and GIS can help answer four basic questions:

1. Where is something located?
2. Where is something concentrated?
3. What kinds of things coincide in a specific place?
4. How is a place changing over time?

The first two questions are primarily descriptive and can be represented by points and shaded areas on maps (or layers of a GIS map). A culturally significant site, for example, can be marked in a GIS map with a point location and a place name, along with "metadata" about the source of this information. Or, a census block with a high concentration of airborne Toxic Release Inventory (TRI) pollutants may be represented by a shaded area. These types of geographic information are the building blocks that enable researchers to explore more complex analytic questions about coincidence and change. To answer those kinds of questions, researchers use GIS to overlay two or more maps. A neighborhood map with overlays of schools, poverty figures, supermarkets, and fast food outlets may reveal patterns related to children's food quality and access. A regional map with overlays of each decade's land use data may show changes such as "greenfield" development on agricultural land.

The forms of community participation in GIS projects typically fall into two categories: "expert-facilitated community GIS" and the "GIS upskilling" approach. Expert-facilitated GIS can be an efficient way to develop alternative maps that community organizations may use to strengthen their position, credibility, and inclusion in policy settings. Expert-facilitated GIS has great potential for PAR because it builds critical spatial thinking among participants. A wide range of people can contribute local knowledge by participating in map-based discussions or walking interviews (sometimes called "transect walks"), in which they might speak about specific locations in their communities. When community members know how to read and interpret maps, they can challenge how public institutions, developers, and competing stakeholder groups represent places on maps. In some PGIS projects, participants have learned that their neighborhoods were not even documented on official city or state maps (McMahan & Burke, 2007). In the process of "groundtruthing" by empirically cross-checking official map data on foot, participants gain firsthand experience in the effects of scale and generalization in maps or the political implications of how data is presented in chloropleth (shaded) maps.

A focus on "upskilling" participants in the technical practice of GIS provides a second model for PGIS projects. The reward of an upskilling focus is capacity building and sustainability: with local experts in residence, local organizations may continue developing their community GIS independent of outside GIS consultants. Another, longer-term advantage of upskilling is the potential for local experts to design counter-maps and new applications that challenge and transform traditional GIS. As we present in a case study of Māori GIS later in this chapter, a new generation of indigenous GIS practitioners is reshaping the relationship between traditional oral knowledge traditions, map-making, and tribal governance. The main disadvantages of the upskilling approach is that mastering GIS software takes time, patience, and good trainers who understand and respond to participants' needs. When projects go beyond the use of user-friendly online mapping applications such as Google Earth™, training participants requires a greater commitment of time, effort, and sustained interest. Peterson and West, in their analysis of a failed PGIS project attempted in New Orleans after Hurricane Katrina, warn that an overly "high-tech" approach can alienate community partners (West & Peterson, 2009). If the main goal of the project is to produce community-driven maps in a relatively short timeframe, expert-facilitated GIS is most likely a better option. Matching the GIS approach to the level of community interest is thus important: simple map elicitation sessions with a facilitator may spur spirited community discussions, while highly technical GIS training aimed at "upskilling" may disaffect those community members it was intended to empower.

In either the expert-facilitated or upskilling approach, the presence of a "GIS champion" is a critical factor in the success or failure of a PGIS project because of the technical demands of the technology. In an evaluation of four public participation GIS projects, Sieber observes that most GIS projects that are sustained over a longer term involve at least one person with strong technical expertise in GIS who is passionately drawn to the technology and—most important in PGIS projects aimed at building technical capacity in community participants—can teach others how to use it (Sieber, 2000).

DOING PGIS: TECHNIQUES

Whether using an expert-facilitated or an upskilling approach, PGIS projects use a wide range of techniques for spatial elicitation, generating new information about places through discussions with community members (Corbett et al., 2006). "Ephemeral mapping," where participants create maps on the ground using sticks and other readily available materials, and "sketch mapping," where participants draw freehand maps on paper, have been used to elicit spatial information throughout the history of social scientific field research. These methods require almost no technology or expertise and can be used spontaneously to represent participants' observations or memories. Unlike ephemeral and sketch mapping, "scale mapping" produces maps with accurate scale or georeferences, using a range of cartographic techniques including GIS.

Participatory researchers use many different methods of generating georeferenced spatial data. One simple method of elicitation is the "map interview," in which facilitators show participants scale maps, allowing them to identify places on existing maps and to discuss land use, traffic patterns, daily habits, and cultural knowledge about specific places (Rattray, 2007). Participants directly mark a transparent film (or sheet of tracing paper) placed over the map using colored pencils or pens. The use of "photomaps" (also known as "ortho-photomaps") depicting aerial or satellite images of the terrain that viewers can more readily identify makes map elicitation even more effective. Since Google Earth™ was released to the public in 2005, Internet users have free access to sophisticated and visually appealing ortho-photomaps. In some cases, researchers and facilitators encounter participants who are already skilled users of Google Earth™, and map interviews are a way of opening up a more active, critical, and dialogic engagement with spatial representations and information.

The map interview is a powerful tool, but it also has drawbacks. Interpreting maps is a socially learned skill, and research participants may need to learn geographic skills to have meaningful discussions of what maps depict. Although the maps themselves may be accurately scaled, participants sometimes find it difficult to mark places on the maps at accurate scale and tend to overestimate the size of places that are more familiar or personally important (Corbett et al., 2006; Rambaldi et al., 2006). Residents of rugged landscapes with steep hills and mountains may find it counterintuitive and frustrating to translate their experiential knowledge of locales onto two-dimensional maps.

Three-dimensional modeling (also known as 3DM) addresses some of the limitations of paper maps for community-based research by enlisting participants in the creation and labeling of a large, three-dimensional, scaled topographic model, typically made of layers of cardboard covered with paper. The process of making the model itself is time-consuming, but the construction process helps to build technical and geographical skills among participants. When model-making is carried out with the help of local teachers and students, the process can be integrated into the school curriculum as a way of teaching social studies to children and youth (Rambaldi et al., 2006). Once constructed, the scale model provides a focal point for group discussions. Participants often enjoy the tactile qualities of the model, marking places on its varied surface using colored yarn, pins, and flags. Facilitators may guide participants through a range of exercises using the model, including "virtual transect walks" where participants describe features, explain place names, and share stories associated with places while tracing a trail with their fingers on the map (Rambaldi et al., 2006). Once the participants have generated data using the model, researchers (and sometimes community members) input the geospatial data into GIS files so that community-elaborated maps can be produced. The 3D model is a large, aesthetically pleasing artifact, and at the end of the project, it is usually displayed in the community (at a library, school, town hall, or other public place) and used in education and public planning for years to come, with locals continuing to add new information and place names.

Map elicitation, 3DM, and GIS usually use existing maps as a starting point. As war historian Carl von Clausewitz famously stated, however, "the map is not the territory." Existing maps may be inaccurate, out of date, and in need of "groundtruthing." In addition to using map elicitation to correct existing official maps, researchers may conduct "walking interviews" or "transect walks" with participants (Ingold & Vergunst, 2008; Low, Taplin, & Scheld, 2005; Pink, 2008). Traversing real physical spaces and making firsthand observations of conditions makes it possible to understand people's embodied practices of avoiding dangerous or unpleasant areas, seeking safe and accessible paths, and engaging with the environment at the human scale (Aporta & Higgs, 2005).

Many field researchers now use global positioning system (GPS) devices or phone apps to collect data from walking interviews. GPS allow users to obtain spatial and time coordinates from orbiting navigation satellites, and using GPS, researchers and participants may capture georeferences while navigating the actual landscape. GPS tracking units are increasingly accessible in cost, size, and ease of use, to the extent that many backpackers now use $120 handheld GPS units in conjunction with traditional maps for weekend camping trips, and some members of traditional hunting and fishing groups are supplementing their "wayfaring" practices with GPS (Aporta & Higgs, 2005). Despite concerns that

GPS may potentially replace and erase forms of traditional environmental knowledge, it can be a useful tool for participatory research in support of the preservation of cultural knowledge. For example, in urban settings, it can be used to understand individual's paths, constraints, and agency in the city.

Once the team has generated new information through spatial elicitation techniques, this data can be organized and used with the help of GIS software. Simple PGIS projects can achieve impressive results using Google Earth™ and related "mash-up" applications such as mapbuilder. net, wayfaring.com, and communitywalk.com. These software applications are available online, are free for noncommercial use, and are relatively easy to learn. Google Earth™ offers free base layers of geospatial information, which is especially important in countries that do not offer free data to the public. The disadvantages of Google Earth™ and related software are advertisements appearing on the margins of the screen and a somewhat limited range of features. For projects requiring more sophisticated GIS applications, researchers should consider using proprietary GIS software such as ArcGIS™ or free and open-source software such as GRASS GIS. ArcGIS™ is considered the "industry standard" for government, business, and university GIS labs in the United States, but licenses start at $1,500, making it an expensive option for community organizations. Free and open-source GIS programs are available at no cost and allow skilled users to access and edit code to improve and expand the software, but they also require considerable technical expertise to use (Table 7-2).

More recently, some practitioners of PGIS have embraced the Internet as a means of making geographic data accessible to the wider public, giving rise to the field of web-based GIS (WGIS). Large projects such as the Neighborhood Knowledge California repository and the Living Independently in Los Angeles (LILA) project, both housed at

Table 7-2 GIS software packages compared

GIS Software	Ease of Use	Technical Capabilities	Cost
Google Maps™, Google Earth™, and related "mash-up" applications	Easiest for laypeople to use	Medium	Free for noncommercial use
Proprietary GIS software such as ArcGIS™ (ESRI)	More expertise required	High	Software licenses start at $1,500
Free, open-source GIS software such as GRASS	Considerable expertise required	High	Free; some applications available for a small fee

the Neighborhood Knowledge Research Center at the University of California, Los Angeles, provide online platforms for community organizations to use and contribute new data and analyses to municipal and statewide GIS (Rattray, 2006). With the proliferation of GPS units on mobile telephones and other common consumer technologies, there is a growing availability of volunteered geographic information (VGI) that might be used for environmental monitoring and other community-based research (Elwood, 2011).

DOING PGIS: ETHICAL ISSUES

PGIS, like other research methods, poses its own specific ethical issues. Maps, GPS, and GIS are cultural technologies, and participants may have other ways of perceiving, imagining, and representing space that researchers should also engage. Indeed, learning about and representing these multiple perspectives on space are primary aims of PGIS research. Reflecting on a PGIS project undertaken with community organizations in Nogales, Mexico, McMahan and Burke write that "the use of maps in the research design phase permitted an additional opportunity for engagement, as it foregrounded issues of representation and data accuracy, and provoked discussions of perceptions about areas in which community members negotiated the representation of their neighborhood" (McMahan & Burke, 2007, p. 38). Participatory and qualitative approaches to gathering spatial information may not only improve the accuracy of data, but also offer insights into the place-based identities and "cognitive maps" of different actors and social groups. Later in this chapter, we discuss a project in post-apartheid South Africa that explored different social groups' perceptions of land use and forced evictions as a path toward strengthening black farmers' land rights.

At the same time, researchers should remain attentive to the ways that maps themselves, as a form of authoritative knowledge, affect participants' perceptions of place. Looking at what is depicted on a map inevitably influences what viewers see and what data is elicited. Participants may neglect their own knowledge of physical features or spatial relationships if these are not visible in a given map (Rambaldi et al., 2006). To address this issue, research teams may cross-check map discussions with walking interviews or participant observation.

As researchers, we must never forget that maps are, among other things, tools for *doing* things. Maps can be used in ways that harm people, even when they represent information that has been generated in an inclusive participatory manner. Teams using participatory mapping and GIS must carefully consider the potential consequences of mapping resources or cultural sites and discuss control over access to geographic information elicited in the research process. Marginalized groups must have access to geographical information and maps and need to develop skills to challenge and to redesign GIS in ways that create openings in policy settings.

Participant confidentiality and privacy pose ethical concerns for PGIS researchers. Indeed, a technology such as VGI also presents new ethical issues related to "sousveillance," or "watching from below," along with its potential for citizen watchdog applications and critical geographic information from the grassroots (Elwood, 2008). WGIS allows nonexperts to contribute to map-making and using maps in public decision-making, but it can also replicate the social hierarchies that shape access to technology. Because participants do not necessarily know researchers personally, it is hard to ensure that the information represents a diverse sample of perspectives (Dunn, 2007).

Publishing GIS data also presents ethical questions about how to protect participants' privacy, particularly in projects investigating hidden and vulnerable populations such as undocumented workers or gays and lesbians (Kwan, 2006). In such cases, revealing locations can place participants at risk and must be avoided. Researchers using GIS must keep up to date on "geographic masking" techniques and practices for projects where location data is sensitive. In the case study of Māori uses of GIS later in this chapter, we address some of the techniques currently being used to protect and secure sensitive geographic information.

In the next sections of this chapter, we present several cases of PGIS projects in action. In one project, geographers worked with residents in South Africa's Mpumalanga Province to create maps that were subsequently used to develop a land reform policy. The second case study discusses Māori communities in New Zealand that are designing GIS to meet the needs of *iwi* (tribe) authorities and to develop a new indigenous cartography. A third case presents the potential of PGIS for bridging social scientific and humanistic approaches to research through "story-mapping." As Kwan states, "when complemented by contextual information on the ground and at microscale (e.g., stories about the lived experiences of individuals), GIS visualizations can establish important connections between large-scale phenomena (e.g., urban restructuring or land-cover change) and the everyday lives of individuals" (Kwan, 2006, p. 141). PGIS can reveal hidden patterns and powerfully represent multiple meanings, practices, and experiences of a place.

CORE STORY 1: COMMUNITY-INTEGRATED GIS AND LAND RIGHTS IN SOUTH AFRICA

One of the earliest attempts to engage marginalized communities in GIS research was undertaken in the Mpumalanga Province of South Africa in the years immediately following the end of apartheid. Acknowledging the past complicity of cartographers and GIS technologies used to maintain the apartheid system, geographers Daniel Weiner and Trevor Harris sought to develop counter-maps through what they called "community-integrated GIS (CIGIS)" (Weiner & Harris, 2003). Weiner and Harris brought together GIS technologies and participatory mapping workshops to create "cognitive maps" that could be layered onto existing maps to present competing "community spatial stories" about land use and the history of forced evictions of black households. Through collaborative research with communities and receptive authorities in the government's Department of Land Affairs, they hoped to introduce voices from the grassroots into the land reform policy process and to pave the way for reconciling land conflicts.

Harris and Weiner facilitated map discussions with focus groups drawn from different settlements, tribal authorities, and other social groups in the region. They placed tracing paper over existing geographical survey maps and asked participants to color code areas on the map with markers and pencils. They asked participants to mark sites of forced evictions of black households and also white settlers, to shade in areas according to land quality, and to designate land use. The group discussions were audio- and videotaped and transcribed.

The project documented histories of forced removals as well as differing perceptions of the extent and specific areas of evictions, filling in gaps in official knowledge left over from the apartheid state. Harris and Weiner also used overlaid maps to show different perspectives on land potential and learned that local residents' perceptions of high-quality land differed from official categorizations that represented the needs of large, industrial farmers over those of black smallholders. These maps also shed light on local people's resentment of the state's placement of forestry plantations on steeply sloped but high-quality lands they saw as well suited for subsistence farming. The overlaying maps produce a visual image of power and conflicts over land that makes it possible to identify needed land reform projects. Despite their success in documentation and analysis of conflicting views, Weiner and Harris state that the project was ultimately limited by the constant institutional reorganizations of the early post-apartheid period. They had hoped to locate the community GIS in the offices of Mpumalanga's provincial government to facilitate ongoing development and use of the database. After the project, however, the local participants with GIS know-how moved to different jobs, and the team was unable to find a "home" for the database that would ensure ongoing community access and development. Without a locally based PGIS champion, it was not possible to maintain a community-integrated database.

CORE STORY 2: DESIGNING "INDIGENOUS INFORMATION SYSTEMS" BY AND FOR MĀORI COMMUNITIES IN NEW ZEALAND

Since the mid-1990s, there has been growing interest in PGIS research in New Zealand, spurred by a wave of new legislation recognizing Māori land claims, autonomy, and the rights of *iwi* (tribes) and *hapu* (subtribes) to take part in public decision-making (Michaels & Laituri, 1999). The 1991 Resource Management Act, for example, states that New Zealand's government recognizes as a matter of national importance "the relationship of Māori and their culture and traditions with their ancestral lands, water, sites, *waahi tapu*, and other *taonga*" (Resource Management Act of New Zealand, 1991, section 6). *Waahi tapu* is the term used for Māori cultural heritage sites, while *taonga* refers to other cultural "treasures." The 1993 Māori Land Act requires government institutions to consult *iwi* and *hapu* authorities on environmental policy and land use planning decisions to ensure that Māori values are taken into account.

In this new policy environment, some Māori *iwi* and *hapu* authorities now use GIS to administer dozens of resource consent applications each week, to conduct cultural impact assessments, and to plan *Puketawai*, or environmental-cultural preservation projects (Harmsworth, Park, & Walker, 2005). Many Māori communities have turned to community-based GIS: "In New Zealand, GIS is a ubiquitous tool among resource managers and government agencies; Māori identified GIS as an enabling technology that would allow them to 'speak the same language' through culturally relevant layers and mapped output" (Laituri, 2002, p. 275).

Although GIS use offers many advantages, Māori critics express several concerns. Does the use of maps and GIS change traditional forms of spatial knowledge and wayfaring? Who has control over and access to *iwi* and *hapu* knowledge? Can one map sacred sites or medicinal plants without exposing them to exploitation by people from outside the community? Māori knowledge is founded on place-based *korero*, or stories, and traditional ways of communicating this knowledge often involve walking through, looking at, or being in specific physical locations in the company of an elder. Writing down Māori knowledge in text and map form affects the quality of cultural transmission and the ability of elders to use discretion in sharing information.

Māori GIS advocates argue that it is possible to design systems that build technological capacity and allow *iwi* authorities and members to efficiently access information while also protecting sensitive information and encouraging users to consult elders when appropriate. "This is an essential caveat in the use of GIS by indigenous people: that the GIS is utilized *by* them *for* their needs. The need to assert self-determination in the research process itself is essential to the success of such efforts" (Laituri,

2002, p. 271). Māori GIS researcher Huia Pacey emphasizes ways to integrate GIS with a research approach based on *Kaupapa Ma-ori* (Māori traditional knowledge systems) and the principle of *ranga-tiratanga*, or autonomy and self-determination. This approach to PAR particularly emphasizes reciprocity, appropriate technology transfer (or "upskilling"), and community peer review (Pacey, 2005). Māori are increasingly working with universities and private GIS consultants to create community GIS and to "upskill" community members so that they build "in-house" expertise within the *iwi* and become less dependent upon *Pakeha* (non-Māori) consultants.

Māori GIS designers typically develop map layers in collaboration with *iwi* elders, not only collecting information but also discussing how the information could be used and how to control access. For example, a layer depicting the location of medicinal plants may be useful to *iwi* authorities considering approval of a resource consent application for a specific site, but making the layer publicly available could invite "biopiracy," the commercialization of traditional ecological knowledge. Māori GIS thus has at least three levels of screens to control access to data: public, restricted or sensitive, and private or highly sensitive (Harmsworth, Park, & Walker, 2005; Pacey, 2005). Public data are information layers that are made available to the general public and typically include national- and regional-level government data on land use, vegetation, water, wildlife, and air quality. Restricted or sensitive data is usually stored in password-protected layers that only *iwi* members may access (Figure 7-1). Outsiders' access to data is controlled in various ways. For example, a sacred site may be indicated on a public GIS layer as a shaded area, rather than as a set of coordinates; this marks its presence without disclosing its precise location. It is also possible to make sites completely invisible on the public area of the GIS. For very sensitive or private information that is not written down within the GIS but is communicated only through elders' stories, Māori GIS designers may indicate a point on the map (or on a password-protected layer) directing the user to the appropriate elders to consult in person. This allows younger generations and outsiders to consult elders for place-based *korero*, while at the same time enabling *iwi* elders to maintain traditional means of transmitting cultural knowledge and to use their own discretion in sharing knowledge.

Huia Pacey sees utopian potential for GIS as indigenous mapmakers use it to create "counter-maps." With the development of indigenous cartography, Māori are challenging the use of dominant Western place names on official maps. Prior to the use of GIS, public discussion was dominated by the practical concern of the length of Māori place names such as *Te Rotorua nui a Kahumatamoemoe* (or Lake Rotorua, in the

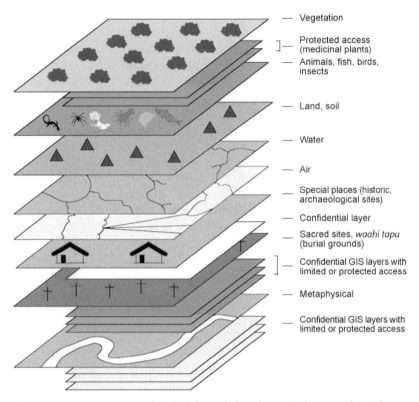

— Vegetation

]— Protected access
(medicinal plants)

— Animals, fish, birds,
insects

— Land, soil

— Water

— Air

— Special places (historic,
archaeological sites)

— Confidential layer

— Sacred sites, *waahi tapu*
(burial grounds)

]— Confidential GIS layers with
limited or protected access

— Metaphysical

— Confidential GIS layers with
limited or protected access

Figure 7-1 Protecting sacred Māori knowledge through the use of GIS layers
(©2005, Harmsworth, Park, & Walker)

English place name). With the possibility of using GIS layers, longer
Māori place names may appear on maps, abbreviated with ellipses with
a link to the full name. Thus, "the cartographic focus will inevitably shift
from how can the software programmer increase the number of charac-
ters available for the label text string or what will be accepted/acceptable
by the New Zealand Geographic Board to the more fundamental one of
scale—how can we fit it all on the map?" (Pacey, 2005, p. 60).

Indigenous cartographers are creatively finding new ways to express
the internal diversity of Māori knowledge in GIS as well. When different
hapu in an *iwi* use different place names, for example, this variety can
be represented by overlaying GIS layers. Using GIS for cultural heritage
mapping can supplement *korero*, oral tradition knowledge, and make it
possible to transmit such knowledge to *iwi* members who have moved

away from their ancestral homeland (Pacey, 2005). Pacey and others also consider participatory Māori GIS as a strategy to "upskill" local Māori in techniques for designing "indigenous information systems" so that *iwi* and *hapu* members have the technical skills needed in a new institutional environment where Māori have a greater voice in public policy and more social resources for cultural preservation.

CORE STORY 3: USING "STORYMAPPING" TO VOICE COMMUNITY PERSPECTIVES ON URBAN PLANNING IN HOUSTON'S THIRD WARD

GIS and maps are also increasingly used in PAR projects focused on place-based stories. This kind of narrative research is sometimes called "storymapping" or locative storytelling and media: "Locative storytelling is distinguished by the powerful ability to enhance a user's connection to a given place. . . . [It] can help participants better envision the past, present and future" (Chang et al., 2008, p. 4). Many storymapping projects involve simple-to-use WGIS applications such as Google Earth™, mapbuilder.net, communitywalk.com, and wayfaring.com to pin audio or video files onto neighborhood maps, creating an online oral history archive with spatial coordinates. Users may then explore an online map or an actual physical space using audio or video tours. Some projects, such as [murmur] in Toronto and Orange, New Jersey, link audio files to telecommunications and street signage, inviting pedestrians to access local stories in situ on their cell phones (murmurtoronto.ca and murmurorange.com). Multimedia scholar and artist Carroll Parrott Blue's "Dawn Project" in Houston's Third Ward offers an example of how storymapping can be used to literally put the history of marginalized communities on the map.

"The Dawn Project" began as a multimedia autobiography and has transformed into a nonprofit organization promoting community-based multimedia arts and urban planning. After years of living and working as a filmmaker and university professor in southern California, Carroll Parrott Blue returned to her hometown of Houston, Texas, to create *The Dawn at My Back*, an autobiography in text, film, and hypermedia form (Blue, 2003). Having grown up in the Third Ward, a historically African-American neighborhood, Blue examined how Jim Crow segregation shaped her parents' lives and her own childhood and adolescence. In the years since the civil rights movement, the Third Ward's black-owned businesses have struggled to survive, urban renewal efforts knocked out houses for highway construction, and Houston's real estate boom caused housing prices to rise, placing pressure on longtime residents. Concerned that the rich history of the Third Ward was dying with the neighborhood's older residents, Blue established the Dawn Project, a nonprofit community creative media organization focused on getting residents involved in neighborhood planning and development.

Third Ward Storymapping was an initiative of the Dawn Project in collaboration with the Center for Digital Storytelling and the University of Houston. Working with a local journalist, Professor Blue and her students collected photos and oral narratives about the Third Ward, filming community members' stories on location and placing them on an interactive online map (storymapping.org/thirdward.html). During the project, the area surrounding a central neighborhood site, Emancipation Park, became a special locus of participants' narratives.

The Third Ward Storymapping project presents the story of Emancipation Park's establishment through a series of video interviews "pinned" onto a Google Map. Thelma Bryant, a 101-year-old resident and local historian, gives a detailed history of Emancipation Park. Named for the Emancipation Proclamation, the park has been the site of Juneteenth celebrations for more than 135 years commemorating the date that enslaved Africans in Texas received the news that President Lincoln had abolished slavery. In 1872, the Reverend Jack Yates led the African-American churches of the Third Ward in a fundraising effort resulting in the purchase of land for a Juneteenth fairgrounds. Emancipation Park was built on these grounds and the community donated the park to the City of Houston in 1916. Bryant's memories of family outings to the park are supplemented by the personal stories of others. In the video clip "Semi-Pro Soft-Pitch Baseball," Friends of Emancipation Park President Bill Milligan shares his childhood memories of attending Monday night baseball games in the park, with teams sponsored by the local department store.

The significance of Emancipation Park as a local landmark and source of community pride is also made visible on the map by a string of stories emanating from the park down Dowling Street, the core of the neighborhood's traditional business district. In another video clip, "Barbershop Stories," three Third Ward residents talk about a barbershop that was a site of African-American men's political organizing for the right to vote in the years leading up to the civil rights movement; the barbershop later served famous African-American musicians and performers visiting Houston.

The Third Ward Storymapping initiative brought together community members to educate residents and policymakers about the unique history of Emancipation Park and its environs. Their efforts influenced the city's revitalization efforts and supported the process of registering Emancipation Park as a historic site. The Dawn Project is working with artists and architects from the University of Houston to develop public art for the METRO Southeast Corridor Transit Line, the renovated Ryan Middle School, and the new Park at Palm Center. Site-specific art installations for these projects are inspired by residents' stories initially collected through the Third Ward Storymapping project.

CONCLUSIONS

The three cases discussed above demonstrate the versatility of GIS in participatory research in terms of documenting and analyzing local spaces, using GIS technologies, and engaging community participants. All three projects seek out "local knowledge" and stories about land to produce "counter-maps" that supplement and sometimes challenge official maps. The process of creating these alternative GIS maps unearths narratives of historical injustice, such as the mass evictions of black South African farmers under apartheid, as well as stories reflecting community assets and cherished sites, as in the stories about Emancipation Park in Houston. All three cases involve community or indigenous groups that are trying to gain more self-determination and decision-making power in land use, urban planning, and environmental policy settings. The PGIS research process may spur spatially grounded discussions of how to create public policy that integrates local knowledge and is more inclusive of marginalized groups.

All three cases included the significant involvement of expert facilitators. This suggests that GIS technologies still have a long way to go in terms of user-friendliness, even with the growing use of Google Earth™ and GPS units by laypeople. Project teams turn to GIS because it allows them to speak to policymakers using the authoritative voice of maps, and the goal of GIS upskilling is only feasible when community members have a strong motivation to learn the technology. Māori *iwi* had strong incentives to invest in GIS upskilling as a result of gaining greater political autonomy that also entailed more bureaucratic demands in land use policy. Even without the goal of upskilling, however, the projects show that the techniques of map elicitation, sketch mapping, and walking interviews offer excellent opportunities for community members to reflect upon and discuss their local environment and the meanings of specific places in their communities. In some cases, the research process results in participants becoming more confident in interpreting and challenging how their neighborhood is represented in maps.

Each of the cases also sheds light on different ethical considerations and power issues. In the South African case, one of the explicit goals of the research was to make past land evictions visible because under apartheid, no geographers had recognized or documented the land claims of black farmers. Similarly, Third Ward Storymapping aimed to make African American history a more visible feature of Houston's urban landscape. But in other cases, visibility is itself an ethical problem. The Māori GIS designers created confidential layers so that their indigenous knowledge would not be shared indiscriminately with outsiders, and so that users would be encouraged to learn about the landscape through the elders' oral tradition.

Finally, the three cases present a range of participatory GIS outcomes and research products. The research in South Africa resulted in many academic publications and influenced the early development of the PGIS field. However, Harris and Weiner were unable to sustain relationships with local policymakers through the early post-apartheid years, and they regret that they were not able to find an institutional home for the community-produced maps that local people could access easily. Nevertheless, their CIGIS research approach influenced other researchers and land reform activist groups in South Africa to seek out local cognitive maps and meanings as the process of land reform unfolded (Jones, 2005; Mearns, 2011).

The PGIS projects in Houston's Third Ward and in New Zealand's Māori communities demonstrate how access to mapping technologies and skills can empower members of groups that have historically been marginalized in public planning. The Dawn Project's Third Ward Storymapping began as a multimedia experiment and led to new opportunities for community participation in the design of new public art installations, park space, and transportation infrastructure. In New Zealand, more and more Māori students are drawn to GIS because of its potential for supporting indigenous autonomy and *iwi* governance. In the process, Māori GIS practitioners transform not just geographic information, but also geographic knowledge itself, critically engaging the colonial underpinnings of map-making. The creation of a Māori and indigenous geographies graduate program at the University of Waikato demonstrates the vital, generative power of counter-mapping and PGIS as a scholarly endeavor.

CHAPTER 8

Participatory Digital Archives and Exhibitions as Research

INTRODUCTION

Today's social scientists work in a scholarly context where once-obscure repositories and collections are being digitized and released to the public on the Internet as "digital archives" or "online museums." This technological shift has opened up new opportunities for the public to participate in collections and archives, not only as information consumers, but also as contributors and lay curators, which is a shift toward "community informatics" (Lenstra, 2011), "participatory archives" (Huvila, 2008), and "virtual museums" (Giaccardi, 2011). As social scientists have gotten involved in creating digital archives, many have come to see the process itself as a new form of participatory action research.

Participatory digital archives present historical documents, images, and media files online and involve community members or the broader public in curating the collection. Archives are a fusion of artifacts and interpretation:

> [A]rchives are comprised of at least two layers: the objects themselves, which carry sensual meanings; and the metadata, which hold the interpretive meanings ascribed by the archivist during the archival process (Labrador & Chilton, 2009).

Digitization is changing the archive in important ways. In a traditional archive, a professional curator or librarian interprets and categorizes objects in a collection. In contrast, digital archives allow decentralized curation, including efforts to include community members in interpretation (Huvila, 2008). "Metadata" now may take the form of group discussions of how to present and interpret items, potentially leading to greater reflexivity about knowledge produced in archives (Huvila, 2008).

Participatory Visual and Digital Methods by Aline Gubrium and Krista Harper, 169–182. ©2013 Left Coast Press Inc. All rights reserved.

Related to participatory archives is the virtual museum, with "virtual" defined as an online extension of "actual" reality (Giaccardi, 2011). Virtual museums and exhibitions consist of multimedia products and websites that are based on either digitized files of existing museum holdings or collections of digital files created by participants. Museums and heritage institutions commonly use virtual exhibitions or archives to duplicate collections, to facilitate locating items, and extend access to a larger number of people. When access is extended to the descendants of the people who produced the original artifacts, this is called "virtual repatriation" (Hennessy, 2009). Online virtual museums often have interactive features, enabling users to recombine objects to create personalized "collections," "trails," or "tours" through the linking of hypermedia texts, images, and film and audio files. Online virtual museums foster creative interaction between tangible artifacts and people's interpretations of and narratives about them. Museum scholar Elisa Giaccardi calls this last quality "iridescence," meaning that our perceptions of cultural artifacts change depending on how they are presented and interpreted from different perspectives (Giaccardi, 2011).

The turn toward participatory digital archives and virtual museums means that nonprofessional users are encouraged to contribute both artifacts (in the form of digital files) and interpretive meanings of the materials presented. This in turn prompts new epistemological debates about expertise and the power dynamics of knowledge produced in museums and archives. In the next section, we explore the "participatory turn" as a way of *democratizing* and *decolonizing* museums and archives shaped by class, race, colonialism, gender, and other historical power relations. We move on from theoretical discussion of participatory archives and museums to sketch a general outline of the production process. Individual projects, however, vary in their goals and approach to collaborative production, interpretation, and audience interactivity. We present three "core stories" of researchers in practice, creating online multimedia archives and exhibitions based on collections from Russia, rural New Hampshire, and a First Nation in British Columbia. Each of these groundbreaking projects reveals exciting possibilities and emerging dilemmas related to participatory digital archives and virtual museums.

DEMOCRATIZING AND DECOLONIZING THE ARCHIVE AND THE MUSEUM

Anthropologists and other social scientists have worked with and deposited materials in museum collections and archives for the past 150 years. Social scientific museum collections originated during the "salvage" movement of the late nineteenth century, when researchers saw their role as documenting and preserving indigenous and later popular folk traditions seemingly destined to disappear under the pressures of colonization and modernization (Kirshenblatt-Gimblett, 2012). Traditional museums and archives served as places for the storage and restricted, scholarly use of collections of written records, material artifacts, photographs, and audio and visual recordings. Academic collectors working in the "salvage paradigm" saw themselves as validating other people's cultures by preserving *authentic* materials from the contaminating influences of not only outsiders, but also younger generations who had adopted new ways of life (Clifford, 1989).

Archives and museums exist as scholarly institutions within larger, hegemonic systems: the nation-state, the colonial empire, and the global political economy. As library scholar Mark Flinn states, the archive "overwhelmingly privilege[s] the voices of those with power and influence in society" (Flinn, 2010). Archives and museums have usually celebrated and given prominence to the stories of powerful groups, such as the dominant racial or ethnic group in a nation or the upper-class or male leaders of a political struggle (Hall, 1999). Hegemony in the archive and museum context also means that subordinated groups, when they appear, do not have the opportunity to tell their own stories. "When these 'others' do appear in the archives," Flinn states, "they rarely speak with their own voice, but rather appear as the objects of official interest and concern" (Flinn, 2010).

Advocates of participatory archives and museums argue that traditional archives and the experts who created them were never neutral, but instead positioned by social power relations (Huvila, 2008). They call for the *democratization* of archives through critical engagement with official archives and through independent production of "community archives," such as the Herstory Lesbian History Archive (www.lesbianherstoryarchives.org).

Efforts to democratize archives and exhibitions preceded the Internet, but with the rise of collaborative web technologies, alternative "memory institutions" have proliferated. Looking at recent projects in the United Kingdom, Mark Flinn holds up the website *My Brighton and Hove* as an example of the wide range of perspectives presented in participatory archives and virtual museums. Visiting the *My Brighton and Hove* living history website (www.mybrightonandhove.org.uk/), the user is greeted with images of the British seaside town and its famous pier and invited not only to explore the site, but also to participate in its ongoing development:

> Through the site, people share their memories, photos, knowledge and opinions about the city—as it is today and as it was in the past. There are over 11,000 pages to explore and it's very easy to add your own. Enjoy!

Browsing the pages, you see not only historical documents and images that would have previously been hidden away in archives, but also snapshots from personal collections showing workers in a butcher's shop, a citizenship ceremony at the town hall, scouting troops, and boxing clubs, often with commentary provided by locals. Delving further, the site offers "personal tours" curated by a broad spectrum of residents to show local history from a wide range of perspectives, including those of deaf people, pensioners, and members of Brighton's longstanding black communities. The "Best of" and "Worst of" pages prompt lively exchanges among users and discussions of the character of the place and how it has changed over time. If the visitor has photos or stories to contribute to the site, they can find directions for submitting materials and get help from local history volunteers. The entire website is digitally archived by the British Library. For Flinn, democratization means coming to grips with "knowledge-rich users," many of who are not professional historians or social scientists, and to make room for their contributions (Flinn, 2010).

Another perspective, rooted in indigenous and postcolonial critique, calls for the *decolonization* of museums and archives. While efforts to democratize the archive focus on increasing the visibility and voice of excluded groups, decolonization focuses on colonized groups regaining control of how cultural materials are used in exhibitions and what stories are told about objects (Atalay, 2006; Battle-Baptiste, 2011). Decolonization is related to the overall movement toward repatriation of collections related to indigenous groups, either through the physical transfer of objects or the "virtual repatriation" of collections that continue to be maintained by museums, universities, and other institutions.

Digital Dynamics, a multimedia collaboration between anthropologist Kimberly Christen and the Warumungu people, disrupts visitors' websurfing habits to critically engage them in thinking about the ongoing effects of colonization. Visiting the site, you are greeted with a pop-up flag that says, "Welcome to *Digital Dynamics Across Cultures*, an interactive project focusing on the cultural protocols of the Warumungu people of central Australia." The flag hovers over a stylized map with sites indicated by Aboriginal dot-painting symbols, delaying access to the website. "Please note that access to certain elements of Warumungu culture is restricted," the text continues. "As such, you may come across images, video, or other content that have been partially or completely blocked from view. . . . Enjoy!"

Digital Dynamics involves participatory production within the community, but interactivity is limited in ways that force visitors to consider how to use the Internet according to Warumungu ethical standards. A video clip of Warumungu elder women telling stories about family members from the "stolen generations"—those forcibly removed and sent to boarding schools—covers the face of one woman with an image of silver duct tape to remind viewers of cultural protocols. Short animations narrated by Warumungu elders explain how prohibitions relate to cultural conceptualizations of death, land, relationships between people, and ownership. In this way, *Digital Dynamics* foregrounds information about curatorial decisions and the production process.

DIGITAL ARCHIVES AND VIRTUAL EXHIBITIONS IN PRACTICE

Participatory digital archives and exhibitions are created when a group of participants work together to create a web-based interface where users may access a multimedia collection of visual, audio, and text files. Goals of participatory archives and exhibitions vary: some projects involve a face-to-face community group compiling materials for online public display, while other projects are directed by curators who seek the active participation and contributions of the audience as a "virtual community." All projects involve the following elements: a collection for display, a design and interpretive team, a process for making decisions about how materials will be presented, and a target audience of users.

The first step in the process is identifying a set of artifacts and images to assemble and curate. All digital archives and exhibitions are based on collections: collections of digital images of objects, digital audio and video files, and text files of narratives, interview transcriptions, and other documents. Many digital archives or virtual museums get started when there is already an existing collection of artifacts, films, and photos, and members of an organization associated with the collection want to make these items accessible to a wider public. A number of recent projects came into being when an ethnographer, facing retirement, decided to "repatriate" research collections to the community studied (Ridington & Hennessy, 2008), or at least to make data available online for others to explore (Fabian, 2008).

In some instances, a researcher or organization assembles a digital archive or exhibition as part of a participatory action research, enlisting community members in building the collection as part of the project. Photovoice researchers may assemble a digital archive so that research participants may use the images on an ongoing basis for educational materials and programming (de Lange & Mitchell, 2012). Other projects assemble and organize existing personal photo collections into a community archive. Social scientists and other scholars are beginning to take family photography seriously (Rose, 2010). Art historian Minh-Ha T. Pham, for example, curates the blog *Of Another Fashion*, which she describes as "an alternative archive of the not-quite-hidden but too-often-ignored fashion histories of U.S. women of color" (ofanotherfashion. tumblr.com/). Contributors may post images from their personal family photo collections along with commentary, and Pham has analyzed these images in her work on race, the body, and fashion in the United States (Pham, 2011). Looking at photo albums and home movies may be a part of "in-person" participatory digital research; for example, digital storytelling often involves participants selecting images from their home collections of photos.

Participatory digital archive projects also demand the commitment of a team of creators. The work of assembling and curating are time-consuming and involve group discussions, and so members of the team must be willing to contribute time and effort and to work toward consensus in decisions about ethics, interpretations, and design. Digital archives require some technical skills to create and use infrastructure for the online interface, so any team needs at least one member with technical skills for building a website and other members who are willing to learn how to use it. If the team is recruiting a web designer to create the interface, they should make sure the designer is comfortable with participatory design processes. The team must work out a plan for maintaining the site over time, and for managing user comments and contributions. Quite often, a library or museum hosting the archive or exhibition will have resources for creating and maintaining online collections, but it is important that collaborators from these institutions understand the goals of community collaborators.

Once the website is assembled, the team's first discussion should address the question of audience since the primary goal of placing archives or exhibitions online is to make materials available to a wider public. A primary goal of many virtual archives and exhibitions is "bringing it back home" to the community where photos and other materials were originally collected. Finding the best strategy to reach this audience is especially critical. "You need to have an organization that will form a base of users, a center of gravity that attracts other users," advises anthropologist Thaddeus Guldbrandsen. "Without partners, you don't have a vision of how real people will use it." When community members are involved as coproducers or consultants, they may offer insights on local media practices that can help guide site design and outreach activities.

Another aspect of "audience" is interactivity. The research team must make decisions about what kinds of responses and actions they would like to elicit from the Internet public and how to design a site accordingly. Some projects seek to elicit information and stories about the photos from a dispersed population of descendants through the web's social media technologies. For this kind of site, the research team must plan ahead so that the site has a moderator and develop policies for what to do when some users post inappropriate or offensive comments.

When the team has established the target audience for the project, they must then establish ground rules on photo permissions and other ethical questions. These may include discussion of how traditional cultural protocols apply to the Internet, an issue that has been especially important in projects involving the "virtual repatriation" of artifacts and images collected in a context of colonial domination (Christen, 2009). Digital archivists must at times limit what is on display to respect an individual's privacy or community norms about artifacts with spiritual significance. Yet digital archives can also be a tool for empowerment and recognition of communities and populations rendered invisible by traditional history (Lenstra, 2011).

The web infrastructure of participatory digital archives and museums must be designed and maintained. In many projects, the research team works together with a web designer on design decisions. In working with a designer, it is important to communicate the goals of the project, cultural protocols about the display of images, and target audiences' technological resources and skills. Project teams may call a community meeting to discuss which images or media files to post online and to develop interpretive materials and framing texts for the designer to place on the site. Once the virtual archive or museum is online, the site must be maintained, and this is where university partnerships can truly benefit communities. University libraries have resources for maintaining digital repositories and skilled librarians who are experts in the work of preserving collections even when technologies change. Again, planning ahead and collaborating with information specialists can help keep the collection available to users for years to come.

Each participatory multimedia exhibition or archive offers new opportunities for bringing together communities and technologies in new ways and encounters new ethical dilemmas of representation along the way. In the core stories that follow, we see how "digital dynamics" play out in specific projects in Russia, northern New England, and a First Nation community in British Columbia.

CORE STORY 1: *KOMMUNALKA*—A VIRTUAL ETHNOGRAPHIC MUSEUM OF THE SOVIET EVERYDAY EXPERIENCE

A team of scholars of Russian language and culture, Ilya Utekhin, Alice Nakhimovsky, Slava Paperno, and Nancy Ries developed the *Communal Living in Russia* multimedia digital museum, which includes Web 2.0 features to encourage user participation in curating the collection (Utekhin et al., 2006). The website is described as an "online ethnographic museum" focusing on the social and cultural aspects of everyday life in a *kommunalka*, or Soviet-style communal apartment. This style of apartment building featured small family quarters arranged around a shared kitchen, corridor, and lavatory. *Kommunalkas* came into being after the 1917 Bolshevik Revolution, and the daily material and social practices of sharing common domestic spaces shaped the lives of millions of Russians. Communal apartment buildings have remained in wide use in Russia in the decades since the end of the Soviet Union, and so Utekhin and others conducted interviews with past and present residents about life in their buildings. The *Kommunalka* website includes short, ethnographic video clips; audio files of interviews in Russian with English transcriptions; digitized photographs; text essays; video clips from Soviet-era movies; and scanned documents ranging from official state notices to residents' handwritten notes reminding other tenants to shut the front gate firmly.

Kommunalka combines elements of "autoethnography" (Pratt, 1992), ethnographic film, and cultural analysis. Nancy Ries described how the project team came together:

> My Russian collaborators were all "natives" in the sense that they had grown up in St. Petersburg's communal apartments. I was interested in the apartments because it is a combination of politics, emotions, and everyday practices, and I have always been interested in the theorization of everyday life.

The four scholars decided to create the virtual museum after seeing many ironic or sentimental references to the *kommunalka* in art exhibitions, restaurants, and popular culture in the late 1990s. Even as nostalgia swelled, *kommunalka* residents were being pressured to leave because the buildings occupy prime real estate in the center of St. Petersburg and other cities. The project team wanted to present real people's varied experiences of communal living and the material culture of shared domestic space. Nakhimovsky and Paperno wanted the site to be an immersive environment for students of Russian language and culture, and so all materials are presented in Russian and English.

Kommunalka draws especially from Utekhin's personal experience and presents self-reflexive ethnography through eight video tours, showing his intimate connection with research participants. Films of Utekhin conducting interviews and guiding his two young children and a videographer through apartments give viewers access to the research process, the personal history and qualities of the ethnographer, and his relationship to the people and places he is investigating. In the clip "Stairwell," he leads a tour of the lobby, telling a story about the elevator operator who worked at the building when he was growing up. In the clip "Nina Vasilievska," Ilya's former neighbor goes through her photo album on camera, sharing her memories from more than 80 years of living in the building. Each clip is labeled with extensive metadata on the filming date, people present in the film and how they are related to one another, and ethnographic notes glossing the cultural significance of household items, such as the samovar or a pot full of stale bread crusts.

The team analyzed the materials as a collective, producing an overarching narrative for the virtual museum and a series of 43 short essays on themes related to citizenship under the Soviet system, the material culture of the communal apartment, and coping narratives of communal apartment dwellers. Each essay is presented in summary, but readers may expand the essay and references by toggling the screen. The essays use hypertext to link back to other media files, an innovative strategy for ethnography. The essay "Housing Policy in the USSR," for example, describes how the Soviet state allotted housing to workers, and when the author refers to the ethnographic example of a woman taking a job as a building janitor to get housing, a hyperlink offers readers the opportunity to switch over to the video clip of the woman telling her story.

The participatory aspect of the website is primarily aimed at its Internet audience: site visitors are invited to contribute as lay curators of the collection. The site's "My Tours" feature allows users to assemble and publish their own "routes" and interpretations of the archive's images, audio and video clips, historical documents, and analytical essays, and to make them available on the Internet. Already, college teachers and students have created and annotated collections in English and Russian on such themes as "Kitchen Conflicts" and "Comfort, Privacy, Security, and Identity," adding their own short essays to the website.

CORE STORY 2: *BEYOND BROWN PAPER*—"OBSERVANT PARTICIPATION" IN A DIGITAL ARCHIVE

The *Beyond Brown Paper* online digital archive uses social tagging and cataloging software to involve past and current residents to identify people and places in a large historical photo collection. The project, headed by anthropologist Thaddeus Guldbrandsen and curator Catherine Amidon, was organized by the Center for Rural Partnerships, the Lamson Library, the Drerup Art Gallery at Plymouth State University in New Hampshire, and the Arts Alliance of Northern New Hampshire. Online since 2006, the website has attracted more than 8 million hits and established a large circle of active contributors.

Beyond Brown Paper presents thousands of scanned photographs taken by photographers employed by the Brown Paper Company between 1930 and 1960. Established in the nineteenth century, Brown Paper built lumber and pulp mills along the Androscoggin Valley in northern New Hamphire and founded the town of Berlin. For more than a century, the social and economic life of the rural "Northern Forest" region was driven by the lumber and paper industry. In the late twentieth century, however, many of the mills were sold or closed down, with devastating effects for rural towns like Berlin. The Brown Paper photo archive, donated to the university in the 1970s, documents the work and leisure activities of a rural industrial population that today is seeking a viable future. The collection consists of photos on paper and on fragile glass plates, which made it difficult to make the collection accessible to a wider public.

In 2006, Plymouth State received a grant to begin digitizing the collection and to create a public interface for accessing the images. Since then, more than 45,000 photos have been scanned and uploaded to the website. The site uses Scriblio, award-winning "mash-up" software developed by Plymouth State computer scientist Casey Bisson that combines a library catalog database with a WordPress blog, making it relatively easy for nonexpert users to search the photos using keywords and to contribute comments.

Once the website was in place, Plymouth State loaned a computer to the historical society in Berlin and helped to arrange Internet access. The team held events where volunteers from the historical society and other local groups could learn how to use the site. Building technological skills was an important part of the project, as Guldbrandsen stated: "The community organizations did not have a computer or members with tech savvy when we started the work. . . . [A] lot of volunteers got on computers for the first time to work on this project." At other local exhibitions around northern New Hampshire, Guldbrandsen and Amidon's team brought computers and demonstrated how to get online to visit the site.

The project uses Web 2.0 applications to foster new forms of collaborative research, which Guldbrandsen and Amidon characterize as "observant participation," analyzing the exchange of comments on a single photograph from the collection. The black-and-white photograph depicts two male mill workers using large wrenches to adjust the bolts on a cylindrical steel machine.

> This single image received thirteen comments regarding papermaking processes, the identities and location of the subjects of the photo, workplace safety, and the significance of books and web pages in the contemporary library. (Guldbrandsen & Amidon, 2009, pp. 29–30)

The photograph elicited posts from former mill workers and their children, who provided detailed descriptions of and workers' terms for different industrial processes used at the mill in the 1940s. "This photo holds itself out as an invitation to these different perspectives," Guldbrandsen commented. The *Beyond Brown Paper* site provides space for "observant participants" to write narratives on family and local histories associated with the images.

The Brown Paper archive combines the goals of democratizing access and virtual repatriation. The photo collection does not depict colonized people, but it does document a white, rural proletariat at a moment when personal cameras were prohibitively expensive for timber and paper workers and photos were precious. When the photos were donated to the library at Plymouth State University, 75 miles to the south, some Berlin residents felt an important resource had been alienated from the rural communities north of the White Mountains. "At Plymouth State, we're considered northern New Hampshire by everyone else," Guldbrandsen explained, "but to locals in Berlin, we're 'Below the Notches,' we're outsiders." The university maintained the Brown Paper photo collection, but it was inaccessible and underused until the online archive was created.

Today, the *Beyond Brown Paper* site serves as a point of engagement and connection between the university and community organizations whose members regularly contribute to the site. Guldbrandsen and Amidon organized "actual" events in conjunction with the virtual archive, including traveling exhibitions aimed at children and secondary school students and an interactive permanent museum exhibition at the St. Kieran Community Center for the Arts in Berlin. They also organized a meeting with presentations on economic change in the northern counties of New Hampshire in the context of an exhibition on "Industrial Explorers." These events use the archive not only as a way of learning about the region's past, but also as an entry point for residents to discuss what they value about life in the northern counties, and how they envision the future. "It's a source of community pride in a region harmed by rural deindustrialization," Guldbrandsen said. "In the context of the archive, it enables people in the community to tell their own stories and have some agency."

CORE STORY 3: DOIG RIVER FIRST NATION—REPATRIATION AND THE CREATION OF A VIRTUAL MUSEUM

Historically, archives and museums originated as scientific institutions within empires, providing knowledge for governing indigenous populations and preserving and reframing artifacts from subjugated cultures within colonial narratives (Edwards, Gosden, & Phillips, 2006; Stoler, 2010). Today, indigenous groups in Canada, Australia, and around the world are pioneering both the use of virtual archives and museums and of participatory planning, production, and curating (Christen, 2009). *Dane Wajich, Dane-ẕaa Stories and Songs: Dreamers of the Land* is a collaborative online museum exhibition produced by elders, youth, and leaders from the Doig River First Nation working together with anthropologists, linguists, and web designers. The exhibition, hosted by the Virtual Museum of Canada (www.virtualmuseum.ca/Exhibitions/Danewajich/english/index.html), represents the rich potential of participatory virtual museums for decolonizing knowledge.

The Doig River Nation, one of several Dane-ẕaa (also known as Beaver Indian) communities in Northeastern British Columbia, lived as hunters, gatherers, and later fur traders until the mid-twentieth century. With the construction of the Alaskan Highway, members of the Doig River Nation were forced to live on reservations and to send their children to Canadian government schools. Despite these wrenching changes, the community elders maintained their language and traditional knowledge.

The virtual museum exhibition began with the repatriation of a large collection of documents and photographs to the Doig River Nation. Anthropologists Robin Ridington and Jillian Ridington began conducting fieldwork in Doig River in the 1960s, and they repatriated their collection to the community when they retired from the University of British Columbia (Hennessy, 2009). Their daughter, Amber Ridington, and their former student, Kate Hennessy, had done cultural documentation projects with Doig River youth, and together they applied for a grant to produce a virtual exhibition based on repatriated items using participatory media training and production with youth.

Hennessy and Amber Ridington spent the summer of 2004 holding planning meetings with elders in Doig River and recruiting parents and youth to sign on for media training and production to take place the following summer. A close partnership with Garry Oker, an artist and the chief at that time, helped Hennessy and Ridington get community members involved and organize events where discussions could take place. The project's multimedia documentation dovetailed with another important community project, building the new band hall, and so word traveled fast and excitement built. Hennessy recalled: "Some parents heard about it and flagged down my car from their garden, saying 'What about my son? He should participate'." The organizers assembled a group of six youth for the media production team and a wider circle of Dane-ẕaa elders as consultants.

In the summer of 2005, the production phase began in earnest. Hennessy invited ethnographic filmmaker Peter Biella to lead a two-week film production course with the youth in Doig River. The group held meetings with elders to identify the most important stories, places, and people to film. The group examined items repatriated from the Ridingtons' research, including a moose-hide Dane-ẕaa *náácḥe* (dreamers') drum from the early twentieth century and many photographs and recordings of drummers. The group settled on the organizing theme of drums and the dreamers who used the drums ceremonially.

Once trained, the young filmmakers traveled with adults on the project team to film elders telling stories on location around the reserve. They spent long days riding in a van, setting up, filming, and striking equipment. It was not always easy to keep the youth committed to filming. "Sometimes a youth who was supposed to be filming had basketball practice," Hennessy said. "People can't drop everything in life to take part in our amazing participatory projects!" After several weeks of training, meetings, and filming, however, the team had assembled a collection of interviews and film footage for the multimedia exhibition. It was time to bring materials back to the community for comment.

The project team used the Doig Days summer celebration as a moment for eliciting Dane-ẕaa people's responses to the videos and other materials planned for the virtual exhibition. Hennessy remembered:

> We put up this exhibition in the community museum space, with videos clips that we shot, and a pinboard mapping out the website, and that's where we talked about the project with elders, and the chief, and other people who walked in. It wasn't a highly organized process, we just let people come in and look, and they could talk to us when they wanted.

Over the next two years, Hennessy and Ridington had designers create prototypes for the virtual museum and then brought these back to Doig River for further feedback and revisions.

Ethical issues related to representation and indigenous intellectual property rights occurred at every step of the production process. Elders determined an overall theme for the exhibition focused on the drum, but as time went on, ways of presenting the drum were renegotiated, as Hennessy explained:

> Elders knew that there were restrictions on showing a dreamer's drum—that it should not be viewed by menstruating women and other specific protocols for maintaining the power of the drum. They had to discuss, "Is a photograph the same as the artifact?" in terms of these cultural protocols.

Aside from the cultural protocols, some elders wondered if it was wise to show the original drum, which was old and torn. Would this image give audiences the impression that the drum and its traditions had been neglected? The group had to decide whether or not to use a picture of the drum that had so inspired Dane-ẕaa elders and youth as they were planning the virtual exhibition. In the end, the project team replaced the photo of the original drum with another showing a contemporary drum, an image representing the ongoing life of the Dane-ẕaa.

While the production process for *Dane Wajich* epitomizes the participatory approach in digital archives, the site is almost entirely closed to user contributions in the Web 2.0 sense. There is no public area for posted comments, only a "Feedback" page where users may write to the webmasters and the Canadian Heritage Information Network (CHIN), which is responsible for the Virtual Museum of Canada. Hennessy reflected on this absence:

> The dynamics and form of Web 2.0 don't necessarily serve the aims of the participatory process in an indigenous community. . . . [W]hat is the benefit to communities whose main goal is to be able to represent themselves after centuries of colonialism?

Doig River Nation participants, when considering interactive uses of the virtual exhibition, chose to focus on audiences being able to learn about and appreciate Dane-ẕaa culture. User resources include lesson plans and classroom materials, as well as an introductory course in the Dane-ẕaa language.

Concluding Thoughts

The three core stories reveal how participatory digital archives and virtual museums are changing the relationship between scholars, communities, and the collections that have historically linked them on unequal terms. The *Kommunalka* virtual museum draws from its producers' autoethnography of growing up in communal apartment buildings, and it invites the public to explore ordinary Russians' domestic lives and spaces in ways that challenge the two narrative frames that dominate contemporary media depictions: jokey irony and rosy nostalgia. The *Beyond Brown Paper* archive applies interactive blogging capabilities to the task of curating a large collection of photos documenting rural workers' lives. The project drew its strength from combining communication in the virtual space of the archive with strong community outreach in the actual space of community centers, schools, and nursing homes. The collaborative production of the *Dane Wajich* multimedia exhibition trained First Nations youth as filmmakers and media producers while inspiring in-depth community discussions on the best ways to virtually repatriate cultural objects and to "tell the important stories" about them. All three are the product of negotiations over representing culture and provide diverse answers to the call to democratize and decolonize scholarly knowledge.

CHAPTER 9

Opening Up Data Analysis, Writing, and Research Products

INTRODUCTION

Traditional qualitative data collection has always involved dialog between the researcher and participants, even when social scientists chose to downplay the interpersonal aspects of the research process in their writing (Marcus & Fischer, 1986). While many researchers are now comfortable with including community members in data collection, fewer have opened up data analysis and writing to research participants (Cashman et al., 2008). This is a missed opportunity. Collaboration in interpreting data and creating research products can be valuable for community members in terms of experiential learning and skills building, and for researchers in terms of increasing the validity, authenticity, and applicability of research findings.

Inviting research participants to analyze data remains unusual. Participatory data analysis poses challenges because it is time-consuming and requires academics to make their methods explicit: researchers must process and present data in forms that are accessible and train community members in specific types of analysis. Engaging participants in analyzing their own words and images also runs up against old taboos in the social sciences: if norms of scientific detachment require researchers to resist "going native" in their analysis, how can the "natives" make valid contributions to analysis? Any social scientist embarking on their first participatory action research (PAR) project will soon discover how ideals of detachment and objectivity persist in professional practice and identity, despite the fact that "insider ethnographers" began to deconstruct the "detached observer" decades ago (Rosaldo, 1989).

Although we are critical of the ideal of objectivity, we remain firmly committed to the quest for *trustworthiness* (Guba & Lincoln, 2005) in the qualitative social sciences. How else can we be sure that we are achieving the goals of qualitative inquiry: to study social practice in a naturalistic mode and understanding participants' emic perspectives—how they make sense of the world? Rather than placing trust in the objectivity of a single scientific observer, the ideal of trustworthiness presents multiple moments for cross-checking data and analysis. These include "reflective commentary" on the research process; triangulation of methods, sources, and participant perspectives; use of "member checks" on data as discussed in this chapter; and the creation of rich, "thick descriptions" that offer audiences enough contextual information to allow comparisons to be made (Denzin & Lincoln, 2007; Guba & Lincoln, 2005; Shenton, 2004). When social scientists take into account these forms of validity, participants' contributions to data analysis and the production of texts may actually improve our research, both empirically and ethically.

We believe that participatory digital research has special potential for opening up the data analysis and dissemination phases of research. By relying on accessible media, participatory digital research invites participants to analyze images as part of a visual elicitation strategy. PAR strategies more generally encourage self-reflexivity, with team discussions of the research process simultaneously generating analytic frames, new data, and action plans. In this chapter, we discuss the following: 1) identifying and analyzing the varied types of data collected in participatory visual research; 2) using collaborative data analysis and dialogic editing strategies; and 3) creating research products—including written texts, videos, and multimedia presentations—that reach both scholarly and popular audiences.

ESCAPE FROM DATA MOUNTAIN: DOCUMENTATION, SITES OF ANALYSIS, AND ANALYTIC QUESTIONS

The first fact of participatory visual research is that researchers collect mountains of data in a very short period of time and need a clear strategy for managing it all. Participatory researchers must make analytic strategies clear to nonacademic partners, guiding them up the slope of "Data Mountain." What kinds of data should we analyze, and to what end? What kinds of data are needed to study the participatory research process self-reflexively? Multiple materials (written, oral, and visual) are available for analysis—those from the media, which may include images, story scripts or voiceovers, or captions—and those from ethnographic data collection, including field notes from participant observation and transcriptions of interviews and focus group discussions. To lead participants through data analysis, we need a clear set of landmarks to help

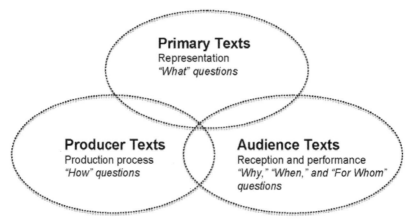

Figure 9-1 Types of data in participatory visual/digital research

them recognize the kinds of documentation (or texts) that serve as sites of analysis for different analytic questions.

Claudia Mitchell (2011) cites Fiske and Neuman's (1987) work, which speaks of three types of texts in participatory videomaking: "primary texts," "producer texts," and the "audience texts." These three types of texts each provide distinctive sites for visual data analysis (Rose, 2007) that map onto characteristic questions (Figure 9-1).

Primary texts are the media produced by participants during the research process. These could consist of Photovoice images, videos, GIS maps, multimedia digital stories, archives, or exhibitions. Scholars working with visual data have noted the difficulty of integrating video and the like into certain qualitative analytic frameworks.

> The quality of the data collected often undermines the development of an analysis; the data collected seeming strangely resistant to analysis. It can then be difficult to codify and categorize video data, to break it apart into fragments that can be subjected to analysis, and transcriptions of visual conduct can seem unwieldy and time-consuming to produce, even for the shortest fragment (Luff & Heath, 2012, p. 258).

Indeed, researchers may need to "transcribe" visual materials before proceeding to data analysis: Mitchell (2011) writes of transcribing video texts as we would transcribe audio texts to convey what is "said and told," and "what's going on" (p. 80). Other components—including visuals, background music, and special effects—also contribute to the telling and interpretation of the materials and should be included in analysis. Gubrium and Turner (2011) present one method for constructing a transcript of a multimodal media production, in this case a digital story, such that multisensory elements of the story—including the visual, emotional, sound, and pacing—are represented in a storyboarded transcript layout for coding and analysis. Knoblauch and Schnettler (2012) argue that beyond analyzing video (or other visual material we might add) for content, visual analysis is decidedly rooted in a hermeneutic approach:

> Video interaction analysis is not a version of content analysis that exclusively takes into account those aspects documented on the videotape. In order to make sense of the recorded interaction—which is indeed the main object of analysis—the *context* it is embedded in has to be considered systematically. . . . Our methodological arguments are the following: (1) video interaction analysis is a fundamentally interpretive method. Therefore, analysing video data has to be considered a *hermeneutic* activity. (2) Video recordings are only tools. The analytical focus lies on the interaction taking place in a certain social situation. Making sense of what has been tape-recorded essentially depends upon additional contextual knowledge. This insight is provided by focused *ethnography*. (3) With the aim of further improving the existing video analytical methods, we need to observe our own practices of video analysis and reflect them methodically. In addition to principles borrowed from established interpretive methods (of verbal or textual data), this reflection may allow us to generate unique new methodical principles specific for video data (Knoblauch and Schnettler, 2012, pp. 335–336).

Taking our analytic cue from these arguments, we describe three types of texts produced in visual and digital projects that may be considered as data for analysis. Primary texts are a key site for analyzing representation, the visual symbols and language participants use to express meanings. Primary texts are ripe for the "what?" questions of thematic and content analysis such as "what issues do research participants define as problems?" and "what aspects of culture do participants especially value?" as well as more interpretive questions such as "what symbols does the producer associate with this topic?" Researchers may analyze primary texts comparatively, juxtaposing images or videos focused on similar topics or produced by similar social groups to uncover patterns and variations, shared and contested meanings.

Producer texts document "how" participants produce media, treating the process itself as a site of inquiry. Using field notes, researchers may document participant "narrative work" focused on the task at hand before, during, and after the production process (Gubrium & Holstein, 2009). After the media are produced, participants may be asked to comment on the message, purpose, and potential uses of the visual material in recorded discussions that may be transcribed as producer texts. As presented in Chapter 4, Photovoice provides a formal method for the creation of producer texts through group discussions using Wang's five "SHOWED" questions (Wang et al., 2004; see Figure 4-1 in Chapter 4).

These questions may be revised by participatory project teams and adapted to participatory filmmaking, digital storytelling, participatory GIS (PGIS), or participatory archive and virtual museum projects. Data analysis of producer texts brings the context behind production and participants' ethical and aesthetic decision-making into focus.

Audience texts document individual and group responses to participatory visual media, including other stories that audience members associate with the particular project on display. Written texts or curricular material accompanying public exhibitions of visual material may also serve as audience texts. Finally, visual media producers' representations of their project to diverse audiences—such as in the workshop, public community exhibition, or through publication—also serve as audience texts. Here, data collection focuses on the moment of performance and audience responses to photographic and multimedia exhibitions, videos, and other digital and visual products.

Researchers may document "audiencing" through audio- or video-recorded discussions, as well as through field notes of observations. Viewer response forms may be distributed to assess audience responses. Do audience members respond as producers anticipated, and if not, what could explain different interpretations of images or stories conveyed in the work? Researchers may also document the responses of the producers/participants themselves, especially upon viewing their work again at a more public event. Documenting "audiencing" is a challenge because researchers are typically busy putting on an event; thus, it is important to plan ahead and get extra help to document audience responses.

Audience texts provide a site for inquiry into the performance and reception of participatory visual media by focusing on "why," "when," and "for whom" questions. The researcher may delve into dialogic/performance analysis (Frank, 2012; Riessman, 2008), a perspective that analyzes image-making and storytelling as socially situated in particular contexts and produced through dialog between producer, researcher, and the viewing audience (Bakhtin, 1981). From this perspective, participatory visual media are not seen as individual productions in their own right, but rather as sites for the dynamic interaction and transformation of participants and their intended audiences.

Taken together, primary, producer, and audience texts afford rich materials for analyzing content, themes, poetic and narrative form, and social interactions. Researchers increase the trustworthiness of their findings by triangulating several types of data. Producer texts provide documentation so that participants may analyze the collaborative research process reflexively. Comparing the responses of participants and audience members subjects findings to multiple "member checks" that can reveal factual discrepancies and conflicting interpretations. A well-documented participatory visual research project provides ample data for systematic and self-reflexive analysis.

WE'VE GOT DATA, NOW WHAT? PARTICIPATORY DATA ANALYSIS IN PRACTICE

Once a research team has collected a body of images, field notes, and transcriptions, participatory data analysis can begin. In Photovoice and Videovoice projects, photographers regularly engage in analytic discussions of images and films. Participants may get involved at later stages of analysis and writing as well. Academic researchers must be prepared to explain data analysis techniques in lay terms and to develop interactive ways to analyze data.

Harper and her research partners Catherine Sands, Molly Totman, and Diego Angarita engaged youth participants in data analysis in a Photovoice project on school lunch in collaboration with the *Nuestras Raíces* youth group, a community development organization in Holyoke, Massachusetts (Harper et al., n.d.). Following the Photovoice project, the team of four adult and ten youth researchers was invited to submit an article to a peer-reviewed journal's special issue on food politics. The youth group's participation in developing the journal article presented a new set of challenges for the group, including their hesitation to present their ideas in a more academic setting. A year after the Photovoice exhibition, however, the youth were more mature and had more experience and confidence in communicating their ideas to the public. Several youth were preparing to apply to college and wanted to develop new academic skills. The adults on the team were surprised, pleased, and proud that the youth felt invested in participating in more scholarly analysis.

Youth who had participated in the Photovoice project attended the data analysis session. Harper reminded the group of milestones in the research project, from its beginning to the present. As she explained to the group, data analysis was the next phase:

> When you took the pictures, that was data collection. We were making new facts by taking pictures and asking questions. Data analysis is making sense of it. Sorting into categories, and making new categories when they don't fit.

Harper and Totman brought in printed transcriptions of quotations from the Photovoice discussions. Two youth participants, Monica and Jonell, cut up the transcriptions into individual quotations with scissors, and each of the youth drew a handful of quotations. Next, the group set out four big sheets of newsprint, and another youth participant, Jazzy, wrote categories at the top of each page. Based on a first reading and discussion of the transcriptions as well as the target journal's special issue theme, Harper and Sands suggested working titles of "learning about policy," "youth doing research," "school lunch experiences," and "other" for new categories generated during coding. Before anyone started working, the group reviewed every category. They discussed and negotiated what might be included in each theme. The youth felt confident with the categories "school lunch" and "youth doing research," but talked at length about how to define policy:

> Catherine: So, what is policy?
> Nick: It's rules and regulations. Who runs what.
> Catherine: Oh, OK. We can also talk about "little p" policies and "big P" policies. Remember when we talked about the Farm Bill? That's a "big P" policy.
> Jazzy: "Little p" policies are like what is served for lunch?
> Catherine: Exactly.
> Nick: When I hear policy, I think we're talking about government and the mayor.
> Krista: Policy could also be about how you get groups of people to change things. After doing this project, did you know more about changing policy?
> Monica: Yes, because I didn't know how school food worked. We have to know what we're trying to change if we're going to move forward and change policy.

As the discussion of policy continued, the youth identified the school committee and two specific food service managers as people with power to enact or implement cafeteria policies. They reached this conclusion based on their detailed knowledge of the school food procurement process, which the youth had acquired over the course of the Photovoice research project.

Once the youth expressed confidence in the categories, they went to work sorting the quotations and taping them onto the sheets of newsprint. They also had extra copies of the quotations in case a quotation fit in more than one category. Once the quotations were all sorted, youth circled the table with felt markers in hand, scribbling notes on each poster and drawing stars, checks, or dots next to the quotations they thought were especially important, following the group's tradition of using "sticker-dot polls" to gauge interest in topics. The free movement, snacks, and graffiti-style writing made data analysis more lively and fun for the youth researchers who had already spent a full day in school.

Harper's team did not use qualitative data analysis (QDA) software such as NVivo, Atlas.ti, or MaxQDA to code the images, but future projects may include training youth to use such software. Each year, new versions are being released that make it easier to create a database of visual images for coding and searching by category. Most QDA software programs have photocoding capabilities, and some offer video- and audiocoding as well. Since even a small Photovoice project can easily produce several hundred images, using QDA software makes it easier to organize and navigate photo collections.

As the group moved from data analysis to drafting the article, they once again retooled the academic tradition of solo expert authorship. Adults on the team wrote drafts based on the group's analysis and brought these back to the youth group for dialogic editing. Some of the youth are preparing to apply to college and take great interest in coauthoring an academic publication. Others are more interested in working on PowerPoint slideshows, photo exhibitions, and other ways of disseminating our research to a wider popular audience in Holyoke and beyond.

DIALOGIC EDITING OF TEXTS, IMAGES, AND FILMS

Since the 1980s, some anthropologists have used dialogic editing to involve research participants in creating ethnographic texts and multimedia products. The term "dialogic editing" originated with anthropologist Steven Feld, who developed this technique in 1982 as a way of creating a more collaborative text with his research participants in Papua New Guinea. He translated sections of his book *Sound and Sentiment: Birds, Weeping, Poetics, and Song in Kaluli Expression* into Kaluli and read these passages aloud to participants as a prompt for discussion. He writes, "Dialogic editing is, then, the impact of Kaluli voices on what I tell you about them in my voice; how their take on my take on them requires reframing and refocusing my account" (Feld, 1987, p. 191). For example, Feld's Kaluli interlocutors were impressed by the level of detail used to describe the use of bird sounds in funeral rituals, but they were puzzled that Feld had not written at all about everyday sounds of the forest. While imitations of bird songs formed a large part of their song repertoire, Feld's participants felt he had neglected the sounds of frogs, insects, and other animals that Kaluli weave into their songs. Through dialogic editing, Feld and his research participants identified an area for further research: depicting the sonic experience of a day in the life of the Kaluli in the rainforest. In the resulting project, *Voices of the Rainforest*, several Kaluli directed Feld in audio-recording sounds and assembling them into a sound narrative. The resulting 30-minute sound collage combined experimental ethnography with musical composition, resonated with Kaluli participants' interest in the senses, and contributed to the burgeoning field of sonic (see also Gershon, 2012) and sensory anthropology.

Dialogic editing may take a variety of forms. Luke Eric Lassiter surveys the many strategies used by collaborative ethnographers in producing texts: involving principal consultants as readers and editors; convening focus groups to review drafts; using collaborative ethnographer/consultant teams; holding community forums to present research findings; discussing drafts with a community-based editorial board; and cowriting texts (Lassiter, 2005, p. 139). While writing his book, *The Power of Kiowa Song* (1998), Lassiter reviewed chapter drafts with individual Kiowa consultants and focus groups. One of Lassiter's key consultants, Ralph Kotay, objected to the detached way Lassiter portrayed spiritual songs, separating the sacred and secular facets of spiritual music. Lassiter changed the text to present his dialogs with Kotay on this topic, and he also shifted to a more phenomenological analysis of participants' embodied experience of religious song. Lassiter explains: "Collaborative reading and editing emerges, like collaborative ethnography itself, as a *dialogue about* a particular ethnographic topic—be it Kiowa song or managing a hotel—not as a final *statement on* any particular ethnographic topic" (Lassiter, 2005, p. 141). In subsequent projects, Lassiter explored other methods of dialogic editing. In *The Other Side of Middletown* (2004), Lassiter and colleagues paired Ball State University students with members of the local African-American community to explore the fraught history of race relations in Muncie, Indiana. As the ethnographer–consultant teams developed individual chapters, they presented these in public forums where a broader segment of the African-American community could participate. Students from a creative writing class created and performed a play based on the oral histories they had recorded, and the research team held a facilitated discussion after the performance to gather community members' responses. Scholars working with indigenous groups increasingly present their research to formally constituted community-based editorial boards to ensure sensitive representation (or, when appropriate, omission) of sacred traditions or intracommunity problems (Lobo, 2002; Wexler & Graves, 2008). Cocreated texts were pioneered by social scientists working within the life-history tradition as a way to share authority with key research participants (Crapanzano, 1985). What all of these approaches to dialogic editing share is a commitment to negotiating ethnographic representations with participants when their interpretations conflict with one another or with that of the researcher.

RESEARCH PRODUCTS AND DISSEMINATION

Participatory visual methods allow for the repurposing of research images and narratives in academic and community-driven texts and media. Collaborative social scientists often come to see their scholarly output as a varied portfolio of academic and popular work, as illustrated by the following story of anthropologist Catherine Besteman. Participatory visual researchers typically turn to images to reach different publics in and out of the academy, and publishers are beginning to reckon with the challenges and new opportunities for multimedia scholarship. Nevertheless, there is still a long way to go before universities acknowledge and reward nontraditional research products in the tenure and promotion process.

In her 2010 article "In and Out of the Academy: Policy and the Case for a Strategic Anthropology," Catherine Besteman narrates her journey into collaborative, multimedia research and the challenges of communicating to diverse academic and popular audiences. When she established herself as an anthropologist in the late 1980s, Besteman conducted traditional ethnographic fieldwork in a Bantu village in Somalia. Over the course of a year, she conducted participant observation, surveyed the villagers, audio-recorded open-ended interviews, and amassed a collection of over 1,000 photos taken by her husband, the photographer Jorge Acero (Besteman, 2009). Upon returning to the United States, she wrote a series of scholarly articles and books based on her research, while trying (with limited success) to gain a foothold in policy circles where decisions about U.S. government interventions in Somalia's civil war were under way (Besteman, 2010).

In 2006, Besteman then came into contact with a group of Bantu Somali refugees living near her home in Maine and made the astounding discovery that many of the resettled Bantu were from the village where she had conducted her fieldwork almost 20 years earlier. They had endured violence and eviction from their farms during the civil war and discrimination in refugee camps before receiving official "persecuted minority" status enabling resettlement in the United States. The Bantu refugee community faced many difficulties in their encounters with social service providers, schools, and hospitals in rural Maine, and they enlisted Besteman in a collaborative project aimed at educating the public about Bantu Somali culture and studying the experiences of the resettled refugees.

To communicate refugees' concerns and experiences, Besteman and her collaborators developed a varied portfolio of research products. The central research product of the collaboration is the multimedia website "The Somali Bantu Experience" (www.colby.edu/somalibantu). Besteman,

Somali community partners, and Colby College students worked together to assemble the website. Together they reviewed Besteman and Acero's collection of photographs from the 1980s, an emotional process for the refugees: "Somali Bantu refugees find both pleasure and grief in the photos, which include images of deceased relatives, plundered farms and family members left behind in refugee camps" (Besteman, 2009, p. 23). The photos show life before the civil war, giving Somali Bantu children and youth a window into their parents' and grandparents' lives and culture. Besteman's team expanded this photographic archive with contemporary images of refugee life in Maine. This digital collection forms the centerpiece of the multimedia website, which also includes resources on Somali Bantu culture and history, digital audio interviews, and classroom material (Besteman, 2010). Other research products from the Somali Bantu Experience project include ethnographic presentations, an ELL (English Language Learner) book, newspaper, radio, and television news stories, op-eds, workshops with service providers and teachers, and meetings to build networks among refugees.

The Somali Bantu Experience project resulted in a prolific array of research products aimed at community members, direct service providers, policymakers, and the general public of Maine. Besteman acknowledges that she was able to respond to the needs of her research collaborators because she had already published enough traditional scholarly works to attain tenure. As she explains, "Ethnography may become a 'byproduct' . . . less important than workshops, community forums, and nonacademic publications undertaken with the goal of identifying, articulating, and resolving specific community concerns" (Besteman, 2010, p. 410).

Besteman argues that the social sciences will have greater public impact if our professional organizations and universities develop guidelines for including policy and advocacy work as part of the tenure and promotion process.

Scholarly publishing is gradually creating spaces for visual and multimedia work. *Visual Studies* and *Visual Anthropology Review* provide space for presenting photographic essays alongside peer-reviewed articles. Well-known peer-reviewed journals such as *Cultural Anthropology* are now publishing multimedia electronic editions. New peer-reviewed multimedia journals such as the interdisciplinary black studies journal *FIRE!* and the religious studies journal *Practical Matters* allow scholars to present text, video, audio clips, and digital images online in the space of a single article. Contributors to Philip Vannini's edited volume and companion website, *Popularizing Research* (www.popularizingresearch.net) offer "show" (multimedia) and "tell" (written narrative) versions of their efforts to communicate research to the public (Vannini, 2012, p. 8). The new Routledge series, "Innovative Ethnographies," combines traditional book publishing with online multimedia illustrations and video, with an eye to ever more seamless integration as tablet computers and e-readers such as the iPad and Kindle gain popularity (Uimonen, 2012; Vannini, 2012).

Such innovations in scholarly publishing are still rare, but they offer a glimpse of the creative potential of online multimedia publishing to present immersive, thick description and to engage wider audiences. One such experiment is heritage scholar Edward Gonzalez-Tennant's Virtual Rosewood Research Project (www.virtualrosewood.com/) and its associated virtual museum located in Second Life, the online gaming world (Gonzalez-Tennant, 2011). The Virtual Rosewood Museum offers interpretive exhibits on the history and archaeology of Rosewood, a Florida town built by African-American freedmen in the 1870s that was burnt to the ground by a white mob in 1923. Visitors to the Virtual Rosewood website and the Second Life online museum may also watch a 25-minute documentary based on the digital stories of survivors of the 1923 massacre and members of Rosewood's descendant community. Gonzalez-Tennant has also posted archival data such as oral histories, census data, and climate records on the Virtual Rosewood website for the benefit of academic and lay researchers. Gonzalez-Tennant's work demonstrates groundbreaking ways to present participatory digital research that go far beyond the written text.

Concluding Thoughts

As the examples in this chapter demonstrate, exciting things can happen when researchers integrate participants in data analysis and the creation of research products. In Harper and colleagues' PAR investigation of an urban school food system, analyzing transcribed discussions allowed the youth to see what they had learned about policy over the course of a long-term project. Sharing control of how a group is represented in text and images, as was the case in Lassiter and colleagues' *Other Side of Middletown* (2004) project, can also help begin to repair community members' negative past experiences with and distrust of academic researchers. Dialogic editing with research participants can lead to new theoretical explorations and experimental ethnographic forms. This was the case when Feld and his Kaluli interlocutors moved beyond Feld's initial analysis of Kaluli song into the phenomenological analysis of soundscapes, a move that broke new ground in sensory and multimedia ethnography.

Scholars journeying down the path of collaborative analysis and authorship/production quickly learn that working meaningfully with others demands organization, time, and creativity. Early in the research process, it is crucial to identify what types of primary, producer, and audience texts might be produced and to consistently document them as data. Participatory visual research can be made more trustworthy, robust, and self-reflexive by triangulating several different types of data with texts or community interlocutors. Researchers must also be prepared to accessibly explain data analysis principles and procedures and to organize the work creatively to keep participants engaged.

Given these multiple demands, should our work be participatory in every moment? There may be times when participants would prefer to highlight the academic authority of the knowledge produced over the collaborative qualities of the research process. During her collaborative research, Besteman learned that activists had used her early traditional ethnographic writing on the Somali Bantu to make the case for resettlement (Besteman, 2010, p. 411). There may be other moments of stress in a grassroots organization, too, when participation becomes a burden upon our research partners. The degree and substance of participation must be negotiated (and periodically renegotiated) so that there is a balance between the needs and contributions of community participants and academic researchers and a shared understanding about using the research in public presentations and publications. Finally, academic researchers and their collaborators must come to explicit agreements about how to give credit for coauthorship, permission to use images, and the distribution of royalties from cocreated academic books and documentary videos (Lassiter, 2005, p. 153).

CHAPTER 10

Conclusion

In this book we've presented numerous case studies of participatory visual research practitioners who are taking advantage of digital technologies to highlight common themes across their projects. Common issues related to community engagement in participatory action research (PAR) include establishing ethical practices, negotiating the terms of participation and collaboration, and developing projects and research products that are useful and accountable to the communities involved. In addition to these concerns, scholars also spoke of the tensions between PAR and academic and disciplinary success. Getting academic institutions to recognize, value, and reward the investment of time and varied outputs from doing this kind of work, as well as the potential for PAR to transform individual scholars and make our disciplines more relevant to the broader public, remains a central challenge.

Carolyn Fluerr-Loban writes about the turn toward collaborative anthropology as an ethical turn, another "experimental moment" in the social sciences (Fluehr-Lobban, 2003; Marcus & Fischer, 1986). Researchers often come to participatory methods through a desire to change power relationships within their own practice, moving from an "extractive" to an "enriching" vision of research (Rhoades, 2006). Yet, once embarked on the collaborative research journey, researchers encounter many "emergent" ethical dilemmas, starting with who asks the research questions and establishes the topic, to tensions between projects aims (such as advocacy versus research agendas), to questions of the control, ownership, and maintenance of research materials. PAR scholars are starting to organize resources to educate institutional review boards (IRBs) and funders to consider ethical obligations to communities involved in research projects beyond simple confidentiality and informed consent agreements (see Campus-Community Partnerships for Health, 2012).

Another cross-cutting theme of the case stories presented is just what kinds of participation or collaboration we hope to achieve in our research,

Participatory Visual and Digital Methods by Aline Gubrium and Krista Harper, 197–200. ©2013 Left Coast Press Inc. All rights reserved.

and to what ends. This is constantly hashed out between research participants, colleagues, funders, and with ourselves as we develop a program of research. Sometimes participatory research provides opportunities for community members to build new skills that they need, while at other times participation may seem like a burden to participants. As researchers, we must negotiate an appropriate division of labor in knowledge production, one that includes participants in ways meaningful to them without seeming like they are participating only to fulfill some external requirement. The cases also show that in PAR projects, researchers must take on the responsibility of explaining the research project in clear, accessible language throughout the course of the project.

Teams should also articulate the uses of the project for those involved and make sure that research products address community needs and that outcomes are tracked consistently (Catalani & Minkler, 2010). While long-term outcomes may be difficult to track, being able to present short-term results may allow community members to use data as evidence in policy settings. The results also provide impetus to continue participation in a project, build participants' confidence in the process, and develop the capacity, financial and otherwise, of a project to continue. Use of participatory visual methods means that community groups may enjoy easily accessible documentation of these outcomes (the web and digital technologies are a boon in this respect).

Participatory visual approaches encourage us to coproduce varied research products with and for our participants. Multipurposing research materials is a major theme cutting across the case studies and affects the terms of participation. In his approach to collaborative filmmaking, Menzies produces both the classic documentary film and deconstructed vignettes that Gitxaala community members may use to teach a younger generation their stories and traditional ecological knowledge. Photos from Harper's Photovoice project in Hungary have appeared in slide shows targeting policymakers in Hungary and the United Nations, in local and national photo exhibitions aimed at networking and discussion, and in academic articles. Weiner and Harris' participatory GIS (PGIS) maps were used to stimulate group discussions in rural South Africa, to document land evictions requiring redress by the post-apartheid government, and were also presented in academic forums. These examples highlight the need for broader and more flexible parameters for evaluating research, including the research process, products, and the multiple ways we communicate and use research findings. This requires a major shift in thinking about what constitutes a body of research.

Researchers who choose to work with participatory visual methods often comment on the challenges of getting academic institutions, as well as funders, to understand, support, and reward community-based research. This speaks to the continued dominance of written text as an academic product, and in particular first-authored books and articles. Catherine Besteman (2010) writes about balancing the demands of PAR with a resettled Somali Bantu community in Maine while maintaining an academic career:

> Although my intent is ultimately to write an ethnography of their experience —a goal shared by community leaders—I also recognize that my inter- locutors are often more interested in dealing practically with immediate issues like getting a job, better classes for their kids, obtaining assistance for family members still stuck in refugee camps in Kenya, and so forth. Ethnographic research can sometimes feel self-indulgent in these circum- stances, and I have not yet found a way to balance these (Besteman, 2010, p. 415).

Besteman ultimately recommends that our professional organizations develop guidelines for considering PAR and public engaged work in the tenure and promotion process. At a more personal level, our case studies also signal a shift in the ways we conceptualize ourselves as scholars and how we build a "core story" (Elder, 2001–2002) around our body of scholarship. We hope that the cases presented in this book demonstrate some ways that social researchers might "compose" (Bateson, 2001) or "construct" an academic life (Richardson, 1997) around participatory visual methodologies.

Our case studies, especially in the context of indigenous research methodologies, reveal the need to decolonize (Smith, 1999) and "de- school" (Illich, 1971) the research process. Learning ethnographic research methods in the academy, we both learned that while ethnogra- phy might be a craft based on improvisation and empirical learning (Van Maanen, 1988), it is also always important to plan ahead. Hennessy and Ridington worked with Doig River Nation youth and elders to produce a multimedia website, but had to choose new images later in response to community discussion of what artifacts should and should not appear online to a worldwide audience. Similarly, Elder and Kamerling's core story on community collaboration tells us that part of "trusting the proc- ess" is to open ourselves to the messiness of lived experience outside the artificial confines of research proposals, particularly to community members' visions of research.

These comments also speak to the ongoing process of learning both new technologies and collaborative approaches. Reflecting on their entry into participatory visual research, several practitioners emphasized the importance of on-the-job training. They had not been formally trained in visual anthropology or in technical aspects of the methods, per se, but rather were introduced to these approaches through their own and their research participants' interest in new media.

How are participatory visual and digital methods changing the qualitative social sciences? In terms of knowledge production, they remain rooted in ethnography's traditional commitment to "emic perspectives": understanding participants' ways of seeing and interpreting the world. The approaches also enhance humanistic and social scientific research. Projects such as PGIS, Photovoice, and participatory video offer rich possibilities for "groundtruthing" and sometimes challenging official knowledge claims, by documenting, for example, deforestation (Zackey, 2007), waste management (Harper, Steger, & Filčák, 2009; McMahan & Burke, 2007), and disaster response (Jhala, 2007) in specific settings. In participatory visual and digital research, these forms of documentation are not naively empirical. The negotiated quality of knowledge is foregrounded because the researcher arrives at knowledge claims through processes of discussion and reflection with research participants.

Participatory visual and digital methods also contribute to building public-engaged ethnography, a critically applied social science that seeks to reach policymakers and the broader public in the twenty-first century. The process changes the research relationship from the academic social scientist and research "subject" dyad to a more coeval model (Fabian, 1983) based on negotiation and collaborative knowledge production. Using digital technologies we can communicate research through accessible, visually appealing media. In this participatory frame, research is recast as an emancipatory process through which participants may reflect on problems and issues in their communities, with possibilities for growth as citizens, activists, and users of technologies.

APPENDIX

Release of Materials Form

Instructions: Please review the contents of this Release, complete it, and return it to us. If you have any questions regarding the release, please contact the Principal Investigator at name@university.edu or xxx-xxx-xxxx. Thank you!

I, the undersigned _____ (please print your name) ("Applicant"), grant the ("Project Partner") permission to use all and/or part of my final project ("Project Materials") in the following ways (please initial):

_____ At the end of the project activities, within the project and confined to project participants and facilitators. Comments or exceptions:

_____ During future project activities or at workshops taught by project team members, as a design example. Comments or exceptions:

_____ At community screenings of project outcomes, intended to discuss and raise awareness about ("research topic.") Comments or exceptions:

_____ At social research and/or advocacy (circle one or both) conferences to generate support for the work of the project. Comments or exceptions:

_____ For social research funders, in order to develop collaborative partnerships for additional workshops. Comments or exceptions:

_____ In social research and other special interest film festivals, to offer visibility to the work of the project. Comments or exceptions:

_____ On the project web site, www.xxx.xxx.

_____ On other strategic communications social networking media forums, such as Facebook/MySpace pages, wikis, and blogs. Comments or exceptions:

_____ As an individual playable DVD of my project product. Comments or exceptions:

_____ As part of a compilation playable DVD of project products, to generate discussion around ("research topic") for the project. Comments or exceptions:

By entering into this voluntary agreement, Applicant releases and forever holds harmless the Project Partner from any and all claims, demands, damages, losses, obligations, rights, and causes of action, whether known or unknown, relating in any way to this activity. Applicant acknowledges that her/his participation in the project was entirely voluntary. *This Release is effective as of ("date specified.")*

_____

Applicant Signature   Date

_____

Permanent Mailing Address (Street, City, State/Province, Postal Code, Country)

_____

Phone   Email

References

Aberley, Doug and Renée Sieber 2002 Principles of Public Participation GIS. Paper presented at the First International PPGIS Conference held at Rutgers University, New Brunswick, NJ, July 20–22. Retrieved August 23, 2012, from www.iapad.org/ppgis_principles.htm.

Aguilera, E. and J. Peterson. 2002 From Berkeley to Brazil through the Fifth Dimension. Retrieved August 23, 2012, from www.uclinks.org/what/newsletter/nl1/nl1.1.pg9.html.

Alexandra, Darcy 2008 Digital Storytelling as Transformative Practice: Critical Analysis and Creative Expression in the Representation of Migration in Ireland. *Journal of Media Practice* 9(2): 101–112.

―――― 2012a Undocumented in Ireland: Our Stories. Retrieved from www.darcyalexandra.com/practice/undocumented-in-ireland-our-stories/.

―――― 2012b Living in Direct Provision: 9 Stories. Retrieved from www.darcyalexandra.com/practice/living-in-direct-provision-9-stories/.

Anthropologies 2012 Anthropologies: A Collaborative Online Project. Retrieved from www.anthropologiesproject.org/.

Aporta, Claudio and Eric Higgs 2005 Satellite Culture: Global Positioning Systems, Inuit Wayfinding, and the Need for a New Account of Technology. *Current Anthropology* 46(5): 729–753.

Appadurai, Arjun 2006 The Right to Research. *Globalisation, Societies and Education* 4(2): 167–177.

Asad, Talal 1973 Anthropology and the Colonial Encounter. London: Ithaca.

Atalay, Sonya 2006 Indigenous Archaeology as Decolonizing Practice. *American Indian Quarterly* 30(3): 280–310.

Baker, Tamara and Carolyn C. Wang 2006 Photovoice: Use of a Participatory Action Research Method to Explore the Chronic Pain Experience in Older Adults. *Qualitative Health Research* 16(10): 1405–1413.

Bakhtin, M. 1981 The Dialogic Imagination: Four Essays. Austin, TX: University of Texas Press.

Banks, Marcus 2001 Visual Methods in Social Research. Thousand Oaks, CA: Sage.

―――― 2007 Using Visual Data in Qualitative Research. Thousand Oaks, CA: Sage.

Bateson, Mary Catherine 2001 Composing a Life. New York: Grove.

Battle-Baptiste, Whitney 2011 Black Feminist Archaeology. Walnut Creek, CA: Left Coast Press.

Behar, Ruth 2003 Translated Woman: Crossing the Border with Esperanza's Story. Boston, MA: Beacon.

Behar, R. and D. Gordon 1995 Women Writing Culture. Berkeley: University of California Press.

Bell, D. and P. Caplan 1993 Gendered Fields: Women, Men, and Ethnography. New York: Routledge.

Ber, Rosalie and Gideon Alroy 2002 Teaching Professionalism with the Aid of Trigger Films. *Medical Teacher* 24(5): 528–531.

Bergan, Renee and Mark Schuller 2009 Poto Mitan: Haitian Women, Pillars of the Global Economy. Watertown, MA: Documentary Educational Resources.

Berger, John 1972 Ways of Seeing. New York: Penguin.

Berry, David M. 2004 Internet Research: Privacy, Ethics and Alienation: An Open Source Approach. *Internet Research* 14(4): 323–332.

Besteman, C. 2009 The Somali Bantu Experience: Using Multimedia Ethnography for Community Building, Public Education and Advocacy. *Anthropology News* 50(4): 23.

———— 2010 In and Out of the Academy: Policy and the Case for a Strategic Anthropology. *Human Organization* 69(4): 407–417.

Biehl, Joao and Torben Eskerod 2005 Vita: Life in a Zone of Social Abandonment. Berkeley: University of California Press.

Biella, Peter 2006 A DVD and a Place to Screen: The Lever of Applied Visual Anthropology. Paper presented at the Society for Applied Anthropology Annual Meeting, Vancouver, British Columbia, March 26–April 2. Retrieved August 23, 2012, from online.sfsu.edu/~biella/biella2006a.pdf.

———— 2008 Elementary Forms of the Digital Media: Tools for Applied Action Research in Visual Anthropology. *In* Viewpoints: Visual Anthropologists At Work, edited by Mary Strong and Laena Wilder, 363–388. Austin, TX: University of Texas Press.

———— In press The Idea of a Field School in Visual Anthropology. *In* Teaching Visual Anthropology in Europe and Beyond, edited by P. I. Crawford and N. Kriznar. Hoejberg, Denmark: Intervention Press.

Biella, P., K. Hennessy, and P. Orth 2003 Essential Messages: The Design of Culture-Specific HIV/AIDS Media. *Visual Anthropology Review* 19(1–2): 13–56.

Biella, Peter, Jeff Himpele, Kelly Askew, and David MacDougall 2002 AAA Statement on Ethnographic Visual Media. *American Anthropologist* 104(1): 303–306.

Blue, Carroll Parrott 2003 The Dawn At My Back: A Memoir of a Black Texas Upbringing. Austin, TX: University of Texas Press.

Boal, Augusto 1979 Theatre of the Oppressed. London: Pluto.

Boellstorff, Tom 2008 Coming of Age in Second Life: An Anthropologist Explores the Virtually Human. Princeton, NJ: Princeton University Press.

Boellstorff, Tom, Bonnie Nardi, Celia Pearce, and T. L. Taylor 2012 Ethnography and Virtual Worlds: A Handbook of Method. Princeton, NJ: Princeton University Press.

Bosak, Keith 2008 Nature, Conflict, and Biodiversity Conservation in the Nanda Devi Biosphere Reserve. *Conservation and Society* 6(3): 211–224.

Bourgois, Phillipe 1997 Confronting the Ethics of Ethnography: Lessons Learned from Fieldwork in Central America. *In* Decolonizing Anthropology, edited by F. Harrison, 111–127. Washington, DC: American Anthropological Association.

Bourgois, Phillipe and Jeffrey Schonberg 2009 Righteous Dopefiend. Berkeley: University of California Press.

Bowrey, K. and J. Anderson 2009 The Politics of Global Information Sharing: Whose Cultural Agendas Are Being Advanced? *Social & Legal Studies* 18(4): 479–504.

Briggs, Charles 1986 Learning How to Ask. Cambridge, UK: Cambridge University Press.

Bruckman, A. 2002 Ethical Guidelines for Research Online. Retrieved December 6, 2012, from www.cc.gatech.edu/~asb/ethics/.

Buchanan, David R. 2000 An Ethic for Health Promotion: Rethinking the Sources of Human Well-Being. New York: Oxford University Press.

Burrough, P. A. and R. A. McDonnell 1998 Principles of Geographical Information Systems. Oxford, UK: Oxford University Press.

Butler, Judith 1990 Gender Trouble: Feminism and the Subversion of Identity. New York: Routledge.

Cammarota, J. and M. Fine 2008 Revolutionizing Education: Youth Participatory Action Research in Motion. New York: Routledge.

Campus-Community Partnerships for Health 2012 Campus-Community Partnerships for Health: Promoting Health Equity and Social Justice. Retrieved from www.ccph.info.

Case, Amber 2012 A Dictionary of Cyborg Anthropology: A Field Guide to Interface Culture. cyborganthropology.com. Retrieved December 6, 2012, from cyborganthropology.com/store/.

Cashman, S. B., S. Adeky, A. J. Allen III, J. Corburn, B. A. Israel, J. Montano, A. Rafelito, S. D. Rhodes, S. Swanston, and N. Wallerstein 2008 The Power and the Promise: Working With Communities to Analyze Data, Interpret Findings, and Get to Outcomes. *American Journal of Public Health* 98(8): 1407–1417.

Castelden, Heather Theresa Garvey and the Huu-ay-aht First Nation 2008 Modifying Photovoice for Community-Based Participatory Indigenous Research. *Social Science and Medicine* 66(6): 1393–1405.

Catalani, C. and M. Minkler 2010 Photovoice: A Review of the Literature in Health and Public Health. *Health Education & Behavior* 37(3): 424–451.

Catalani, C., A. Veneziale, L. Campbell, S. Herbst, B. Butler, B. Springgate, and M. Minkler 2009 In Harmony: Reflections, Thoughts, and Hopes of Central City, New Orleans. Retrieved online at ces4health.info/find-products/view-product. aspx?code=5P3GZ4HT.

——— 2012 Videovoice: Community Assessment in Post-Katrina New Orleans. *Health Promotion Practice* 13(1): 18–28.

Chalfen, R. and M. Rich 2004 Applying Visual Research Patients Teaching Physicians Through Visual Illness Narratives. *Visual Anthropology Review* 20(1): 17–30.

Chang, Joyce, Ki Mae Heussner, Amy Lee, Hope Needles, Hilary Powell, and Satta Sarmah 2008 Locate Chicago 2016: Using Location-based Technology to Enhance Journalism. Project report, Medill School of Journalism, Northwestern University, Chicago, IL.

Chavez, Vivian, Barbara Israel, Alex J. Allen III, Maggie Floyd DeCarlo, Richard Lichtenstein, Amy Schulz, Irene S. Bayer, and Robert McGranaghan 2004 A Bridge Between Communities: Video-Making Using Principles of Community-based Participatory Research. *Health Promotion Practice* 5(4): 395–403.

Checker, Melissa, David Vince, and Alaka Wali 2010 A Sea Change in Anthropology? Public Anthropology Reviews. *American Anthropologist* 112(1): 5–6.

Christen, Kimberly 2008 Archival Challenges and Digital Solutions in Aboriginal Australia. *SAA Archaeological Record* 8(2): 21–24.

——— 2009 Access and Accountability: The Ecology of Information Sharing in the Digital Age. *Anthropology News* 50(4): 4–5.

Clifford, James 1989 The Others: Beyond the "Salvage" Paradigm. *Third Text* 3(6): 73–78.

Clifford, James and George E. Marcus, eds. 1986 Writing Culture: The Poetics and Politics of Ethnography. Berkeley: University of California Press.

Coleman, Gabriella 2010 Ethnographic Approaches to Digital Media. *Annual Review of Anthropology* 39(1): 487–505.

——— 2012 Phreaks, Hackers and Trolls and the Politics of Transgression and Spectacle. *In* The Social Media Reader, edited by Michael Mandiberg pp. 99–119. New York: New York University Press.

Collier Jr., John 1957 Photography in Anthropology: A Report on Two Experiments. *American Anthropologist* 59(5): 843–859.

Collier, Malcolm 1986 Visual Anthropology: Photography as a Research Method. Albuquerque, NM: University of New Mexico Press.

Collins, Patricia Hill 1998 Toward an Afrocentric Feminist Epistemology. *In* Fighting Words: Black Women and the Search for Justice, edited by Patricia Hill Collins, 124–154. Minneapolis: University of Minnesota Press.

——— 2000 Black Feminist Thought: Knowledge, Consciousness, and the Politics of Empowerment. New York: Routledge.

Combahee River Collective 1983 The Combahee River Collective Statement. *In* Home Girls: A Black Feminist Anthology, edited by Barbara Smith, 264–274. New York: Kitchen Table Press.

Contando Nuestras Historias n.d. Spanish Language Projects. Retrieved August 23, 2012, from www.storycenter.org/casestudies.html.

Cooke, Bill and Uma Kothari, eds. 2001 Participation: The New Tyranny? London: Zed Books.

Corbett, J., G. Rambaldi, R. Olson, M. McCall, J. Muchemi, P. K. Kyem, D. Weiner, and R. Chambers 2006 Mapping for Change: Practice, Technologies and Communication. *Participatory Learning and Action* 54: 13–20.

Crapanzano, Vincent 1985 Tuhami, Portrait of a Moroccan. Chicago, IL: University of Chicago Press.

Creed, Gerald W., ed. 2006 The Seductions of Community: Emancipations, Oppressions, Quandaries. Santa Fe, NM: School for Advanced Research on the Human Experience.

Crowe, D. M. 1996 A History of the Gypsies of Eastern Europe and Russia. New York: St. Martin's Griffin.

Davis, Angela 1981 Women, Race and Class. New York: Vintage.

de Lange, Naydene and Claudia Mitchell 2012 Community Health Workers Working the Digital Archive: A Case for Looking At Participatory Archiving in Studying Stigma in the Context of HIV and AIDS. *Sociological Research Online* 17(1). Retrieved on August 23, 2012, at www.socresonline.org.uk/17/1/7.html.

de Lange, Naydene, Claudia Mitchell, and Jean Stuart, eds. 2007 Putting People in the Picture: Visual Methodologies for Social Change. Rotterdam, the Netherlands: Sense Publishers.

de Leeuw, S. and I. Rydin 2007 Migrant Children's Digital Stories Identity Formation and Self-Representation Through Media Production. *European Journal of Cultural Studies* 10(4): 447–464.

Debrecen University School of Public Health 2004 *Telepek És Telepszerü Lakóhelyek Felmérése* [Survey of Settlements and Settlement-Type Residences]. Report presented to the Hungarian Ministry of Environment.

Denzin, Norman and Yvonna Lincoln, eds. 2007 Strategies of Qualitative Inquiry (3rd edition). Thousand Oaks, CA: Sage.

Dicks, Bella, Bambo Soyinka, and Amanda Coffey 2006 Multimodal Ethnography. *Qualitative Research* 6(1): 77–96.

Downey, G., J. Maud, P. Nyiri, J. Timmer, and L. Wynn 2012 Culture Matters: Applying Anthropology. Retrieved from www.culturematters.wordpress.com.

Doyle, Heather 2004 Improving Access of Roma to Health Care Through the Decade of Roma Inclusion. *Roma Rights* 3/4: 42–45.

Dunn, C. E. 2007 Participatory GIS—A People's GIS? *Progress in Human Geography* 31(5): 616–637.

Dupain, M. and L. L. Maguire 2007 Health Digital Storytelling Projects. *American Journal of Health Education* 38(1): 33–35.

Edwards, E., C. Gosden, and R. B. Phillips 2006 Sensible Objects: Colonialism, Museums and Material Culture. New York: Berg.

El Guindi, Fadwa 1998 From Pictorializing to Visual Anthropology. *In* Handbook of Methods in Cultural Anthropology, edited by H. Russell Bernard, 459–512. Walnut Creek, CA: AltaMira Press.

Elder, Sarah 1995 Collaborative Filmmaking: An Open Space for Making Meaning, a Moral Ground for Ethnographic Film. *Visual Anthropology Review* 11(2): 94–101.

———— 2001–2002 Images of Asch. *Visual Anthropology Review* 17(2): 89–109.

Elwood, Sarah 2008 Volunteered Geographic Information: Future Research Directions Motivated by Critical, Participatory, and Feminist GIS. *GeoJournal* 72(3–4): 173–183.

———— 2011 Participatory Approaches in GIS and Society Research: Foundations, Practices, and Future Directions. *In* The Sage Handbook of GIS and Society, edited by Robert McMaster, Timothy Nyerges, and Helen Couclelis, 381–399. Thousand Oaks, CA: Sage.

Emerson, R. M., R. I. Fretz, and L. L. Shaw 2011 Writing Ethnographic Fieldnotes, 2nd edition. Chicago: University of Chicago Press.

Fabian, Johannes 1983 Time and the Other. New York: Columbia.
_____ 2008 Ethnography as Commentary: Writing from the Virtual Archive. Durham, NC: Duke University Press.
Feld, Steven 1987 Dialogic Editing: Interpreting How Kaluli Read Sound and Sentiment. *Cultural Anthropology* 2(2): 190–210.
Fielding, N., R. M. Lee, and G. Blank 2008 The Internet as a Research Medium: An Editorial Introduction to the Sage Handbook of Online Research Methods. *In* The Sage Handbook of Online Research Methods, edited by G. Blank, R. M. Lee, and N. Fielding, 3–20. Thousand Oaks, CA: Sage.
Fine, M. 1994 Dis-Stance and Other Stances: Negotiations of Power Inside Feminist Research. *In* Power and Method: Political Activism and Educational Research, edited by Andrew Gitlin, 13–35. New York: Routledge.
Fine, M., M. E. Torres, K. Boudin, I. Bowen, J. Clark, D. Hylton, M. Martinez, M. Rivera, R. A. Roberts, P. Smart, and D. Upegui 2004 Participatory Action Research: From Within and Beyond Prison Bars. *In* Working Method, Research and Social Justice, edited by L. Weis and M. Fine, 95–119. New York: Routledge.
Fisch, A. L. 1972 The Trigger Film Technique. *Improving College and University Teaching* 22(4): 286–289.
Fish, A., A. Golub, C. Kelty, D. Wax, J. Sosa, K. Friedman, M. Thompson, R. Anderson, T. Strong, and C. McGranahan 2012 Savage Minds: Notes and Queries in Anthropology —A Group Blog. Retrieved from www.savageminds.org.
Fiske, J., P. Harding, and W. R. Neuman 1987 New Directions in Mass Media Audience Research. Cambridge, MA: MIT Press.
Flicker, Sarah, Robb Travers, Adrian Guta, Sean McDonald, and Aileen Meagher 2007 Ethical Dilemmas in Community-Based Participatory Research: Recommendations for Institutional Review Boards. *Journal of Urban Health: Bulletin of the New York Academy of Medicine* 84(4): 478–493.
Flinn, Andrew 2010 "An Attack on Professionalism and Scholarship"?: Democratising Archives and the Production of Knowledge. *Ariadne* 62. Retrieved from www.ariadne. ac.uk/issue62/flinn.
Flores, Carlos Y. 2007 Sharing Anthropology: Collaborative Video Experiences Among Maya Film-Makers in Post-War Guatemala. *In* Visual Interventions: Applied Visual Anthropology, edited by Sarah Pink, 209–224. New York: Berghahn.
Flores, Kim Sabo 2008 Youth Participatory Evaluation: Strategies for Engaging Young People. San Francisco: Jossey-Bass.
Fluehr-Lobban, C. 2003 Ethics and the Profession of Anthropology: Dialogue for Ethically Conscious Practice. Lanham, MD: AltaMira Press.
Forests and Oceans for the Future 2012 Sustainable Forestry, Traditional Economies, and Community Well-Being. Retrieved from www.ecoknow.ca/communityvids.html.
Forte, M. C., M. J. Hanifi, E. J. Darling, and J. Allison 2012 Zero Anthropology. Retrieved from www.zeroanthropology.net.
Foucault, Michel 1979 Discipline and Punish. New York: Vintage.
Fox, Richard G., ed. 1991 Recapturing Anthropology: Working in the Present. Santa Fe, NM: School for Advanced Research.
Frank, A. 2012 Practicing Dialogical Narrative Analysis. *In* Varieties of Narrative Analysis, edited by J. F. Gubrium and J. A. Holstein, 33–52. Los Angeles: Sage.
Freire, Paulo 2000[1970] Pedagogy of the Oppressed. New York City: Continuum.
Fyfe, Hamish 2007 "Habits of the Heart" Storytelling and Everyday Life. George Ewart Evans Centre for Storytelling Research Seminars. Retrieved on August 23, 2012, from storytelling.research.glam.ac.uk/documents/download/5/.
Gershon, W. 2012 Sonic Ethnography as Method and in Practice. *Anthropology News* 53(5): 5, 12.
Giaccardi, Elisa 2011 Collective Storytelling and Social Creativity in the Virtual Museum: A Case Study. *Design Issues* 22(3): 29–41.

Ginsburg, Faye 1995 The Parallax Effect: The Impact of Aboriginal Media on Ethnographic Film. *Visual Anthropology Review* 11(2): 64–76.

Gonzalez-Tennant, E. 2008 Rethinking the Digital Age. *In* The Media and Social Theory, edited by D. Hesmondhalgh and J. Toynbee, 127–144. New York: Routledge.

——— 2011 Archaeological Research and Public Knowledge: New Media Methods for Public Archaeology in Rosewood, Florida. Ph.D. dissertation, Department of Anthropology, University of Florida, Gainesville.

González, E. R., R. P. Lejano, G. Vidales, R. F. Conner, Y. Kidokoro, B. Fazeli, and R. Cabrales 2007 Participatory Action Research for Environmental Health: Encountering Freire in the Urban Barrio. *Journal of Urban Affairs* 29(1): 77–100.

Gready, Paul 2010 Introduction: "Responsibility to the Story". *Journal of Human Rights Practice* 2(2): 177–190.

Green, L. W., M. A. George, M. Daniel 1995 Study of Participatory Research in Health Promotion. Ottawa: Royal Society of Canada.

Greenwood, Davydd and Morten Levin 2005 Reform of the Social Sciences, and of Universities Through Action Research. *In* Handbook of Qualitative Research, 3rd edition, edited by Norman Denzin and Yvonna Lincoln, 43–64. Thousand Oaks, CA: Sage.

Greenwood, Davydd and José Luis González Santos 1992 Industrial Democracy as Process: Participatory Action Research in the Fagor Cooperative Group of Mondragón. Assen-Maastricht, the Netherlands: Van Gorcum Publishers.

Gregory, Sam, Gillian Caldwell, Ronit Avni, and Thomas Harding, eds. 2005 Video for Change: A Guide for Advocacy and Activism. London: Pluto Press.

Guba, Egon and Yvonna S. Lincoln 2005 Paradigmatic Controversies, and Emerging Confluences. *In* Handbook of Qualitative Research, 3rd edition, edited by Norman Denzin and Yvonna S. Lincoln, 191–216. Thousand Oaks, CA: Sage.

Gubrium, Aline 2006 I Was My Momma Baby. I Was My Daddy Gal: Strategic Stories of Success. *Narrative Inquiry* 16(2): 231–253.

——— 2009a Digital Storytelling: An Emergent Method for Health Promotion Research and Practice. *Health Promotion and Practice* 10(2): 186–191.

——— 2009b Digital Storytelling as a Method for Engaged Scholarship in Anthropology. *Practicing Anthropology* 31(4): 5–9.

Gubrium, Aline and Krista Harper 2009 Visualizing Change: Participatory Digital Technologies in Research and Action. *Practicing Anthropology* 31(4): 2–4.

Gubrium, Aline and M. Idalí Torres 2011 "S-T-R-8 UP" Latinas: Valorizing a Negative Gender Identity. *American Journal of Sexuality Education* 6: 281–305.

Gubrium, Aline and K. C. Nat Turner 2011 Digital Storytelling as an Emergent Method for Social Research and Practice. *In* Handbook of Emergent Technologies in Social Research, edited by Sharlene Nagy Hess-Biber, 469–491. New York: Oxford University Press.

Gubrium, J. F. and J. A. Holstein 2009 Analyzing Narrative Reality. Los Angeles: Sage.

Guldbrandsen, T. C. and C. Amidon 2009 Beyond Brown Paper: Reflections on Web 2.0. *Practicing Anthropology* 31(4): 27–32.

Hajdu, Gábor, Árpád Kostyál, Eszter Kovách, György Málovics, Linda Mohay, and Szentistványi István 2010 *Környezeti Igazságosság Magyarországon* [Environmental Justice in Hungary]. Budapest, Hungary: Védegylet Association.

Hale, Charles R. 2008 Engaging Contradictions: Theory, Politics, and Methods of Activist Scholarship. Berkeley: University of California Press.

Hall, Stuart 1999 Un-Settling "the Heritage", Re-Imagining the Post-Nation: Whose Heritage? *Third Text* 13(49): 3–13.

Haraway, Donna 1988 Situated Knowledges: The Science Question in Feminism and the Privilege of Partial Perspective. *Feminist Studies* 14(3): 575–599.

Harmsworth, G., M. Park, and D. Walker 2005 Report on the Development and Use of GIS for Iwi and Hap: Motueka Case Study, Aotearoa-New Zealand. Retrieved on August 23, 2012, at icm.landcareresearch.co.nz/knowledgebase/publications/public/ICMMaoriGISreport.pdf.

Harper, Douglas 2002 Talking About Pictures: A Case for Photo Elicitation. *Visual Studies* 17(1): 13–26.

Harper, Krista 2012 Visual Interventions and the "Crises in Representation" in Environmental Anthropology: Environmental Justice in a Hungarian Romani Neighborhood. *Human Organization* 71(3): 292–305.

Harper, Krista, Catherine Sands, Molly Totman, and Diego Angarita n.d. Youth Engagement in School Food Systems Policy: Photovoice in Holyoke, Massachusetts. Unpublished manuscript.

Harper, Krista, Tamara Steger, and Richard Filčák 2009 Environmental Justice and Roma Communities in Central and Eastern Europe. *Environmental Policy and Governance* 19(4): 251–268.

Harrison, Faye, ed. 1997 Decolonizing Anthropology: Moving Further Toward an Anthropology for Liberation. Washington, D.C.: American Anthropological Association.

Hartley, John 2009 TV Stories: From Representation to Productivity. *In* Story Circle: Digital Storytelling Around the World, edited by John Hartley and Kelly McWilliam, 16–36. Malden, MA: Wiley-Blackwell.

Hemment, J. 2007 Public Anthropology and the Paradoxes of Participation: Participatory Action Research and Critical Ethnography in Provincial Russia. *Human Organization* 66(3): 301–314.

Hennessy, Kate 2009 Virtual Repatriation and Digital Cultural Heritage: The Ethics of Managing Online Collections. *Anthropology News* 50(4): 5–6.

Hergenrather, Kenneth C., Scott Rhodes, Chris Cowan, Gerta Bardoshi, and Sara Pula 2009 Photovoice as Community-Based Participatory Research: A Qualitative Review. *American Journal of Health Behavior* 33(6): 686–698.

Hill, Amy L. 2010 Participatory Media Help Ugandan Women Who Have Experienced Obstetric Fistula Tell Their Stories. *MAZI: The Communication for Social Change Report* 21. Retrieved from www.communicationforsocialchange.org/mazi-articles.php?id=417.

———— 2011 Digital Storytelling for Gender Justice: Exploring the Challenges of Participation and the Limits of Polyvocality. *In* Confronting Global Gender Justice, edited by Debra Bergoffen, Paula Ruth Gilbert, Tamara Harvey, and Connie L. McNeely, 126–140. New York: Routledge.

Hine, Christine 2005 Virtual Methods: Issues in Social Research on the Internet. New York: Berg.

———— 2008 Virtual Ethnography: Modes, Varieties, Affordances. *In* The Sage Handbook of Online Research Methods, edited by N. Fielding, R. Lee, and G. Blank, 257–270. Thousand Oaks, CA: Sage.

Holstein, James and Jaber Gubrium 1995 The Active Interview. Thousand Oaks, CA: Sage.

House, J. S. 2002 Understanding Social Factors and Inequalities in Health: 20th Century Progress and 21st Century Prospects. *Journal of Health and Social Behavior* 43: 125–142.

Howes, D. 2005 Empire of the Senses. New York: Berg.

Hull, G. 2003 At Last: Youth Culture and Digital Media: New Literacies for New Times. *Research in the Teaching of English* 38(2): 229–233.

Hull, G., J. Zacher, and L. Hibbert 2009 Youth, Risk, and Equity in a Global World. *Review of Research in Education* 33(1): 117–159.

Humphreys, M., A. D. Brown, and M. J. Hatch 2003 Is Ethnography Jazz? *Organization* 10(1): 5–31.

Hussey, Wendy 2006 Slivers of the Journey: The Use of Photovoice and Storytelling to Examine Female to Male Transsexuals' Experience of Health Care Access. *Journal of Homosexuality* 51(1): 129–158.

Huvila, Isto 2008 Participatory Archive: Towards Decentralised Curation, Radical User Orientation, and Broader Contextualisation of Records Management. *Archival Science* 8(1): 15–36.

Hymes, Dell, ed. 1974 Reinventing Anthropology. New York: Vintage Books.

Illich, Ivan 1971 Deschooling Society. New York: Harper & Row.

Ingold, Tim and Jo Lee Vergunst 2008 Ways of Walking: Ethnography and Practice on Foot. Burlington, VT: Ashgate.

Israel, Barbara A., Eugenia Eng, Amy J. Schultz, and Edith A. Parker 2005 Methods in Community-Based Participatory Research for Health. San Francisco: Jossey-Bass.

James, N. and H. Busher 2006 Credibility, Authenticity and Voice: Dilemmas in Online Interviewing. *Qualitative Research* 6(3): 403–420.

Janelle, D. G. and M. F. Goodchild 2011 Concepts, Principles, Tools, and Challenges in Spatially Integrated Social Science. *In* The Sage Handbook of GIS and Society, edited by Robert McMaster, Timothy Nyerges, and Helen Couclelis, 27–45. Thousand Oaks, CA: Sage.

Jhala, Jayasinghji 2007 Emergency Agents: A Birthing of Incipient Applied Visual Anthropology in the "Media Invisible" Villages of Western India. *In* Visual Interventions: Applied Visual Anthropology, edited by Sarah Pink, 177–190. New York: Berghahn.

Johns, M. D., S. L. Chen, and G. J. Hall 2004 Online Social Research. New York: Peter Lang.

Jones, Jennifer L. 2005 Transboundary Conservation: Development Implications for Communities in Kwazulu-Natal, South Africa. *The International Journal of Sustainable Development and World Ecology* 12(3): 266–278.

Kamerling, Leonard 2004 A Quiet Life. 42opus 4(1). Retrieved on August 23, 2012, at www.wou.edu/~mcgladm/Geography%20107%20Cultural%20Geography/optional/ Kamerling%20_%20A%20Quiet%20Life.PDF.

Kelty, C. M. 2008 Two Bits: The Cultural Significance of Free Software. Durham, NC: Duke University Press.

Kirshenblatt-Gimblett, Barbara 2012 From Ethnology to Heritage: The Role of the Museum. *In* Museum Studies: An Anthology of Contexts, edited by Bettina Messias Carbonell, 199–205. Malden, MA: Wiley.

Knoblauch, H. and B. Schnettler 2012 Videography: Analysing Video Data as a "Focused" Ethnographic and Hermeneutical Exercise. *Qualitative Research* 12(3): 334–356.

Krause, E. L. 2012 "They Just Happened": The Curious Case of the Unplanned Baby and the "End" of Rationality. *Medical Anthropology Quarterly* 26(3): 361–382.

Kwan, Mei-Po 2006 Feminist Visualization: Re-Envisioning GIS as a Method in Feminist Geographic Research. *In* Emergent Methods in Social Research, edited by Sharlene Nagy Hesse-Biber and Patricia Leavy, 131–163. Thousand Oaks, CA: Sage.

Labrador, Angela and Elizabeth Chilton 2009 Re-Locating Meaning in Heritage Archives: A Call for Participatory Heritage Databases. Conference Proceedings of the 2009 Computer Applications in Archaeology Annual Meeting, Williamsburg, Virginia, March 22–29. Retrieved on August 23, 2012, from www.caa2009.org/articles/ Labrador_Contribution386_c%20(1).pdf.

Laituri, Melinda 2002 Ensuring Access to GIS for Marginal Societies. *In* Community Participation and Geographic Information Systems, edited by W. Craig, T. Harris, and D. Weiner, 270–282. New York: Taylor & Francis.

Lambert, Joe 2006 Digital Storytelling: Capturing Lives, Creating Community. Berkeley, CA: Digital Diner.

––––––– 2010 Digital Storytelling Cookbook. Berkeley, CA: Digital Diner.

Lassiter, Eric Luke 1998 The Power of Kiowa Song: A Collaborative Ethnography. Tuscon, AZ: University of Arizona Press.

Lassiter, Eric Luke 2005 The Chicago Guide to Collaborative Ethnography. Chicago, IL: University of Chicago Press.

_____ 2006 Collaborative Ethnography Matters. *Anthropology News* 47(5): 20–21.

Lassiter, E., H. Goodall, E. Campbell, and M. N. Johnson, eds. 2004 The Other Side of Middletown: Exploring Muncie's African American Community. Walnut Creek, CA: AltaMira Press.

Lenstra, Noah 2011 E-Black Champaign-Urbana: Community Informatics and Cultural Heritage Information in a Low-Income Community. Certificate of Advanced Study in Library and Information Sciences, University of Illinois at Urbana-Champaign. Retrieved from eblackcu.net.

Lewin, Kurt 1946 Action Research and Minority Problems. *Journal of Social Issues* 2(4): 34–46.

Lobo, Susan, ed. 2002 Urban Voices: The Bay Area American Indian Community. Tuscon, AZ: University of Arizona Press.

Low, Setha, Dana Taplin, and Suzanne Scheld 2005 Rethinking Urban Parks: Public Space and Cultural Diversity. Austin, TX: University of Texas Press.

Luff, P. and C. Heath 2012 Some "Technical Challenges" of Video Analysis: Social Actions, Objects, Material Realities and the Problems of Perspective. *Qualitative Research* 12(3): 255–279.

Lunch, N. and C. Lunch 2006 Insights Into Participatory Video: A Handbook for the Field. Oxford, UK: InsightShare.

Lundby, Knut 2008 Introduction: Digital Storytelling, Mediatized Stories. *In* Digital Storytelling, Mediatized Stories: Self-Representations in New Media, edited by Knut Lundby, 1–17. New York: Peter Lang.

Lykes, M. B. 2010 Silence (ing), Voice (s) and Gross Violations of Human Rights: Constituting and Performing Subjectivities Through PhotoPAR. *Visual Studies* 25(3): 238–254.

MacClancy, Jeremy 1995 Brief Encounter: The Meeting, in Mass-Observation, of British Surrealism and Popular Anthropology. *Journal of the Royal Anthropological Institute* 1(3): 495–512.

MacDougall, David 1997 The Visual in Anthropology. *In* Rethinking Visual Anthropology, edited by Marcus Banks and Howard Morphy, 276–295. New Haven, CT: Yale University Press.

Marcus, George 1995 Ethnography in/of the World System: The Emergence of Multi-Sited Ethnography. *Annual Review of Anthropology* 24: 95–117.

_____ 2008 The End(s) of Ethnography: Social/Cultural Anthropology's Signature Form of Producing Knowledge in Transition. *Cultural Anthropology* 23(1): 1–14.

Marcus, George and Michael M. J. Fischer 1986 Anthropology as Cultural Critique: An Experimental Moment in the Human Sciences. Chicago, IL: University of Chicago Press.

May, Shannon 2010 Rethinking Anonymity in Anthropology: A Question of Ethics. *Anthropology News* 51(4): 10–13.

McIntyre, Alice 2003 Through the Eyes of Women: Photovoice and Participatory Research as Tools for Reimagining Place. *Gender, Place, and Culture* 10(1): 47–66.

McMahan, Ben and Brian Burke 2007 Participatory Mapping for Community Health Assessment on the US-Mexico Border. *Practicing Anthropology* 29(4): 34–38.

McNiff, Jean 1988 Action Research: Principles and Practice. New York: Routledge.

Mead, Margaret and Gregory Bateson 1977 On the Use of the Camera in Anthropology. *Studies in the Anthropology of Visual Communication* 4(2): 78–80.

Meadows, Daniel 2003 Digital Storytelling: Research-Based Practice in New Media. *Visual Communication* 2(2): 189–193.

Mearns, K. F. 2011 Ekaluka Farmers' Association and the Land Reform Programme: Expectations and Success Factors. *Development Southern Africa* 28(2): 241–254.

Menzies, Charles 2002 Working in the Woods: The Story of the Tsimshian and Forestry [film]. Forests for the Future. Vancouver, B.C.: University of British Columbia Press.

———— 2004 Putting Words Into Action: Negotiating Collaborative Research in Gitxaala. *Canadian Journal of Native Education* 28(1/2): 15–32.

———— 2011 Butterflies, Anthropologies, and Ethnographic Field Schools: A Reply to Wallace and Hyatt. *Collaborative Anthropologies* 4: 260–266.

Menzies, Charles and Caroline Butler 2011 Collaborative Service Learning and Anthropology with Gitxaala Nation. *Collaborative Anthropologies* 4: 169–242.

Michaels, Eric 1985 New Technologies in the Outback and Their Implications. *Media Information Australia* 38: 69–72.

Michaels, Sarah and Melinda Laituri 1999 Exogenous and Indigenous Influences on Sustainable Management. *Sustainable Development* 7(2): 77–86.

Milne, E. J., C. Mitchell, and N. de Lange 2012 Handbook of Participatory Video. Lanham, MD: AltaMira Press.

Minkler, M. and N. Wallerstein 2008 Community-Based Participatory Research for Health: From Process to Outcomes. San Francisco: Jossey-Bass.

Mitchell, Claudia 2011 Doing Visual Research. Thousand Oaks, CA: Sage.

Mitchell, Claudia and Sandra Weber 1999 Reinventing Ourselves as Teachers: Beyond Nostalgia. London: Falmer.

Mizen, Phil and Yaw Ofosu-Kusi 2010 Unofficial Truths and Everyday Insights: Understanding Voice in Visual Research With the Children of Accra's Urban Poor. *Visual Studies* 25(3): 255–267.

Murthy, Dhiraj 2008 Digital Ethnography: An Examination of the Use of New Technologies for Social Research. *Sociology* 42(5): 837–855.

Nabudere, D. W. 2008 Research, Activism, and Knowledge Production. *In* Engaging Contradictions: Theory, Politics, and Methods of Activist Scholarship, edited by Charles Hale, 62–87. Berkeley: University of California Press.

Nakamura, K. 2008 A Case Against Giving Informants Cameras and Coming Back Weeks Later. *Anthropology News* 49(2): 20.

Nyerges, T., R. McMaster, and H. Couclelis 2011 Geographic Information Systems and Society: A Twenty Year Research Perspective. *In* The Sage Handbook of GIS and Society, edited by Robert McMaster, Timothy Nyerges, and Helen Couclelis, 3–21. Thousand Oaks, CA: Sage.

Otañez, Marty 2012 Sidewalk Radio: Anthropology as a Resource to Promote Health, Labor Rights and Visual Media. Retrieved from www.sidewalkradio.net/.

Pacey, H. A. 2005 The Benefits and Barriers to GIS for Maori. MA thesis, Department of Indigenous Planning, Lincoln University, New Zealand.

Packard, J. 2008 "I'm Gonna Show You What It's Really Like Out Here": The Power and Limitation of Participatory Visual Methods. *Visual Studies* 23(1): 63–77.

Peterson, Jeffery Chaichana, Mary Grace Antony, and Ryan J. Thomas 2012 "This Right Here is All About Living": Communicating the "Common Sense" About Home Stability Through CBPR and Photovoice. *Journal of Applied Communication Research* 40(3): 247–270.

Peterson, Jeffrey Chaichana and Aline Gubrium 2011 Old Wine in New Bottles? The Positioning of Participation in 17 NIH-Funded CBPR Projects. *Health Communication* 26(8): 724–734.

Pham, Minh-Ha T. 2011 Blog Ambition: Fashion, Feelings, and the Political Economy of the Digital Raced Body. *Camera Obscura* 26(176): 1–37.

Pink, Sarah 2007 Doing Visual Ethnography. Thousand Oaks, CA: Sage.

———— 2008 An Urban Tour. *Ethnography* 9(2): 175–196.

Pittaway, Eileen, Linda Bartolomei, and Richard Hugman 2010 "Stop Stealing Our Stories": The Ethics of Research With Vulnerable Groups. *Journal of Human Rights Practice* 2(2): 229–251.

Pratt, Mary Louise 1992 Imperial Eyes: Travel Writing and Transculturation. New York: Routledge.

Prins, Esther 2010 Participatory Photography: A Tool for Empowerment Or Surveillance? *Action Research* 8(4): 426–443.

Radley, A. 2010 What People Do With Pictures. *Visual Studies* 25(3): 268–279.

Rambaldi, G., R. Chambers, M. McCall, and J. Fox 2006 Practical Ethics for PGIS Practitioners, Facilitators, Technology Intermediaries and Researchers. *Participatory Learning and Action* 54: 106–113.

Rattray, N. 2006 A User-Centered Model for Community-Based Web-GIS. *URISA Journal* 18(2): 25–34.

———— 2007 Evaluating Universal Design: Low- and High-Tech Methods for Mapping Accessible Space. *Practicing Anthropology* 29(4): 24–28.

Reed, Amber and Amy L. Hill 2010 "Don't Keep it to Yourself!" Digital Storytelling With South African Youth. *Seminar.Net* 6(2): 268–279. Retrieved on August 23, 2012, from seminar.net/images/stories/vol6-issue2b/Reed_prcent_26Hill-Don_prcent_26_prcent_23039_prcent_3BtKeepIttoYourself.pdf.

Resource Management Act of New Zealand, Section 6. 1991 Retrieved on August 23, 2012, from www.legislation.govt.nz/act/public/1991/0069/latest/DLM231907.html.

Rheingold, Howard 2003 Smart Mobs: The Next Social Revolution. New York: Basic Books.

Rhoades, Robert 2006 Development With Identity: Community, Culture and Sustainability in the Andes. Cambridge, MA: CABI.

Rich, M., J. Patashnick, and R. Chalfen 2002 Visual Illness Narratives of Asthma: Explanatory Models and Health-Related Behavior. *American Journal of Health Behavior* 26(6): 442–453.

Richardson, L. 1997 Fields of Play: Constructing an Academic Life. New Brunswick, NJ: Rutgers University Press.

Ridington, Amber and Kate Hennessy 2008 Building Indigenous Agency Through Web-Based Exhibition: Dane-Wajich–Dane-Zaa Stories and Songs: Dreamers and the Land. Conference Proceedings from Museums and the Web 2008, Montreal, Canada, April 9–12. Retrieved June 19, 2012, from www.museumsandtheweb.com/mw2008/papers/ridington/ridington.html.

Riessman, Catherine Kohler 2008 Narrative Methods for the Human Sciences. Thousand Oaks, CA: Sage.

Ritchie, Jane and Liz Spencer 2002 Qualitative Data Analysis for Applied Policy Research. *In* The Qualitative Researcher's Companion, edited by A. M. Huberman and Matthew Miles, 305–330. Thousand Oaks, CA: Sage.

Rosaldo, Michelle Zimbalist and Louise Lamphere, eds. 1974 Women, Culture, and Society. Stanford, CA: Stanford University Press.

Rosaldo, Renato 1989 Culture and Truth: The Remaking of Social Analysis. Boston: Beacon.

Rose, Gillian 2007 Visual Methodologies: An Introduction to the Interpretation of Visual Materials. Thousand Oaks, CA: Sage.

———— 2010 Doing Family Photography: The Domestic, the Public, and the Politics of Sentiment. Burlington, VT: Ashgate.

Ruby, Jay 1995 The Moral Burden of Authorship in Ethnographic Film. *Visual Anthropology Review* 11(2): 77–82.

———— 1996 Visual Anthropology. *In* Encyclopedia of Cultural Anthropology, edited by David Levinson and Melvin Ember, 345–351. New York: Henry Holt and Company.

———— 2000 Picturing Culture: An Exploration of Film and Anthropology. Chicago, IL: University of Chicago Press.

———— 2007 Digital Oak Park: An Experiment. *Critical Arts: A Journal of South-North Cultural Studies* 21(2): 321–332.

Said, Edward 1979 Orientalism. New York: Vintage.

Salmons, J. 2010 Online Interviews in Real Time. Thousand Oaks, CA: Sage.

Scharf, Barbara 1999 Beyond Netiquette: The Ethics of Doing Naturalistic Discourse Research on the Internet. *In* Doing Internet Research, edited by Steve Jones, 243–256. Thousand Oaks, CA: Sage.

Schensul, S. L., J. J. Schensul, and M. D. LeCompte 1999 Essential Ethnographic Methods: Observations, Interviews, and Questionnaires. Lanham, MD: AltaMira Press.

Schrum, Lynne 1995 Framing the Debate: Ethical Research in the Information Age. *Qualitative Inquiry* 1(3): 311–326.

Shenton, A. K. 2004 Strategies for Ensuring Trustworthiness in Qualitative Research Projects. *Education for Information* 22(2): 63–76.

Sheridan, D. 1994 Using the Mass-Observation Archive as a Source for Women's Studies. *Women's History Review* 3(1): 101–113.

Sheridan, D., B. V. Street, and D. Bloome 2000 Writing Ourselves: Mass Observation and Literacy Practices. Cresskill, NJ: Hampton.

Sieber, R. E. 2000 GIS Implementation in the Grassroots. *URISA Journal* 12(1): 15–29.

Singhal, A., L. M. Harter, K. Chitnis, and D. Sharma 2007 Participatory Photography as Theory, Method and Praxis: Analyzing an Entertainment-Education Project in India. *Critical Arts* 21(1): 212–227.

Smith, Linda Tuhiwai 1999 Decolonizing Methodology: Research and Indigenous Peoples. London: Zed.

Sonke Gender Justice Network 2012 Digital Stories. Retrieved from www.genderjustice. org.za/digital-stories/tools/digital-stories.

Spivak, Gayatri 1988 Can the Subaltern Speak? *In* Marxism and the Interpretation of Culture, edited by Cary Nelson and Lawrence Grossberg, 271–315. Urbana, IL: University of Illinois Press.

Stacey, J. 1988 Can There Be a Feminist Ethnography? *Women's Studies International Forum* 11(1): 21–27.

Stedman, Richard, Tom Beckley, Sarah Wallace, and Marke Ambard 2004 A Picture and 100 Words: Using Resident-Employed Photography to Understand Attachment to Place. *Journal of Leisure Research* 36(4): 580–606.

Stoler, Ann 2010 Along the Archival Grain: Epistemic Anxieties and Colonial Common Sense. Princeton, NJ: Princeton University Press.

Summerfield, Penny 1985 Mass-Observation: Social Research or Social Movement? *Journal of Contemporary History* 20(3): 439–452.

Szélenyi, Iván and János Ladányi 2005 Patterns of Exclusion: Constructing Gypsy Ethnicity and the Making of an Underclass in Transitional Societies of Europe. Boulder, CO: East European Monographs.

Tang, Shirley S. 2008 Community-Centered Research as Knowledge/Capacity Building in Immigrant and Refugee Communities. *In* Engaging Contradictions, edited by Charles Hale, 237–264. Berkeley: University of California Press.

Tedlock, Dennis 1991 From Participant Observation to the Observation of Participation: The Emergence of Narrative Ethnography. *Journal of Anthropological Research* 47(1): 69–94.

——— 1995 Interpretation, Participation, and the Role of Narrative in Dialogical Anthropology. *In* The Dialogic Emergence of Culture, edited by Dennis Tedlock and B. Mannheim, 253–287. Champaign: University of Illinois Press.

Torre, M. E. 2012 The Public Science Project: Participatory Action, Research & Design for a Just World. Retrieved from www.publicscienceproject.org.

Tsing, Anna Lowenhaupt 1993 In the Realm of the Diamond Queen: Marginality in an Out-of-the-Way Place. Princeton, NJ: Princeton University Press.

Tucker, Genevieve 2006 First Person Singular: The Power of Digital Storytelling. *Screen Education* (42): 54–59.

Turner, Terence 1992 Defiant Images: The Kayapo Appropriation of Video. *Anthropology Today* 8: 5–15.

———— 1995 Representation, Collaboration and Mediation in Contemporary Ethnographic and Indigenous Media. *Visual Anthropology Review* 11(2): 102–106.

Uimonen, Paula 2012 Digital Drama: Teaching and Learning Art and Media in Tanzania. New York: Routledge.

Utekhin, Ilya, Alice Nakhimovsky, Slava Paperno, and Nancy Ries 2006 Communal Living in Russia (Kommunalka): A Virtual Museum of Soviet Everyday Life. Retrieved on June 19, 2012, at kommunalka.colgate.edu/.

Van Maanen, John 1988 Tales of the Field. Chicago: University of Chicago Press.

Vannini, Phillip, ed. 2012 Popularizing Research. New York: Peter Lang.

Wadsworth, Yvonne 1998 What is Participatory Action Research? Action Research International, Paper #2. Retrieved on August 23, 2012, from hdl.handle.net/1959.3/244.

Wallack, Lawrence, Lori Dorfman, David Jernigan, and Makani Themba 1993 Media Advocacy and Public Health: Power for Prevention. Thousand Oaks, CA: Sage.

Walther, J. B. 2002 Research Ethics in Internet-Enabled Research: Human Subjects Issues and Methodological Myopia. *Ethics and Information Technology* 4: 205–216.

Wang, Caroline 1999 Photovoice: A Participatory Action Research Strategy Applied to Women's Health. *Journal of Women's Health* 8(2): 185–192.

Wang, Caroline and Mary Ann Burris 1997 Photovoice: Concept, Methodology, and Use for Participatory Needs Assessment. *Health Education and Behavior* 24(3): 369–387.

Wang, Caroline, Mary Ann Burris, and Xiang Yue Ping 1996 Chinese Village Women as Visual Anthropologists: A Participatory Approach to Reaching Policymakers. *Social Science & Medicine* 42(10): 1391–1400.

Wang, Caroline, Yuan Yan Ling, and Feng Ming Ling 1996 Photovoice as a Tool for Participatory Evaluation: The Community's View of Process and Impact. *Journal of Contemporary Health* 4: 47–49.

Wang, C. C., S. Morrel-Samuels, P. M. Hutchison, L. Bell, and R. M. Pestronk 2004 Flint Photovoice: Community Building among Youth, Adults, and Policymakers. *American Journal of Public Health* 94(6): 911–913.

Weiner, Daniel and Trevor Harris 2003 Community-Integrated GIS for Land Reform in South Africa. *URISA Journal* 15: 61–73.

Wesch, Michael 2009 Youtube and You: Experiences of Self-Awareness in the Context Collapse of the Recording Webcam. *[EME]* 19–34. Retrieved on August 23, 2012, from krex.k-state.edu/dspace/handle/2097/6302.

———— 2012 Mediated Cultures: Digital Ethnography with Professor Wesch. Retrieved from www.mediatedcultures.net.

West, Jonathan and Kristina Peterson 2009 Reflective Learning From Project Failure in a University/Agency/Community Partnership. *Practicing Anthropology* 31(4): 33–37.

Wexler, L. and K. Graves 2008 The Importance of Culturally Responsive Training for Building a Behavioral Health Workforce in Alaska Native Villages: A Case Study from Northwest Alaska. *Journal of Rural Mental Health* 32(3): 22–33.

White, Shirley, ed. 2003 Participatory Video: Images that Transform and Empower. London: Sage.

White, Shirley, K. Sadanandan Nair, and John Ascroft, eds. 1994 Participatory Communication: Working for Change and Development. Thousand Oaks, CA: Sage.

Whitehead, Neil and Michael Wesch 2009 Human No More: Digital Subjectivities in a Post-Human Anthropology. *Anthropology News* 50(9): 12.

York, J. C. 2012 Published Works. Retrieved from www.jilliancyork.com/work.

Young, Lorraine and Hazel Barrett 2001 Adapting Adapting Visual Methods: Action Research With Kampala Street Children. *Area* 33(2): 141–152.

Zackey, Justin 2007 Peasant Perspectives on Deforestation in Southwest China: Social
Discontent and Environmental Mismanagement. *Mountain Research and Development*
27(2): 153–161.
Zimmer, Michael 2010 "But the Data is Already Public": On the Ethics of Research in
Facebook. *Ethics and Information Technology* 12(4): 313–325.

Index

Page numbers *in italics* refer to illustrations.

217

youth as, 39, 75–78, 83–89, 111,
126, 180–181, 188–190
research products
analysis of, 65
ethics of, 54–57
negotiating, 48
multipurpose, 13, 198–199
quality of, 63
researchers
as facilitator, 48, 129, 136, 140,
146–147
multiple roles of, 66, 113, 143–144
as point person, 41
relationship with subjects, 24–25,
46
Returning to Gitxaala (Menzies), 111,
112–113
Rich, Michael, 98–99
Ridington, Amber, 99, 180
Ridington, Jillian, 180
Ridington, Robin, 180
Ries, Nancy, 175–177
Robinson, Mary, 66
Rouch, Jean, 32, 97
Roma/Romani (Gypsies), 18, 82
Ruby, Jay, 41
Rwanda, 76, 80
Rydin, Ingegerd, 125

S
Sajó River Association for
Environment and Community
Development (SAKKF), 82
salvage paradigm, 171
Sandall, Roger, 100
Sandles, Shamia, 118
Sands, Catherine, 188–189
Santos, José Luis González, 31
schools, research on, 108–109
self-reflexivity, 24, 42, 63
visual, 34–35
self-representation, 60, 61, 63
sexual assault education, 137–138
"SHOWED" questions, 72, 186–187
Silence Speaks, 49
Sisters of Color United for Education,
143
Slovakia, 83
smoking, 142
social capital, 34
social context

matching methods to, 39, 74
of research production, 48
social media. *See* Internet; technology
social sciences
extractive model of, 31
research training in, 13–14
See also anthropology;
ethnography; fieldwork
socialism, 82–83
Society for Applied Anthropology
(SfAA), 112
sociology, Chicago School of urban,
28
software
cataloging (Scriblio), 178
data analysis, 42, 189–190
GIS, *158*, 158–159
open-source, 56
solidarity movement, international, 58
Somali Bantu Experience project,
192–193
Somalia, 192–193
Sonke Gender Justice, 137–138
Sound and Sentiment (Feld), 190
sound, documenting, 190–191
South Africa, 76, 77, 137, 160–161
spirituality, 105–106
St. Lawrence Island, 102
Steps for the Future, 121
stigma, of HIV/AIDS, 77–79, 88–89
stories
ownership of, 64
place-based, 162, 165–167
strategic use of, 58
storyboards, 94, 96, 136
storymapping, 165–167
storytelling
locative, 165–167
photo elicitation and, 69–70
representation and, 63
visual methods and, 57–58
Subject to Change (Sandles), 118
Surviving Arctic Climate Change
(Elder), 106–107
Swahili (language), 120
Swaziland, 75

T
Tanzania, 108, 117, 119
teaching, university, 116, 117,
132–134, 143, 149–150, 176–177

About the Authors

Aline Gubrium is an Assistant Professor of Public Health (Community Health Education) and a medical anthropologist at the University of Massachusetts Amherst. Gubrium uses participatory, digital, visual, and narrative methods to study the sexual and reproductive health knowledge and decision-making of marginalized women and youth. From early research with African-American women living in a southern rural community, to work with women using Depo-Provera contraception, and more recent projects working with Latino/a youth to address barriers to sexual communication and sexuality education, the driving question across the board is how research participants view their sexual and reproductive health experiences, particularly how they make sense of, respond to, and confront the many influences that shape their sexuality. For the past six years Gubrium has conducted ethnographic fieldwork at an alternative school for pregnant and parenting young women to explore students' embodied perspectives on contraception, mothering, and sexuality.

Krista Harper is an Associate Professor in the Department of Anthropology and the Center for Public Policy and Administration (CPPA) at the University of Massachusetts Amherst. As an ethnographer, Harper explores issues related to the cultural politics of the environment, cities, and food systems. She is the author of *Wild Capitalism: Environmental Activists and Post-Socialist Political Ecology in Hungary* (2006). Harper has led projects using participatory digital research methods such as Photovoice to study environmental issues in a Hungarian Roma (Gypsy) neighborhood and to investigate school food programs with youth in western Massachusetts. In her current research projects, Harper studies civic organizations working on urban gardens and heritage preservation in Lisbon, Portugal, and western Massachusetts.

green press

INITIATIVE

Left Coast Press, Inc. is committed to preserving ancient forests and natural resources. We elected to print this title on 30% post consumer recycled paper, processed chlorine free. As a result, for this printing, we have saved:

2 Trees (40' tall and 6-8" diameter)
1 Million BTUs of Total Energy
159 Pounds of Greenhouse Gases
863 Gallons of Wastewater
58 Pounds of Solid Waste

Left Coast Press, Inc. made this paper choice because our printer, Thomson-Shore, Inc., is a member of Green Press Initiative, a nonprofit program dedicated to supporting authors, publishers, and suppliers in their efforts to reduce their use of fiber obtained from endangered forests.

For more information, visit www.greenpressinitiative.org

Environmental impact estimates were made using the Environmental Defense Paper Calculator. For more information visit: www.papercalculator.org.